THE BEST:

CONVERSATIONS WITH TOP TRADERS

THE BEST:

TRADING MARKETS^{SM}.COM

CONVERSATIONS WITH TOP TRADERS

Kevin N. Marder
Marc Dupée

M. GORDON PUBLISHING GROUP

Los Angeles, California

ISBN 1-893756-08-4

Printed in the United States of America

Cover design by Conrad Kalil using an image from Bryan Reinhard/Masterfile. The book was typeset in Garmond by Judy Brown.

*To my parents, who gave
me all that mattered.*

Kevin N. Marder

*To Barbara Dupée, my mother,
for her enduring enthusiasm
and gentle encouragement.*

Marc Dupée

Contents

The Interviews

ON THE CUSP

FOREWORD

This book is all about great traders. How they started, how they took their hard knocks, and how they arrived at a strategy to conquer the markets. In short, how they *became* great traders.

Consider this: One trader's personal account appreciated 70,000 percent in the 4 1/2-year period ended June 30, 2000.

Another grew his account by 3,270 percent in the 18 months ended June 30, 2000.

Another was the former head of trading at Fidelity Capital Markets from 1990 to 1997. He had 94 traders reporting to him each day.

Another, after losing 90 percent of his account in the 1973–1974 bear market, turned his career around enough to be ranked by Nelson's Best Money Managers as the No. 1 hedge fund manager in the world for global macro strategy in the five-year periods ended 1997 and 1998.

Another was the biggest S&P 500 futures trader, a man that all other traders in the S&P futures pit feared so much that they felt compelled to keep an eye on him at all times.

Another, after a calamitous start that included a $20,000 loss in his first nine days as well as his boss' comment that he was "redefining the definition of bad luck," earned $1.8 million in only his second full year of daytrading, exceeding the seven-figure threshold in each of the next two years.

Another won the U.S. Investing Championship three times before opening up his own hedge fund.

Another set a record return for the U.S. Investing Championship, then proceeded to catapult his hedge fund into the top 1 percent of all hedge funds for the three years ended May 2000.

When I began my trading career in 1986, there was no one to turn to for advice, no Internet, and precious few books that were written from the perspective of some of the world's top traders. Today, most traders find our era's information overload downright overwhelming. In 1986, however, if you were an aspiring trader, you ached for it.

In any of life's pursuits, whether it be playing tennis, cooking, or playing a musical instrument, the quickest route to success is to learn from someone better than you. Of course, the absolute best way is to learn from the very best in a particular field. In the case of trading, though, how often do you get a close-up peek at what goes on in the minds of some of the world's top traders? Specifically, how often do you learn how some of the world's top traders enter a position, sell a position, or add to a position?

If you're like most people, the answer is probably "not very often."

For unless a trader is fortunate enough to have a top trader in his or her circle of friends or acquaintances, the chances are slim that he or she will come in contact with one. Even then, it's sometimes difficult to know exactly who the top traders are. Many of them deliberately shun the public eye, preferring to lead a low-profile existence. After all, what do they have to prove?

This book, then, presents an opportunity for traders, both aspiring and professional, to benefit from the experiences—both good and bad—of some of the top traders in the world. Some of the interviews represent the first time a trader has consented to a full-length interview detailing his strategy of consistently pulling money out of the market.

I learned a lot from interviewing the traders in this book—indeed, far more than I'd imagined when I began putting it together with Marc Dupée. Although I've read scores upon scores of books since I began trading in 1986, I walked away from each and every chapter of this book with something I can integrate into my own plan of attacking the markets.

My hope is that you will, too.

Kevin N. Marder
Los Angeles, California
July 10, 2000

Trade with the best. There is nothing that has helped me more in the financial markets than learning directly from experienced traders: how they think, what they do, and how they trade.

When I began trading, I had trouble finding successful traders who would share details of how they traded. The few books that were available on the subject, I felt, fell short of adequately describing the specifics of what successful traders did and how they traded. By compiling these interviews, I believe we have provided to traders of all stripes a source that allows readers to get inside the minds of victorious traders: traders who are down in the trenches taking money out of the markets almost every day.

Differing ideas, approaches, and techniques are what make a market. We have assembled a cross-section of top traders, who, despite their differing approaches to the market, have experienced unusual success. And herein lies one of the enduring benefits of this book. Whatever your temperament, time frame, or experience level, there is something from the conversations that you can take and immediately apply to make you a better trader.

In short, we have sought to create a manuscript that mentors. My hope is that the combination of technique and candor shared by the traders in this book will help you achieve greater success in the trading markets.

Marc Dupée
Los Angeles, California
July 9, 2000

ACKNOWLEDGMENTS

Thanks to Toni and Jim Kaplan for being my first believers and for making it all possible. Thanks to Larry Connors, a trader's trader if ever there was one. Thanks to Bill O'Neil for changing my entire life. Marc Dupée and Eddie Kwong, friends and colleagues, thanks for your help in making this book a reality. Greg Kuhn, thanks for the inspiration. Jeff Cooper, thanks for the vote of confidence. David Ryan, thanks for all of your encouragement. Gil Morales and Christian Kacher, thanks for all of your sharing. Danilo Torres and Marianne Winfield, thanks for all of the behind-the-scenes work. Cedd Moses, thanks for setting the example early on. Dave Baker, thanks for the zeal.

Long live the California Momentum School.

Kevin N. Marder

Books are collaborative efforts and I would like to extend my gratitude to everyone involved. I would also like to give a special thank you to the following:

To the traders interviewed, for sharing their knowledge. To Larry Connors, whose vision and drive bring to life projects such as these. To Kevin Marder, for his friendship, insight, and editorial judgment. To Suzie Stubbs, for her patience and understanding. To Mark Etzkorn, for his contribution to the Manuel Ochoa, Kevin Haggerty, and William Greenspan interviews. To Eddie Kwong and Marianne Winfield, for their levity and assistance with charts and the manuscript. To the TradingMarkets.com team, for their support and dedication throughout.

Marc Dupée

GIL MORALES
AND
DR. CHRISTIAN KACHER

THE DISCIPLES

By Kevin N. Marder

You would be hard-pressed to find a trader with a more outstanding track record than either Gil Morales or Dr. Christian Kacher. Simply, these guys are monsters. Gil took a personal account of his and grew it by 3,270 percent in the 18 months ended June 30, 2000. Not to be outdone, Chris's personal account swelled by 70,472 percent in the 4 1/2 years ended June 30, 2000. I verified both sets of results with brokerage account statements.

Gil and Chris are portfolio managers for William O'Neil + Co., managing the company's internal investment account. Gil also runs the institutional services division of the company, which provides research for institutional investors. I first met Gil and Chris in November 1999 through my friend Greg Kuhn, who introduced us at an O'Neil investment seminar.

Some top traders don't like to share their secrets and findings with others. Gil and Chris, on the other hand, couldn't be more different, as you will see in the following conversation which took place in December 1999, January 2000, and July 2000.

Kevin N. Marder: Gil, how did you get started in the stock market?

Gil Morales: I first became interested in the financial arena at Stanford where I majored in economics and took some courses in investment analysis. Ironically, absolutely none of what I learned about investments in college do I use today. Right after I graduated from Stanford I received a job offer from Caterpillar Tractor in Peoria. Instead of taking the job, I took the advice of my advisor, John Cogan. He thought I should do something crazy, so I decided to publish in book form a collection of comic strips titled "Dupie" that I had drawn for *The Stanford Daily* while I was in school. That sold fairly well and then Ballantine Books in New York came along and asked me to do a second book. They got me a publicist and were billing me as "the next Doonesbury." I was doing interviews on talk shows, CNN, CBS News Radio, etc. to promote the book, and the Los Angeles Times Syndicate was looking at picking up the strip for distribution. So here I was, right out of college and I was a professional cartoonist with a Stanford economics degree. I spent the next several years as a cartoonist, illustrator and graphic designer, which was about as far away from the stock market as you could be.

The big turn occurred in 1987, when I moved to Maui, Hawaii to start my own graphics firm. That failed miserably, and I limped back to Palo Alto, California in October 1987. Since I was broke, I was staying with one of my best friends, David Schneider. Dave was in the market pretty heavily at the time and he asked me what I thought of the market. I just kind of blurted out, "Sell everything!" Well, the truth is, I didn't have a clue what I was talking about. But Dave followed my advice which ended up saving him a lot of money, since the market crashed a few days later. From that point on he became a constant influence, telling me I should become a broker and that he thought I was smarter than his broker, etc. So Dave planted that seed in my head.

One thing led to another, and I found myself back in Los Angeles in 1991. I took a temp job at a Dean Witter office in San Marino, a suburb of Los Angeles. After a while, the manager, Scott Hennington, suggested that I apply for a broker position with Dean Witter. So I took this test that you had to pass to become a Dean Witter broker, and failed it! Incidentally, Bill O'Neil took the same test when he was first looking for a job as a stockbroker, and he failed it as well. Well, Dean Witter wasn't going to hire me because I failed their test, so I got mad and finally ended up walking into Merrill Lynch in Beverly Hills where I landed a broker trainee position.

Anyway, I started reading everything I could get my hands on, but nothing really got me excited. Finally I came across Bill's book, *How to Make Money in Stocks*, and a light went on in a big way.

I can relate. When I first read Bill's book in 1990, I got to page 70 or so, and a giant light bulb went on in my head. I was so excited that I'd finally come across a book that made it all come together! And I remember putting the book down at that point, pacing the living room floor, getting very excited.

I made all kinds of notes in the book and carried it around with me wherever I went. One day the book is sitting on my desk and this little old guy, a senior broker at Merrill by the name of Harry Wayne, comes waddling by, points at the book on my desk with Bill's picture on it, and says, "I hired that guy." As it turned out, Harry was Bill O'Neil's first boss and the guy who hired Bill into the business when he was first looking for a job. So Harry and I became good friends and I would give him stock ideas which he would do some nice business with. Harry introduced me to Bill, and I had several opportunities to talk with Bill at investor meetings for Bill's old New USA Fund, Harry's birthday parties, etc.

In 1994 I left Merrill and went to PaineWebber, where I began to focus entirely on catering to investors who were interested in Bill's methodology, CANSLIM. So I chucked my entire Merrill Lynch client base, which consisted of mutual funds, wrap accounts, insurance, and financial planning . . . all that boring financial consultant baloney. My wife Linda thought I was crazy throwing away the client base I had spent the last three years building in order to try this new idea. Anyway, Harry told Bill about my plan, and I remember my first day at PaineWebber. Bill called me up and gave me a little pep talk which helped allay my nervousness about starting at a new firm with this crazy idea of only managing CANSLIM accounts. As it turned out, my crazy plan ended up blossoming nicely as my business shot up to over $1 million in commissions a year and I became one of the quickest million-dollar producers ever at PaineWebber.

Bill had been casually following my progress through Harry, who had retired and then become a client of mine. In September of 1997 I went out to lunch with Kathy Sherman, the head of communications and public relations at *Investor's Business Daily*, and a couple of her friends who wanted to open accounts with me. After lunch, Kathy told me that Bill asked if I wouldn't mind stopping by their offices to chat with him. So I stopped by and talked with Bill for a while, where he sprung this whole idea of recruiting me to run his Institutional Services group and manage internal money for him. Needless to say, it was an offer I couldn't refuse, because here I am.

And, Chris, how did you first become involved in the stock market?

Dr. Christian Kacher: I think it's always been in my blood. When I was in elementary school, I was interested in stamps and coins. I collected them as tools of speculation, not because they looked pretty, like most kids would. At a young age, I think I had an innate sense of the ability for things to appreciate in value. I attempted to actually make money in stamps in elementary school. This was back when the price of stamps was surging. I mean every three months these things would go higher and higher in price. Then when I was 11, I began to track price movements of precious metals. My mom was a top-grossing broker for Merrill Lynch and she received a Bill O'Neil product, *Daily Graphs,* as well as *The Wall Street Journal* in the mail. I would clip the listings of precious metals' spot prices from *The Wall Street Journal* each day and paste them in a notebook. This was in '79 and '80 when gold and silver were making huge moves. This was very fascinating for me.

And then at age 12, I bought my first stock, which was Apple Computer. It just started to gain momentum . . . the whole concept of how stocks seemed to be the ultimate vehicle for being able to buy and sell and make money off price movements. I would say my interest in stocks really took off after reading Bill's book. That really made me understand that it was actually possible to consistently score big gains in the market. I started devouring *Daily Graphs* each week in college. I would scrutinize each of the charts in *Daily Graphs* on the weekends. I began to carry a copy of the latest issue of *Daily Graphs* with me wherever I went so I would always have a chance to look at charts. At that point, my trading started to work. Prior to that point, I was just dabbling and I would carry a position for years. I wasn't really a trader. I had an interest in the market but I wasn't really making much headway.

After reading Bill's book, I started reading a number of other books on the market that were also helpful in trading. I remember telling my mom once that you can't beat the markets because they're all fairly efficient. I bought that school of reasoning. But Bill's book kind of broke through the ice and really made me understand that the markets are not purely efficient and that there is rhyme and reason to these chart patterns.

Once you got out of college, was the O'Neil Co. job your first gig in the business, or were you somewhere else before you came to O'Neil?

Kacher: I finished my BS degree in chemistry at Berkeley and I went right into the graduate program at Berkeley. It was the Ph.D. program in nuclear chemistry. At that point, I didn't feel that I had a real trading methodology. My interest in the market was definitely building. But I didn't feel confident that I could strike out and go right to a job as a professional trader or a market maker or anything like that. I had very strong ties to chemistry, so it was a natural progression to go from chemistry in undergrad to nuclear chemistry in grad school. In graduate school, my interest just completely took off. At the end of my first year in grad school, I finally understood what a base breakout was, that it wasn't just arbitrary, that there was some sense to it. I just totally immersed myself in the business library, where we had archived copies of *Daily Graphs* and many other publications. I started to devise all of these econometric models in my attempts to time the market. I came up with these crazy models with Excel spreadsheets and I finally came full circle and realized that none of those models really worked. I came back to the basics of just looking at chart patterns and using those chart patterns to anticipate moves in the market.

About halfway through grad school I almost quit because my interest in the market was so great. I just wanted to quit and go trade the market. I would have taken a junior analyst position anywhere just to get my foot in the door in this field. But I realized quickly that most places weren't going to hire me in that situation. I didn't have any formal training or experience in economics or business or any of that. So I decided to stick it out and finish the degree and then decide, figuring that the degree would open a lot of doors for me, which it did. So it was the right decision.

In my third year of grad school, I started a Web site called The Virtues of Selfish Investing. It was designed to help investors pick good stocks using the CANSLIM method. I started investing successfully in 1991, and by the time I put the site up in 1995 I had a nice little track record. I was beating the market every year. I put all of my trades up on the site just for the record. It was a subscription-based service and, lo and behold, the $90 checks started coming in on a daily basis. All of a sudden I found that I was making some pretty good cash for a graduate student, just setting up a Web site that cost me absolutely nothing and giving people advice on what my stock picks were.

At the same time, I was prospecting for a job in the field, knowing that I wasn't going to go into nuclear chemistry as a career. A year and a half before I was going to graduate, I knew what the odds were of getting into this field—they were pretty slim. I was frantically cold-calling money managers across the U.S. I must have called 300 of them. I went into an informational interview with a guy in L.A. who was one of the big fund managers for Trust Company Of The West. We had our nice little interview and he gave me some friendly advice. We parted, and two weeks later he called me at Berkeley and said, "I want to try something new that we've never done in the long history of Trust Company of the West. We're going to hire you while you're still in grad school. And you're going to advise me on which stocks I should play. You're going to be one of my advisors." I signed something like a million different forms and I became an employee of Trust Company of the West while still a grad student. They paid me this nice salary and I was an advisor to Charlie Larson, who I would say really gave me my start in the business. I worked for him for about a year, advising him on my picks.

This was in 1995 when we were in a great market. I happened to hit some pretty big ones. He was very open to giving me any kind of letter of recommendation I needed and helping me along once I graduated so that I could get a permanent job in the field. He knew what my whole strategy was and he said that I, without question, should apply to William O'Neil + Co. He thought that would be the perfect fit for me and pushed me into that direction. I interviewed with the O'Neil company and they made me an offer, which I accepted. As far as all of the other job offers that were pending, I didn't even want to hear about what they were going to offer me dollar-wise. I knew that this was the place for me. Money was not an issue. I just wanted to be able to work here.

What did you start doing for the company?

Kacher: They started me off in data research, which is kind of like the bottom rung in the organization. I came to work here with this incredible passion. I'd have to say that since I started working here Jan. 22, 1996, there hasn't been one day that I've gotten up in the morning and not wanted to come to work. Whereas in grad school there were many, many days when I just didn't want to get up and go into the lab. It was like night and day. My whole life just took a dramatic turn for the better by coming here and being in the environment that I'm supposed to be in.

I met some fascinating people. In three months of being here, I met one of the traders who worked for Bill, Dan Morris, who later retired at the age of 33. He had that same passion for the markets that I had. We used to talk long into the evenings and sometimes we'd have these nine-hour marathon talks about the market. It was pretty intense. I knew this was the place for me. I traded my own account, hoping that Bill would notice eventually. After working for three months, they gave me a promotion to sell WONDAs, an O'Neil database product. So I had the opportunity to fly around the country and talk to money managers about this product that I used to make money in the market. So it was something I totally believed in. In the process of flying around the country, I had several job offers thrown at me. Of course I didn't take any of them.

One of the fascinating people I met was Ed Seykota, who's interviewed in one of the *Market Wizards* books. He's always been one of my favorite interviews because he's so intense on the psychological aspects of trading. I spent an entire day with him and it was a day I'll never forget. I constantly refer to that day because we basically talked for the whole day. There's so much that I learned just in that one day sitting with him and talking with him. He had such an impact on me because he wanted to psychologically analyze me. He said he could judge how effective people would be at trading the markets by just sitting and talking with them and picking their brains. He asked my permission first and said it could get very intense, which it did. He's a very strong personality and was very probing in his questions about my early life experiences and things. I found the whole process fascinating and at the end of the day he said he didn't really see any impediments to me becoming a world class trader. That meant the world to me, the fact that he would give me that kind of validation. At that point, I really didn't know Bill very well and had only talked with him once. So this was the first real validation I got from someone I'd truly respected.

A few months later, I ended up getting a job offer in San Diego. This company basically said it was going to roll the red carpet out for me. They said, "we'll give you whatever you want, come trade for us, you have a great track record." Nineteen ninety-five was the first year I scored a triple-digit gain in the market. In 1996, I scored a triple-digit gain of 218 percent. And in 1997, when I was still selling WONDAs, I had already run my account up over 100 percent. Dan Morris, who was still at O'Neil + Co. at the time, said, "it'd be a shame for the firm to lose you because you trade just like Bill trades." And on the day that I was packing my stuff up, getting ready to leave, he went to talk to Bill on my behalf. Bill called me into his office and made a counteroffer, something that I couldn't refuse. Naturally, I knew this was the place.

Then I started trading money for him two weeks before the market topped out in October 1997. So I had just enough time to get on full margin when the market absolutely topped and I had to completely reverse my positions! Fortunately, I finished that segment from October through the end of the year off a couple percent. Nineteen ninety-eight was really the first year that I traded for Bill. I was up 140 percent that year. And then 1999 was really the great year, being up 566 percent.

That's not your personal account, but the account that you manage for the company?

Kacher: Right. It's much larger than my personal account. What was interesting was that even though I traded different stocks for each account during the year, the percentages were very close, since my personal account was up 584 percent. That comes back to what Ed Seykota said, that everyone gets what they want out of the market. I had wanted to get over 500 percent in both of my accounts. And that's pretty much what happened.

That's phenomenal!

Kacher: Thanks, Kevin.

Let's say your account is 100 percent long. How many positions will you typically have open with that much of an invested position?

Kacher: If it's 100 percent long, that means we're either starting a rally or we're coming off a peak. That means I would probably have about six positions, maybe seven.

And if you're 200 percent long?

Kacher: I'll typically have anywhere between 10 and 15.

When you initially open a position, is your goal to start off with 10 to 12 percent of your account in that position?

Kacher: Something like that. It depends on the stock, too. If the stock is very liquid and it's a top-quality name—an institutional name—and it's got a perfect breakout, then I will try to ramp into that thing pretty fast . . . you know, because it poses very little downside risk. But if I'm playing something a little thinner than that, I don't want to get stuck in the position, so maybe my maximum size is only going to be 12 percent of my account.

Whereas the first example of the more-liquid, institutional-quality name would be, what, up to 20 percent?

Kacher: I'd say usually up to 25 percent. My thinking is that if I have 25 percent in top-quality names, then I'll have eight positions at 200 percent invested. And that's where I'm always trying to get my account to—eight positions. But in reality, I always find that I'm playing more than eight. Because what happens is I'll land into a stock and I'll go 25 percent in that stock and realize it's deficient or maybe it's slower. And since I want to get as much juice out of the market when it is trending, I'll quickly cut that position back. I want to make room for something else that is just breaking out, especially if I'm 200 percent margined. So what I'll do is I'll cut that position back. Maybe I'll go from 25 percent and reduce it to 15 percent and then use that extra buying power to initiate a new position in a new stock that's breaking out. So when all is said and done, I don't have eight positions. I have 12 or 13 or 15.

How about you, Gil? If your account is 100 percent long, how many positions will you have open at that point?

Morales: Anywhere from five to 10. And maybe as few as three to four. As we progress through a market cycle, I whittle things down.

So you might have up to 35 percent or so in one position if you really feel good about it?

Morales: Yeah. And that's how you make your big money. I did that in '98 when my big money was heavily into Schwab. In '99, I was heavily into VerticalNet, Verisign, Ariba, Oracle, and Sun.

What were your results in 1999?

Morales: I ended up 518 percent and Chris Kacher was up 566 percent.

You two guys hit the ball out of the park as well as anybody in the entire U.S. stock market in 1999. Can you touch on the basics of what you look for in your trading strategy?

Kacher: We use tools like WONDA (William O'Neil Direct Access, a William O'Neil + Co. research product) to screen out stocks with certain characteristics. We look for stocks that are in leading groups that are near new price highs that have high relative strength that have either a really solid, accelerating earnings track record, or a sales track record. A lot of these new companies don't have earnings and some of them are not going to be earning money for maybe another year or so. But their sales are ramping up very nicely, with high, triple-digit, quarter-over-quarter sales growth. So we look for one or the other.

What percentage weighting do you place on your fundamental analysis versus your technical analysis of a particular stock?

Kacher: That's a great question. The way we approach it is we don't buy stock just on a technical basis. It's got to have good, solid fundamentals. We want to buy stocks that are going to lead their space. So we look first for those stocks that have the strongest fundamentals. And then from there we look at those stocks that are close to their old highs and are forming sound bases.

Morales: I ask myself a very simple question whenever I'm going to buy a stock: If it's got the technical formation and the earnings or sales that we're looking for, does this company dominate its industry or does it have the potential to dominate its industry? And that requires a little bit of putzing around on the company's Web site, maybe looking at some other analyst reports, assessing an industry. And right now, that's quite a challenge because you have a lot of emerging industries, what with e-commerce and all.

But I am asking myself that question because we do know that, with the biggest winning stocks, probably the No. 1 characteristic is that they dominate their industry. Cisco, Microsoft, Dell, Home Depot, Wal-Mart, you can go down the line. And that's really what we're looking for. You don't find very many of those. But by asking that question we do position ourselves in the right stocks. And we have the potential to maybe have one or two of these massive winners. I made more money in the six weeks ended Dec. 7, 1999 percentage-wise than I've ever made in any other period in the market since I started in this business in 1991.

Kacher: I would have to say the same thing. It's been phenomenal.

Morales: The real question for us now is whether we are looking at compressed time frames. In 1999, stocks were going up in six weeks as much as they normally would move up in six to eight to 12 months. We're wondering if this is a sign of power or a sign that we're in these compressed time frames, and maybe we'd better start looking at taking some off the table here. That's a question we're grappling with right now. We don't really have an answer for that. But as long as the trend is our friend, we're going to stay with it.

Kacher: This is a very exciting time. Actually, it's the most exciting time I can remember to be in the market because there's all these new, emerging technologies like storage area networking, business-to-business, e-commerce, and fiber optics. We're trying to figure out what the next big name is going to be in each of these areas and we use a lot of fundamental analysis to figure those things out.

Morales: We're just trying to answer the question of "who is the next Cisco or Home Depot?" We think that we own a couple of them. We're not sure yet which ones they are, since you would know it all only in hindsight. But at the time, that is what we're trying to do. That really drives the fundamental side of our stock selection.

Gil, just getting back to the earnings side of things, a lot of these Internet companies have not earned any money yet. Would that turn you away from buying a stock even though the potential is there and it could be the leader in its space?

Morales: Initially, it was very difficult for us to get a handle on the whole Internet thing and to assess it. At the outset, we weren't putting a lot of the names, like Yahoo and AOL, on our buy list because they didn't have earnings. But we had to think about this more from a fundamental aspect. And also, we had to consider that the stock market is really just a big pricing mechanism—you have the cumulative mind of the stock market representing all of these people that are participating, their opinions and their knowledge about where they're going to put their money.

So I see the market as a pricing mechanism. No. 1, it recognized that there is definitely a significant economic development going on in the Internet. Then the problem became why some of these had no earnings. But the market sensed or could tell that this was going to be big. And so now, the market being a pricing mechanism, it has to grasp onto some way to price it. And since there were no earnings, the next best thing, as far as we could tell, was top-line sales growth. We've studied these models now, since we've got a lot of recent models of these types of big-winning, Internet stocks. We know that the primary characteristic, or the characteristic that's replaced earnings, is a huge sales ramp-up. So we're looking now for companies in these spaces that have huge sales ramp-ups. And the market is using the sales growth as a way to gauge these companies and function as a pricing mechanism to put a value on these companies.

I also think that the market is trying to assess the overall value of the Internet as a whole. Sometimes what happens is you get some companies that have no earnings and maybe in the long run they don't have great potential. But right here, right now, they become representative of a new emerging industry. And so the market grasps onto these companies as well, to try and assess the value and put a price on everything. Our job is to find out what the market's keying on, and what we've discovered is that it is the huge sales ramp-ups. And I mean significant ramp-ups. Not $200,000 this quarter and then $500,000 next quarter, which looks like 150 percent. We're looking for $10 million last quarter and now $26 million this quarter. That's the type of ramp-up we want to see—significant, big sales.

Kacher: It's interesting because the market does function like a pricing mechanism. You can find these things either by looking for high sales rates, high earnings-per-share rates, or even high relative strength. A relative strength of 99 represents the absolute top across the board, because a stock with a relative strength of 99 probably is running for a reason. You can further investigate it using WONDA.

A lot of the great stock performers just really don't give you much opportunity to enter at the beginning of their big advance. Sometimes they'll come out of little, two-week congestion areas. Given that these are coming out on big volume, is that the kind of situation that you would bend the rules for and hop into, or would you stick pretty rigidly to your discipline of buying a stock with a base of at least six weeks?

Kacher: That's a really good question. You can take Qualcomm in this market cycle or you could take AOL in the last market cycle earlier in 1999. When the market corrects you have all of these market indices going lower and lower, but these really strong stocks resist the tendency to go lower. So what happens is that they do correct a little bit, but then they're also the first to spring back up when the market has a good day. What happens is that they tend to form what we call ascending bases, where the stock seems to want to get dragged down, but doesn't. It resists, and actually goes higher and higher by a little bit during the period that the market's actually going lower. Now when the market finally turns around and gets that 1 percent confirmation day in a major average, these stocks, with the weight of the market off, just spring right on out of there.

Morales: The ascending base is telling you that they want to go higher. To give you an example of two of them, if you look at the chart patterns of AOL and Schwab between January 1999 and the end of February 1999, they both made the same type of pattern. Neither made a classic O'Neil base, but they made an ascending pattern. It's almost like you took a base and tilted it up slightly. AOL and Schwab both formed these ascending bases. And when they break out of the top of these ascending bases, we will be buying these stocks, and generally with success. That is a very powerful pattern. The stock is telling you that the weight of the market is trying to hold the stock down, but the stock still wants to keep creeping slightly upward.

Ascending Base: America Online (AOL), Daily

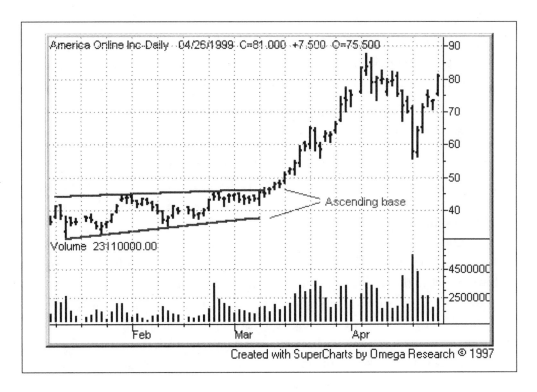

Kacher: And Qualcomm did the same thing in the last market cycle.

Morales: All through the four months of the summer of 1999 when we were weak in June, July, August, and September, Qualcomm just kept going higher and higher. You could actually see that as it's ascending all the way up to 220 and then it breaks out at about 230. And that's a pivot point, actually, and we're buying the stock there.

As far as money management goes, if you're wrong you obviously cut your losses. Do you have any preset percentage limit that you use or do you play

each situation a little bit differently depending on how the general market is acting?

Morales: I use a 5 percent stop loss. I know Bill O'Neil says 7 or 8 percent, but at this stage in the development of my career, I should be good at picking stocks at the right point. So I should be up right away with a position.

Right away, meaning the first day?

Morales: Within the first hour or the first couple of days. My stops are generally 5 percent. I don't let them get too much further than that . . . 8 percent at the most. But when it's down 5 percent, I'm looking at just getting rid of it. Chris might do something different.

   Kacher: I would say that if a stock is not behaving right, yeah, I generally cut the position within 5 percent. A lot of my sells are actually 2 or 3 percent losses. Probably the majority of them are like that. Because we trade size, it's important not to get stuck in a stock that's a little thin. So when you're trying to get out of it, sometimes we're going to be selling it at an average of 8 to 10 percent off where we bought it if it's not working out. We're pretty quick to see when a stock's not working out, so we immediately try to sell at that point.

How do you add to a winner on the way up? Do you double down at a certain point?

Morales: I use a simple rule. Let's say I have $1 million that I want to allocate to this one stock, and it's a $100 stock. So if the stock breaks out, I put one-half the money in it and I buy 5,000 shares. If it goes up 2 percent from my buy point, I put in another $250,000. And then if it goes up another 2 percent from there, I put in the next $125,000. And then the last bit I kind of use at my discretion as to where I want to add to the position. But that's how I pyramid a position right away and get my full position. If it moves up like that, I'll be in right away and get my full position. I'll be in right away and I'll be in deep, heavy. That's how I do it. Now Chris might have a different way.

Kacher: What I do is, when you get to the pivot point and if the volume's there, I'll buy one-half of a full position outright on the breakout. Say that very same day the stock closes at the top end of its range. As long as it's not too extended from the base and did not run up excessively that day, I will buy another one-quarter position at the end of the day. So now I've got three-quarters of my full position intact at the end of that first breakout day. Now as a stock runs up, I'm not going to touch it. But what often happens is, after breaking out, these things will come back on lower volume for a few days before running up again. I will go ahead and sometimes add another one-quarter and get my full position that way.

Another way to do it is, let's say the stock came back a little bit, everything looked good, I bought that last quarter, and now I've got my full position. If the stock then runs up another 50 percent, what happens during a one-month market setback is that these stocks will sometimes come back to the 50-day moving average line. If they're institutional quality, what I find is that a lot of mutual funds that own the stock will come in and support the stock at the 50-day moving average. You can actually use the 50-day as another pyramid point. That's assuming, though, that you already have a lot of cushion in the stock. If it comes all the way back down to the 50-day, and if you're up appreciably in the stock, then there's very little risk to you to add to your position at that level.

So a lot of institutions are really watching that 50-day, then.

Kacher: Yes. You can see that with companies like Qualcomm. Every time Qualcomm hits the 50-day it tends to bounce. Sometimes it'll go below the 50-day, but it's very quick to bounce above it, usually within a day or two. And JDS Uniphase, remarkably, every time it hit the 50 it bounced. It's also an institutional quality stock.

Chris, what would be one or two of the things you'd be looking for that would first give some sort of indication that the market is putting in some sort of intermediate-term top?

Kacher: When we get these nice long trends, and we're seeing a lot of these tech stocks go up dramatically, often the last day of the run is accompanied by huge climax buying, where a lot of stocks go through the roof. A lot of the leaders like Exodus, Verisign, or Qualcomm, will run up huge. This is what happened in the April 14, 1999 top. That was the day when companies like NetBank, AOL, Schwab, and all of those leading names went up huge that last final day . . . and then we went into a correction. So we do look for that. There's no way to tell how long the correction is going to be, but that is an indication that you do have some sort of correction on the way.

Morales: It's pretty much like an across-the-board ebullience. You look at all of the leading names and they'll all be running all at the same time.

Kacher: Also, in addition to the percentage move, since in this market some stocks will move 100 to 200 percent in a few weeks, what we look at is a time frame. When a stock breaks out of a base and runs up 150 percent over the next six or seven weeks, that doesn't mean it's topped. Usually, a stock will make its final topping action three months to four months down the line after the break-out, if it's going to top at all.

To me, the toughest decision is the sell-to-nail-down-a-profit decision. The sell-to-cut-a-loss decision is much simpler, while I think the buy decision might be somewhere in between. What would your advice be to intermediate-term traders to better time their exit points?

Morales: Basically, there are three ways a stock will top. First, you will either be making new highs on less and less volume, which we call wedging. Or you will have a climax, blow-off type of move where the stock has its biggest one-day range from the time the market turned—in other words, from the day that you had the follow-through in the big averages. The stock will have gone on a tear and at the very end of it you're gapping up on huge volume and you've got the widest spread, almost as if there's a rush to get into the stock. At that point, it's almost capitulation on the buy side. We're looking for that, a climax type move. And you had that in a number of the leaders recently. For instance, you saw Sun when it got up above 80, it was up 7 1/2 points in one day which was the biggest

Climax Top: Sun Microsystems (SUNW), Daily

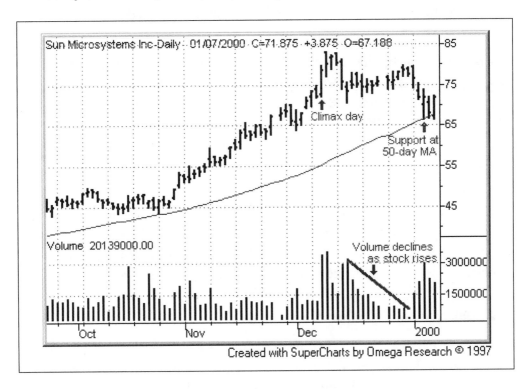

one-day point rise throughout the move. So we kind of got a signal there to start losing some of the position.

Kacher: Not only that, but after it made that huge, 7-point move, it came in and then started to wedge over the next few weeks.

Morales: Right. In other words, you rallied from that low at 70 1/2 upward 80 and your volume was declining pretty much daily. And so that's giving you some signs. In the case of a stock like Sun, it's an institutional-quality company. They're a key to the build-out of the Internet infrastructure. It's possible the stock will have to go through a period of base-building. But in any case, we think the stock has topped for now.

Kacher: Our whole take is this: Why have your money in a stock that at best is going to go sideways and base-build for a number of weeks?

I know that Bill O'Neil likes to say that big gains need a lot of time to build. Now when you say that you don't particularly want to sit in a stock that's forming a base, does that mean you would exit the position now and then if it rebuilds and maybe breaks above 80 you might get back in?

Kacher: I wouldn't exit here. It's easy to sell early—it's hard to sell late. Early would have been to sell—

Morales: —into the climax move at about 80 and into the wedge.

Kacher: Or you could easily have sold into the wedge in the mid-to-high-70s. Now, it's right at the 50-day. So I wouldn't be selling right here because you're at support and it might bounce. If it bounces up into the low-to-mid-70s, I'd probably be selling off the rest of my position.

How would you have handled JDS Uniphase?

Morales: JDSU came out of a narrow base and broke out at about 135, ran up very rapidly, and then you finally had one last day where you had the biggest one-day point move since the breakout. That's sort of like capitulation buying. So it's kind of like it works in reverse for selling. And then the stock picked up volume for three days in a row. And that stock, in our view, has topped. Now that doesn't mean it's dead and it's going to collapse to 40 or something like that. What it means is at best it's going to have to build a whole new base and set up again. At worst, it has topped and could go into a long-term decline, the severity of which you can't really gauge and we're not even going to try to.

Realizing that you do not own the stock, let's hypothetically say you did and let's say you bought it coming out of that October breakout there, around 68 or 69. Now let's just say you held onto the position and it formed that base in November and early-December and then it broke out again a couple of weeks

ago. Right now would you be tempted to just hang on to the thing and hope that it forms a base with say 150 or so as the low?

Morales: It depends on my cost basis.

Let's say you got in at around 69 or so and you have a pretty good profit.

Morales: At 69? You might try to hold it. Let's say I have a position at 69 on the breakout and I've ridden that thing all the way up. I would probably sell half of the position here, and then let the market tell me what to do with the rest of it. If it starts to come under severe distribution, and there's no rally, then maybe I'd lose it all. There's nothing wrong with making money. And that means nailing down profits. People shouldn't feel that they have to sit with everything forever. Now we know people who've owned Home Depot and Cisco for 10 years and of course they've had to sit through all of this. But they've been fortunate that they have a low cost basis. Buying right when the market turns and not hesitating on an O'Neil follow-through day (following a market sell-off of at least 10 percent, a session in which one or more of the big averages rises at least 1 percent on increased volume, and occurs on the fourth through tenth day of rally) is key because you have a low cost basis in most of your stocks and you can afford to maybe sit and watch a little bit here.

Kacher: Whether to hold is a very personal decision and has to do with your time frame. Some people like to have a very long-term orientation with the market and ride through these little corrections that we experience. With something like JDSU, it's had a series of little corrections all the way up from 20. So some fund managers might have gotten in very, very early and have held it the entire way and they're not going to be selling it here because they've got much longer horizons, and the company is a leader in its space. Other traders might have a little shorter-term orientation. Personally, had I bought it at 65 or 70, I would have already sold at least one-half of the position because the tone of the market has changed. We were in a nice up trend on the Nasdaq. The Nasdaq has broken that trend to the downside. That tells me the color of the market is different now. I don't want to have all my money on the table. I'd be taking at least half of it off, if not all of it.

Was there one particular day on the Nasdaq in January 2000 that you thought was the turning point?

Kacher: Tuesday, Jan. 4, 2000. If you looked at the S&P, the Dow, the Nasdaq, and the Internet index, they were all down huge. That's one of the signals. On April 13 or 14, 1999, the Nasdaq and the Internet indices got clobbered after these huge run-ups. I was looking for that kind of sign in this market. And Jan. 4's sell-off was that sign.

    Morales: And on Jan. 4, the other thing you saw was a number of the big leaders get clipped. Oracle was down 10 and Sun was down something like that. A lot of coincidental factors all occurring together kind of gave us a sign that we had to start selling. It doesn't necessarily mean that you run to cash right away. But you do start cutting back and you nail down some profits. We've been very fortunate and we sat through those questionable days when people were nervous in November and we got those powerful moves through December. When I look at where I stand right now, I'm pretty much back to where I was a week before the end of the year even after taking it on the chin just a little bit as I'm selling out of my positions here.

That's pretty significant, then.

Morales: For us, it is.

You're saying two or three days of losses took away a couple weeks of gains, then?

Morales: Yeah, but you were getting tremendous gains.

    Kacher: The nice thing about this style is that you can run your account up a few hundred percent in a good market and then give back maybe 10 percent of all those gains you've made. Basically, if you're quick to exit, you can hold on to the majority of your gains and just sit. Actually, the best thing right now—and this is what takes a lot of discipline on my part, which is what I fail to adhere to time and time again—is to stay out of the market. The tone has changed. The best thing I can do is to not trade until the market sets up again. But I can tell you right now I'm going to get my feet wet, put my toe in the water here and there, just because I like to feel that I'm still playing the market. But at least I will play it with very small positions. That way, if I am wrong, and I probably will be wrong in this topsy-turvy, choppy market we're going to be in, I won't get my head handed to me.

So that means that you might extend yourself up to 30 to 40 percent long instead of 100 to 200 percent long?

Kacher: Or I might go more like 10 percent long and 10 percent short, just kind of dabbling here and there. If I see something that looks good and I feel like I can scalp some profits, I might do that. It's really meaningless. I never make a killing when the market gets choppy like I feel it's going to. I find it's tough for me to short and make real money on the short side. That's not my forte by any means. So I try not to play hard.

Meanwhile, back at the ranch, Gil never finished his discussion on the three ways a stock can top.

Morales: I gave you an example of a climax top, which can be thought of like capitulation selling or capitulation buying. And that will be the final move in a stock. The other one is where you get wedging activity. In other words, the stock continues to move higher but your volume is declining. An example is Verity, which I bought on the breakout in September at around 26. It ran all the way up pretty rapidly to 60 or so. But you'll notice that as the stock was going to the 48 level up into that last final move up to 60, you had no volume. That stock is actually wedging up. I sold into that move up. I didn't get out at the top, but I saw that wedging and that was danger. And then of course the stock breaks once and makes one final attempt to rally to new highs which

Wedging Top: Verity (VRTY), Daily

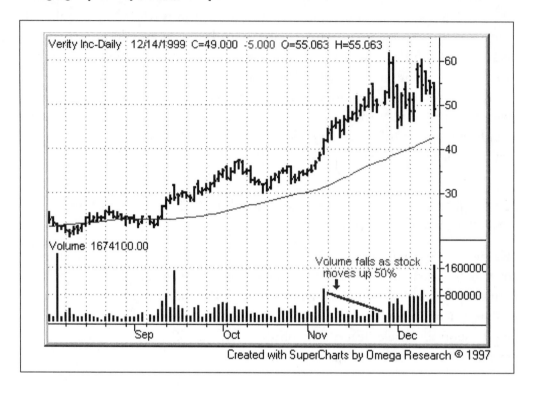

Verity Inc-Daily 12/14/1999 C=49.000 -5.000 O=55.063 H=55.063

Volume: 1674100.00

Volume falls as stock moves up 50%

Created with SuperCharts by Omega Research © 1997

you'll often see, and then it just blows apart and comes out with poor earnings and that's the end of it.

The third way stocks will top is a failed, late-stage breakout. A good example is Razorfish from December 2000. Here's a stock that broke out down around 20, ran up and then tried to set up again, and tried to break out again. It was very choppy and you'll even notice that the failed breakout occurred as the stock wedged up toward 50 late in December. There was no volume there. Once that thing starts to come back into its base it should be sold. So those are the three ways stocks will top and that's what we're looking for. It's tricky and I think people

Failed Breakout: Razorfish (RAZF), Daily

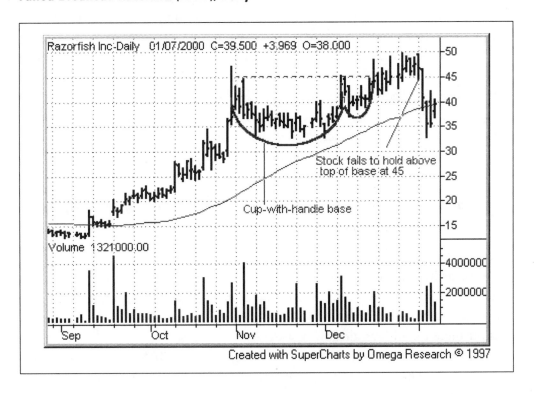

should study Bill's book, *How to Make Money in Stocks*, where he goes over every single one of his sell rules. I think his new book is a much more succinct and simpler explanation of how these things top. It's a good starting place.

And the new book is called what, Gil?

Morales: The new one is called *24 Essential Lessons for Investment Success.*

Actually, I have it right here on my desk.

Morales: A lot of people make the mistake of giving up on the market when in fact this is your time to be culling through and finding out where the new strength lies. To us, that's the beauty of corrections or bear markets—

Kacher: —to weed out the weaklings, essentially. Right now you can look at it as forming the left-hand side of cup-shaped bases. We're right in that process. The strongest stocks will form the left-hand side of that cup, but their cups aren't going to be quite so deep. They're going to be resistant to selling off and they're going to form these pretty-nice cups and it's going to be pretty obvious who the next leaders are going to be when the market turns back around.

When you say we're forming the left side of the cup, Chris, are you talking about looking at the Nasdaq Composite, in general?

Kacher: You can take a look at the market indices or individual stocks. A lot of these stocks have corrected 20 to 30 percent off their peaks. That is the left-hand side of the cup. Now we don't know how deep this cup is going to go. Some of the weaker names are going to be off more than that, especially if the market comes off more than it has already.

Morales: And right now you don't know for sure if in fact those are left sides of cups. They still have to form the right side. Some of those will just go into down trends.

Kacher: Right. Some of these stocks will not form cups at all. It's over for the real weak ones.

Let's talk about the short side for a second. What's interesting to me is how many people think shorting stocks is just as easy as going long. All you do, according to them, is just switch the parameters that you're looking for technically. My take on that is that shorting is many times more difficult because you're dealing with the emotion of fear, which is a much more extreme human emotion than, say, greed or hope. This means your timing on a short sale must be more precise.

Kacher: That's a good point, actually. Interestingly, you can see that to some degree on the chart. If you look at a chart right-side up and you look at the up trend, a lot of these up trends are pretty nice and have a normal rhythm to them. It doesn't take a whole lot to be able to sit in a position on these up trends. If you take a stock that's breaking down and you turn its chart over, you will actually see a cup as well, but it will be a lot more choppy. The volatility on a declining stock is much, much greater than the volatility of a stock that's in an up trend. That's kind of a general rule that you can actually see on the charts.

So wouldn't that make the timing of a short sale so much more critical, then, as opposed to the long side?

Kacher: Exactly. And you can also get whipped out of your position that much more easily. Because on the short side, when a stock drops, it will violently lurch back up, shaking you out of your position.

Morales: Our studies show that the optimal time to be shorting is three to four months after a stock has topped. This is precisely what Chris is talking about. If you take a stock that's gone into a decline, and you flip the chart upside down so that now it's like you're looking at the chart in reverse, a lot of times these things make these upside-down, cup-and-handle patterns. It may take three to four months to form that whole pattern. And that's generally when the optimal time to short is. Generally, the type of pattern we look for is a stock that has topped, based on the three criteria that I mentioned earlier. Once a stock has topped, it will go through the 50-day moving average on huge volume, and then you'll get kind of a wedging rally, in other words a rally where the volume is declining on the way up, back up to or through the 50-day moving average. Then when that stock goes back through the 50-day moving average on volume . . . that's your shorting point.

So that's the way we would short. But the market goes up a lot more than it goes down. I've never made much money shorting and neither has Bill O'Neil. And he's been in the market 45 years. Bill will tell you he's never made big money shorting for the simple reason that it's easy to get run in. And it's much more violent to the downside. The trends are more violent and volatile and you can get shaken out. You can study any stock that's been in a prolonged downtrend: You get these violent rallies and they'll run the stock right up your nose and you've got to be covered.

If you look at Razorfish, it gave us all the topping signs we look for, up in the 45–50 area. Then the stock broke the 50-day, down to 35, goes through 35, finds support, then rallies back up to the 50-day, then reverses on huge volume. So as soon as that stock reversed back to the 50-day today, you could have shorted that stock. That's a good example of how shorting should be done. But, again, I don't really recommend it as a way to try and make big money in the market because it's just too difficult.

Kacher: There's another problem with shorting some of these stocks, especially some of the thinner ones like Razorfish. Let's say you try to get on board a short position at 42 when it was topping. Well, because of the uptick rule, whereby you can only short on an uptick, you might not get that uptick until 39, 3 points from where you initially saw it. Often when a stock does uptick, it'll run 2 or 3 points beyond where you've shorted it. Now you're 2 or 3 points in the hole and that can scare you right out of the position. So in five minutes you can already be down a few percent and get scared out. In fact, some of my shortest plays in the market have been on short positions.

Morales: Some of my biggest and fastest losses have been on the short side! I don't think I've ever lost big money faster than when I tried to short CNET back in April 1999. I remember that. I shorted the stock, walked away from my desk, came back 20 minutes later, and the thing was 22 points up on me.

Whoaaa.

Morales: So that's what can happen.

Kacher: There might be some people out there that are really good on the short side. I'm sure there are people that are consistently good. But shorting is a totally different animal. I think that when you're playing the markets your personality is oriented a certain way—toward either being really good on the long side or really good on the short side or playing the market on a short-term level or a long-term level. It all has to do with your personality. To be able to change your personality is like trying to change the color of your eyes—it's a very difficult thing to do. So to be able to switch gears from going long to all of a sudden going short . . . unless you're a really short-term trader and you're doing all of these daytrades, I think it's pretty tough to do for most people.

Morales: Even then, it's not very much and it's not worth the trouble. You go through 50 bottles of Tums and Rolaids, and what's the point? For 10 or 20 percent? I'd rather go to cash, study my mistakes from the previous up cycle, and be ready to go when that market turns.

Generally, when we get an important intermediate bottom, such as we saw in October 1999, and a powerful advance follows with great leadership and potent volume, the first pullback is a pullback that can be bought, though this shouldn't be done blindly, of course. Is that the way you see this?

Morales: If you have a stock that's acting well and has strong fundamentals and has pulled back to what looks like a logical point and it's not undergoing huge distribution, maybe you could add to your position, say on a move down to the 50-day. In general, when we get this type of action, we just have to become very defensive. Especially, when people make as much money as they've made, you want to keep that. So that's primarily what we're concerned about at this point, keeping what we've made.

Kacher: Again, we're seeing a lot of leaders coming down very fast from their peaks. Whenever we see that kind of action across the board in top-quality names, that's a serious caution flag. You had better be at least off margin in this kind of market environment otherwise you can get your head handed to you. A lot of these big leaders are already 15 to 20 percent off their highs. So if you're on margin, you double that loss off your peak, which is devastating. You don't want to get into that position. If you run your account up quite a bit, you have a lot more cushion. But the whole idea is to give back as little as possible.

Morales: Your question is related to duration. In other words, we're only about 12 weeks out from the follow-through day. You're saying is this about the right duration to go through an initial short- or intermediate-term correction? In most cases, yes. Right now, all we can say is that we're certain we're in a short- to intermediate-term correction. It could be a broader top, but—

Kacher: —the markets are actually a lot faster today than they've ever been before. So the cycles are compressed.

Morales: Right. And maybe they are. And given the fact that they could be compressed, you can't get into the business of telling the market what to do.

Kacher: You've just got to look at the averages and the leaders and they're going to tell you what to do—when to get out and when to get back in.

Morales: Also, if you've been in the market for a period of time, you can get a sense of what the market's going to give you, going from bull market to bull market. How much can these things go up? One way that we can gauge a move in a stock is to look at the P/E ratio expansion. Our studies show that the average P/E expansion is 120 to 130 percent. So we're looking at the P/E ratios of the leaders when the big averages staged their most recent follow-through, in this case on Oct. 28, 1999. What were those ratios and what have they expanded to today? Some of them are even greater than 130 percent—200 percent, 250 percent, and more. But once we're at that number, we're starting to ask ourselves how much further can this really go. Also, we're mindful of the fact that our objective is to make money and keep it.

And again, Bill will tell you this: There's nothing wrong with taking profits. You're either going to sell too early or too late. Accept that. You're not going to get everything the market gives you, but you can get a good chunk of that and you should be grateful for that. We certainly are.

Kacher: Trading the markets is very Zen activity. Gil and I always talk about that, just in having the right mental balance that will give you the right balance on when to sell and when to buy. The whole thing is you don't want to sell too early in the run-up and you don't want to sell too late after the market has peaked. It's like walking a tightrope. And you've got to have a lot of concentration and focus and you don't want to let your emotions get involved because then you're not focused anymore. These markets are so sharp and so much more volatile than they've ever been, that timing and your window of opportunity to get in or get out of the market is so much shorter than it's ever been.

The optimal window of opportunity to get out of this market was about a day, maybe a couple of days. You can catch the bounces if you don't get out on the first day; the market will rally back and there will be some more exit points. But if you wait, say a week, your account could be devastated. This was exemplified by April 1999, when in one week the averages came unglued by 20 percent or something. If you were in some of the highflying Internet stocks, some of those things were off 40 percent from their peak—in one week.

So it's really critical that you've got day-to-day focus on the market and you don't get carried away by your profits. Ego is another problem. Ego can be devastating. I firmly believe that if you have an ego when you're trading the markets, you will potentially give back what you've made. Ego will keep you in when you're supposed to get out.

Morales: Make sure you're operating with a system that has a set of rules. You operate on that so that you're outside of your own head and outside of your own emotions. I saw a lot of people get very ebullient in the last week or so going into the end of 1999. There was a lot of euphoria. Everybody was talking about quitting their jobs. In fact I went to the doctor on Jan. 3 and he even told me he was thinking about quitting his practice and daytrading. And I thought "Oh boy, we're in trouble now." And sure enough, the next day was the top.

When you feel like you're God and you can print money on demand, that's probably the time to be selling.

It's been real. Thanks for your time.

KEVIN HAGGERTY

TRADING WITH THE GENERALS

By Laurence A. Connors

When the evening news tells you why the big rally or drop occurred in the stock market today, that's one thing. When trader Kevin Haggerty tells you, that's another thing altogether.

As senior vice president and manager of equity trading at Fidelity Capital Markets (a division of Fidelity Investments) from 1990 to 1997, Haggerty had a close-up view of how things really work on Wall Street. In charge of U.S. institutional equity trading, he oversaw trading operations and accounted for a significant percentage of the company's volume on the New York Stock Exchange on a given day.

His unique insight on trading is the direct product of this quarter-century career on the institutional side of the stock market, through which he gained a subtle understanding of the way institutional traders, specialists, program traders, and other market forces shape price action.

One of the most interesting aspects of his story is that he has used his understanding of longer-term position trading strategies as the basis of a short-term stock trading approach he now uses to manage his own money.

Haggerty got into trading as a stockbroker in the early 1970s after a short stint in banking. He began hanging out in his firm's trading department, where he was exposed to various hedging techniques—long convertible bonds and short stock, long warrants and short stock, etc.—designed to make money regardless of whether the market was up or down.

Such a multi-dimensional approach made sense to Haggerty, who began using these techniques with a great deal of success. They were especially appealing when the stock market was bottoming in 1974. He moved on to a number of other equity and convertible trading positions on the Street, as well as exchange board positions and his successful stint at Fidelity, the fund colossus of the 1990s.

One of the greatest advantages of his career path was that he was exposed to a wide variety of ideas and was able to become intimately familiar with the strategies and tactics of institutional portfolio managers and traders—how they put trades on and took them off, common patterns they reacted to, and the kinds of opportunities they looked to exploit in the markets—information that would prove invaluable when he began developing and trading shorter-term strategies.

Beyond all of this, he is also the father of two sons who have played in the National Hockey League.

Haggerty trades fast and talks even faster. His enthusiasm for the market is obvious, and there isn't an aspect of his profession that he doesn't seem familiar with or hold an opinion on.

Larry Connors: How would you describe your general approach to short-term stock trading?

Kevin Haggerty: You develop your skills over the years. I started looking at short-term techniques from day one. I've been a position trader my whole life, working large orders on the institutional level. You get to see what a multitude of accounts are doing, how they do it, and you get the opportunity to try these things yourself. It soon becomes apparent that in order to be successful, you have to understand short-term trading techniques to be able to maneuver in and out of the market.

I like to work from the long side, for the most part, although I have strategies to play the short side, mostly using options. I stay in the most active names . . . it doesn't matter if they're big-cap or small-cap. I just want to make sure I'm in an area I know the institutions are going to be interested in.

I also pay close attention to volume. In stocks, you'll definitely see volume precede price. I want to see a trade break out with no news rather than news. I want the breakout to occur, then have news follow . . . that's the better trade. If a stock has been going down, then stops, and volume builds up, I'll put it on my watch list. The stock may have reached a tradeable level.

I trade a lot of pullbacks off the opening move, or any other intraday patterns—congestion patterns, and so forth—that give me low-risk entry points when I see market dynamics pointing in a certain direction.

How did your short-term trading approach grow out of your institutional background?

The edge I've gotten from being in the institutional side of the business for so long is to understand the dynamics of individual stocks and recognize what's "real" buying or selling and what's not . . . when a price move has something backing it up and when it doesn't.

There are a lot of practical things that average investors don't understand about institutional trading. For example, the institutions won't admit it, but they are very technical and many are momentum-oriented. They'll try to break stocks out of patterns and accelerate the stock to higher levels. They're not supposed to be "traders," but sometimes it's part of the overall process to beat the S&P 500 . . . or it might simply be the style of a particular money manager. The specialists and floor traders are aware of technical levels and patterns, too.

Another example is when analysts at big firms put out recommendations on stocks based on technical developments. If a traditionally popular stock has been in a slump for a while, but has recently made a move back above, say, its 50-day moving average, an analyst might put out a "buy" on it. It's a good gamble for them to take, because if the market does run up at that point they look like geniuses, and the fact that it's a big-name stock that institutions traditionally like to hold puts the odds in their favor, too.

How do you try to take advantage of this kind of behavior?

It's a matter of aligning yourself with what the major market forces are doing and finding a pattern that gets you in with a defined risk. Big institutions can't hide—you can always hear an elephant coming—and what they do results in some fairly easy-to-spot patterns.

Say a stock only opens down slightly on a big, down opening and holds its ground in the face of heavy selling in the overall market. There's a reason for this—somebody has to be holding up this stock. So I'll go long when the stock gives an indication it's ready to take off to the upside . . . when it makes a move back above the opening, for example. Those can be great trades.

Another example is if a market-leading stock opens up much lower, but on very light volume . . . what I like to call a "trap door" scenario. The light volume tips you off that the selling isn't for real. Institutions often look at this as an opportunity to pick up shares at a lower price or run up a stock, and the turnarounds in these situations can be explosive.

It's apparent there's a strong discretionary element to your trading. If you're trading a pullback situation, for example, where do you look to enter your trade?

I don't have set points or rules. I'll take a shot at any point in the pullback if I see the dynamics pointing in my direction—larger bids and a series of new highs, for example. If a strong stock pulls back, I don't care if it's a four-day move or a one-day move . . . when the dynamics change and that stock moves above its previous high, I want to be there. The specific pattern, or entry point for that matter, isn't important, as long as it indicates a shift in the stock. The only thing I won't touch is a strong gap move.

What's the most important lesson you've taken out of the markets in the last 25 years?

Without question, risk management. It doesn't matter if your other trading skills are great or so-so. If you don't manage your positions correctly, you'll never make it. Everybody talks about risk management, but sometimes it's difficult to know exactly where they're coming from.

In my case, it's simple: I shoot for a 2:1 reward/risk ratio on every trade and I never take a position home overnight unless I'm protected by options. I almost always limit my risk to three-eighths of a point or less on an intraday trade.

Why don't you like to hold positions overnight?

There is too much manipulation in the market these days to go home na-ked . . . too many out-of-proportion responses to news items. There's no advantage to exposing yourself to the kinds of two- or three-day swings that are common now. It's unnecessary.

I learned my lesson a long time ago: You never know what's going to happen overnight. Early in my career I was short a stock that kept rising even though the rest of the stocks in its group were going down. I held it one day after another, and it kept gapping up until I finally covered with a significant loss. To make a long story short, the reason the stock was rising was because of a stock-loan fraud case involving a buy-in. But it didn't matter that the reason for the move wasn't legitimate. I still lost money. From then on, price action alone was my idol.

How do you reconcile your recognition of the high degree of volatility in the market with the tight stops you use?

A big part of my strategy is being able to take many trades on a given day and get in and out of positions quickly. Getting stopped out doesn't bother me. I can get right back in when the market moves through that stop level again in the opposite direction. I'll still have two or three more chances to trade throughout the day.

The point is to not let the losers be the big trades. If I get a quick half-point or 5/8-point gain on a trade, I'll take profits on half my position and follow up on the rest of the position with a trailing stop.

But I'll get out of a trade almost immediately if it doesn't go in my direction right away and the dynamics of the market change. If I'm long and a bid disappears or a size offer comes in, I get out . . . sometimes I can break even on the trade.

Basically, you like to stress that you cannot be successful without money management. Can we talk a little about that?

Sure, this is key, especially with the volatility in the marketplace. Regardless of how long you've been trading, it's very difficult to adhere to that discipline of cutting your losses short. You try to do it, and a stock looks like it's only going to tick down 1/8. All of a sudden, it's off of there and you miss your stops.

To avoid that, I put my sell stops in at the levels that equate to the volatility of the stock, and go from there. But I also do not wait for the stop to get hit. I let the market dynamics take me out of a trade. Say I've got a 3/8 stop in a $50-$60 stock, and that stock has done nothing in a short period of time. All of a sudden it becomes offered, and if I see some down ticks on the NYSE ticks, and it looks like the up volume/down volume and the overall market dynamics are starting to fade a little bit, I'll scratch that trade, down 1/8 or maybe flat if I'm lucky. But I will not wait. I'll cancel my order and cancel my stop if I see the market dynamics change.

So you're being proactive throughout the trade?

I am, because if I go in saying that the market has to prove me right, then I have to really stick to that discipline on the way out. As soon as that trade turns on me, why should I give the market 3/8 or 1/2 or 1/4? That's my feeling on it.

Now one of the things we were talking about recently was that you got a chance to see people who are new to trading make the same mistakes over and over again. And that is where they are maybe risking 2 to 3 points on a trade or maybe are just afraid to pull the trigger to get out of a trade when it goes against them.

Good point. That is the most common thing. I run a trading office, so I have a dynamic updating on everyone's trades that come through as each trade is taken. I've learned more about trading just by watching the results and how people buy and sell and how they actually enter and exit the trades. And what I see happen with a lot of new traders is they really don't get in and trade certain patterns or inflection points, or trade with discipline.

A lot of them will get in when they see something up 2 to 3 points . . . they'll jump in and try to play that trade. And of course, as happens often, you see the momentum, and all of a sudden it's not there anymore. Unfortunately a lot of the time the new traders are in over-the-counter stocks . . . Internet stocks or something similar. These are situations where there is no depth on the bid or the offer, depending on whether they are long or short. So there might be an inside bid of, say 1/8, and below that there may be a 3/8 or a 1-point spread market. So by the time they are able to hit that button and get out, they're already down 1/2 or 5/8 just based on their original trade. Coupled with a little momentum, you're down 1 point or 3/4 of a point before you even react. I just think those are the wrong stocks for beginners, or for any kind of trader.

You have to define your losses based on the amount of money that you've decided that you can risk in the business. Let's say I'm working with a new trader who has $50,000 in capital. I like to tell the trader something like this: "Okay, make the commitment. What have you committed to buy this business that you're willing to lose should that happen?" And they might say, "I'm willing to lose 20 percent of that." A reasonably new trader, learning what they should be doing once they get live, is saying, "Look, I need at least 50 or 60 trades." Well, I'll say, "Are you going to lose 50 in a row?" They'll say, "No way, based on what I've done in my pre-trading plans, paper trading, and trading with a small amount of shares." They say, "No, my ratio is good."

So I tell them fine, we don't know how the loss trigger is going to work, but at least their stock picking has reached a reasonable level. So what you do is divide 50 trades into the $10,000 that they've committed to the business. That tells you they can lose $200 per trade, or whatever the number happens to be. And then they decide whether they are going to trade 200 shares and risk 1 point or trade 400 shares and risk 1/2 point.

So any way you combine it, it still comes down in my mind to a money stop. But the commitment has to be there to say "I am going to invest this amount of money in this business." It doesn't mean you have to lose it. And that's not the $50,000 capital or whatever capital you put up to support the trades. But you do have to make a financial commitment and you have to be willing over time to trade that. That's risk-taking, and that's one of the reasons why Goldman Sachs is one of the best traders in the business. There are going to be peaks and troughs, but over time, their risk-taking is going to make money.

So, you know, trading runs in cycles and you want to be consistent with your money management and the volatility in the stocks that you choose. And there's nothing wrong with choosing a volatile stock, in conjunction with how much you've committed to the business versus your total capital . . .

You just have to trade fewer shares of a more volatile stock.

Exactly right.

One of the popular money-management theories, at least in the futures markets—and you don't see this in the stock market and I'm going to ask you why—is where you risk 1 to 2 percent per trade. For instance, you'll see someone with a $100,000 account risk $1,000 per trade or maybe $2,000 per trade. But you don't see this method of risk management as much in the equity markets.

No, you don't. You know I think, Larry, part of it has to do with the fact that you don't want to risk $1,000 per trade, 2 percent of your $50,000 in capital. I don't know that that makes a whole lot of sense. But I think people have to adjust their size according to their experience, which is really a better way to do it. I think in the equities business everyone gravitates toward money stops and then adjusts the size according to the amount of money and the amount of shares, versus how much money you can lose.

One of your beliefs about successful trading is that you have to be inside the mind of a large money manager and that you want to be trading in the same direction as the large money managers. One of the things that you use to guide you in your trading is the moving average—the 200-day and the 50-day moving averages. Why are those so important for traders to focus on?

First of all, there have been many tests psychologically and historically that have proven that the 200-day and the 50-day moving averages are two of the best things out there. The institutions are very cognizant of the 200-day and 50-day, especially when they add to positions. What usually happens is that when a stock pulls back to its 200-day, usually it's a stock that has had a good run and the 200-day is a 30-to-40-percent retracement of the run. For some reason the institutions will come in and add to positions at these levels. These are also the levels where the brokerage firms and analysts like to come in and say, "this is a reasonable support level." Then if a stock starts to base a little bit, it's a good point for them to come in and reinvent the wheel and re-recommend the stock. You know, somebody comes in and makes the comment that they're going to make a new widget, or whatever. And the 200-day or 50-day moving average is a good level for it.

Let's talk about the ways that you use the 200-day moving average. You've talked about it when a stock is pulling back to the average. What if it is crossing the 200-day moving average after a sustained downturn?

I call it a cross and a re-cross. The trade I like is when a stock comes from down below the 200-day moving average. Usually, it will back off, go back down below it, then re-cross again. But what usually happens is you get a base period. And the breakout from that base period just at, or above or below, the 200-day is usually a very powerful move.

So far we've discussed tight money management, that you want to have a limited amount of money you're willing to risk on a per-trade basis. We've also discussed that you want to be trading in the direction of the trend. Do you like to see the stock trading above both the 200-day and the 50-day average?

Absolutely, because I think you have a much better edge by staying in strongly trending stocks with high relative strength and where the +DMI component of the ADX indicator is above the –DMI component.

How does volume play into this whole thing?

Volume gives away the buyers. It gives away how aggressive they are. There are also many good trades where you can get in without monster volume coming in, usually out of consolidation. Sometimes they start that way without breaking out of a wide-range bar or a thrust or a runaway move. They'll sneak out of there for a couple days and give you entry.

Another noticeable thing about volume is when you get some narrow-range bars and the stock is not going down. The volume is increasing and you see the thrusts getting smaller and smaller, the bars getting narrower. Volume increases and usually that *portends a change in direction*. The same thing happens on the upside. Someone recently mentioned that they mostly hear me talk about longs. Well, you know, in a bull market you don't run around in shorts. But the reality is you can short these things every day when you get a change. Usually volume will precede price on both ends.

You're not advocating that people avoid shorting stocks. You're saying in a bull market you want to try to be more long than short.

Absolutely. The motors . . . let me give you some examples. Recently, General Motors and Ford both broke down below their 200-day moving averages, looked awful, and were excellent shorts—declining 200-day, declining 50-day. But lo and behold, they've turned around, they've run right back up over the 200-day again, and are no longer great shorts. So you've got to be very careful in a bull market. There are a lot of institutions, hedge funds, and momentum players that spend a lot of money studying liquidity factors of sectors to squeeze. From a daytrading standpoint, you don't have a problem. From an overnight standpoint, a naked short on a stock, regardless of how bad it looks in a bull market, can be difficult, obviously.

Do you find that most of your intraday trades are above or below the highs of the day, or do you feel that it doesn't make a difference? Do you want to enter above yesterday's high on the long side?

Good question. On the long side, if you've selected a trade from the prior day's daily charts, most of those entries are above the prior day's high. Or if it is a gap opening—say, for instance, yesterday's high was 50 and today the stock opened at 50 3/4, pulls back and holds at the 50 level or somewhere just above it—that's good entry above the prior day's high at 50. And also if the stock opens the other way around, if it opens below 50 but trades back up through 50, you're going to enter 1/8 above the prior night's close. That's assuming it's a daily chart, trading-plan entry.

And that's not much different than what Jeff Cooper has discussed in his books. I know that (TradingMarkets.com Director of Research) Dave Landry is also looking for a stock to take out the prior day's high for longs or prior day's low for shorts.

Absolutely. On the daily bars for sure. I'm always looking for early entry, but there are also a lot of head fakes—especially with this volatility—similar to the search-and-destroy missions futures traders run on the opening range. So you see a lot of head fakes early in the morning in stocks above their prior night's close, high, and low.

So the second entries above those highs and lows usually prove to be the best entries. I love the pullback trade because you don't have as much competition: This is where it opens above, pulls back down, and then comes back up. Or else you get in, you get stopped out down 3/8, a 1/4, whatever your number is, and you re-enter the second time. Then the head fake is out of the way, at least in the listed stocks, and you have a very, very good probability on the second entry, assuming the dynamics on both the market and the stock are good.

After doing your nightly chart work with your relative strength screens, explosion lists, pullback lists, etc., how many names will you ultimately focus on as target stocks for the following day? It would appear that you're looking at 150-plus charts a night. Also do you set alarms on those stocks throughout the day or do you just continually scroll your five-minute charts? How many trades will you average on any given day and how many positions will you carry at one time, intraday?

Well, in answer to the question on the number of positions, on a strongly trending day you want to take advantage of as many of the entries as you can get and that you can handle from a capital standpoint. You're right; I'll look at more than 150 charts. I segregate the charts and pre-screen them according to volume and take those that have traded the most volume. Then I'll take those stocks that closed above the mid-point or in the top of the range. I'll go through each chart individually and take the ones that have the best setups. And then I relate those to relative strength and to what their group is. And after you start going through them every night, you know exactly which are the strong groups and which aren't.

One of the things you and I were talking about yesterday was getting familiar with a stock. You tend to trade the same names over and over. I know General Electric is one of your favorites. Talk about that. It's getting to know the personality of a stock.

It is. I think one way you can trade, especially starting out, is to pick four or five stocks in the different industries, like GE, a multi-industry stock. And pick a bank, pick a tech, pick a financial, and what have you, and get to know the character of those stocks, because certain specialists will trade certain stocks in certain ways.

One quick aside, EMC happens to be a stock that is not as much fun now that it has split . . . they never are. An EMC specialist likes to open that stock as the last possible stock on the New York Stock Exchange. He takes advantage of every little bit of information that he can get . . . you know, on the tape, whether the S&P is really up or whether it's going to fade. What you'll see with EMC is that the S&P 500 and the futures are up, and all of a sudden they start to fade. And then EMC suddenly pops up and it opens up 2 points. Well that stock will never see above that opening level again because I just happen to know how that specific specialist trades EMC. So I'm very comfortable when I get an indication or get word that it is going to be opened up, to fade EMC on the opening. In other words, if that stock gaps up, I'll sell stock if I see the market deteriorating right in front of me. If it gaps down, I'll buy stock if I see the market improving. That's the character of the stock.

And General Electric, it's a *classic* trader. If anybody is into geometric, or Fibonacci or 50 percent retracements, the stock is a *classic* stock that trades by the numbers. And the good thing about it is that it's got a good range, you know 3 to 4 points a day. But it is also a $100 stock that can explode when they want to mark it up and the programs kick in. Yet it trades at a teeny (1/16) or 1/8-point spread. Sensational stock.

The only way to get to know the personality of a stock, though, is to trade it over and over and over again. And on the other side, I'm sure you have stocks that—we all do—that you're just *not* going to trade. There's just no way you're going to make money in those stocks. They just don't trade the way that they should, or at least the way that you think they should.

(*Chuckles*) I've got a few of those.

So it's about becoming comfortable with those stocks that have been good to you and just staying with those stocks until proven otherwise.

That's correct.

This question comes into the TradingMarkets.com office a lot. I don't know if there is a right answer to this but let's try to attack it. What is the best time to purchase stock at the opening? Should orders be placed prior to the opening?

As long as I've been in the institutional business, and trading now, and in different ways, I've never made money before the opening or at the opening. There's always an exception, but I very rarely do it. I don't think I've made three trades in the last two years outside of regular trading hours.

So you don't have a resting order to be there on the opening. Is that correct?

That's correct. Unless I have a position-trade in and I'm trying to get out of it for some reason.

So even if stocks are going up, you'd still advise to let these stocks open up and see where they settle before you enter.

Absolutely, because you'll have lots of choices. Stocks all come back sooner or later, but there are always other choices . . . you always have another selection. The only time I'll put it in at the opening is if I want to fade the opening. I have a Trac Data quote machine. So on Trac Data I hit a certain thing and it tells me all the stocks that are being indicated opening up above the limits or with an order imbalance on one side, either the buy side or the sell side. So then I can make a decision whether I want to sell stock on the opening—fade that opening—or buy stock if it looks like it's going to be a real down opening. Those are the times that I will trade the opening to fade it. And you have to put a market order in to sell short at the market or buy at the market because you're not entitled to stock with a limit order on the openings.

But you're fading the opening moves. If it indicates 5 points higher, you're not looking to buy it, you're looking to short that stock.

Absolutely. If it's a big gap down opening I want to buy it and vice versa.

What do you use intraday to keep you in the trend? And what do you do to recognize that there has been a change in the trend and that you need to get out?

I keep a little, simple market table and I update it every 15 or 20 minutes—or less, if in fact it's a real dead day and nothing is really changing.

What market table are you referring to?

The market table is just a little tool that takes a look at the futures, the S&P 500 cash and the New York Stock Exchange ticks, which is the difference between the number of stocks advancing and the number of stocks declining—the up ticks minus the down ticks. And then I'm looking at the up volume and the down volume to see how that changes.

Up volume/down volume can be especially helpful when used with the NYSE ticks. For instance, say the NYSE ticks suddenly go from plus 200 to minus 400, and I see that up volume stays the same while down volume changes by 10 million. And then all of a sudden those stocks are rallying back and I know what the premium was—the difference between the futures and the S&P 500 cash—because I have that right on the screen. Well now I know where the programs are or where somebody is operating at a certain level, and that helps me for the rest of the day!

I'm also looking at the difference between advancers and declines, and I'm looking at the sectors. In other words, if I've got the averages up and I just see the futures moving and the S&P 500 cash is really not moving and most of the sectors are red (down) on the screen, that tells me that this is just some funny money out there playing games in the futures trying to get something going or maybe some of the allocation programs doing something.

But really your best long trades are in up markets and vice versa. So there-fore, when you look at the dynamics, those are the times where you are going to get stocks that explode out of patterns, especially going back above the opening or out of a consolidation. Everything on full-bore together is what makes a good trade.

On neutral days, nontrending days, those are days that can get you into trouble and you have to cut your profit parameters in half. On these days, stocks just take out the highs and the lows in a narrow range. But those are also the days where you really get to do well in a stock like GE or some stock that you really understand. You understand how it reacts to programs and how it moves when certain buyers and sellers are in there.

Looking at a bar chart, a higher low would be when the current bar's low is higher than the previous bar's low. A lower high would be when the current bar's high is lower than the previous bar's high. What do you think of playing off higher lows for longs and lower highs for shorts as the main criteria for a play, both daily and intraday? Do you use that as a criterion?

Oh, absolutely. Price bars relate to each other. The strongest thing that can hap-pen is that on the first day a stock closes in the top end of the range after open-ing in the bottom. And then the second day is another up day with a higher low and a higher high and also the low is above the high of the prior day on increas-ing volume. That's the strongest thing that can happen in any market when you are looking at a bar and then from there it goes to a little different level.

Let's also reverse it and say you had the higher high and the higher low and then it closed *below* the open. Well that wouldn't tell me a whole lot. That does-n't confirm anything. I always want to see the close above the open in addition to having the higher high and higher low, and vice versa for sells.

And you'd like to see some increasing volume with the higher high?

Most of the time . . . we're assuming reasonably liquid stocks now. It's a different game when you get into the mid-cap and the small-cap stocks that don't trade.

But institutions—and you can trust me on this one—they're not going to reach in price unless they can get volume. Sometimes there is someone out there—some momentum player or what have you—that is trying to get the stock to a level to see how far they can take it. But in the normal course of business, when the mutual funds and the money managers are buying, they won't reach for size unless they can get volume. So volume becomes paramount when I look at expansion of range.

Is it more bullish if the bid size is larger than the ask size over the course of a day? And conversely, while in a short, would a larger ask size over bid size be more profitable?

Definitely. If I'm short, I want to see a larger ask size. If I'm the person that's long, I want to see a larger bid size. Absolutely. Where the stock is trading is also important. If you are a buyer or if you're looking to buy, it's very bullish when a stock trades at the mid-point and on the offered side if that is where most of the volume is. And vice versa on the sell side—that stock is weak if it is trading below the mid-point and on the bid side. And if you are watching these, you're going to see that dynamics change right in front of you immediately, as soon as it happens. Because what does happen is an institution can scale down if they are the only player in the game. If the market is a little weak and the institution is a buyer, you won't see that institution. They'll be down there doing what they call a volume weighted average price, scaling down a little bit at each price, a little bit every 15, 20 minutes—and nobody really sees them. And vice versa going the other direction.

But if the market firms up a little bit and things are looking pretty good and everyone's getting a little excited, other buyers show up and now they've got to compete with each other and they can't scale down. Now they're getting aggressive, they're telling their brokers on the floor, I have to be there, I have to be part of that volume, you better protect me on the book. And all of a sudden the broker has to put a bid for 10, 15, 20, 50,000 on there because he's in competition with other buyers. Those are the stocks that *we're* looking for because that's when we notice that the Generals (large institutional investors) are there. And we want stocks where buyers are competing with each other—or vice versa, sellers are competing. And if that's the case and the programs and the accelerators such as the front-runners and the hedge funds and all of the rest that try to get in there in front of size kick in, those are the stocks that make the best moves.

So tying this together, you have a strongly trending stock and all of a sudden you're seeing that the bid has been increasing throughout the day. You also see that volume is beginning to pick up and that the stock is beginning to uptick. It's probably a safe bet that there is a pretty low-risk trade there. You put your stop in there right under the bid and see where they take it.

Absolutely. We have several traders I know at our firm who, before they split the eighth, would do that with the program traders. And I know one or two of them that were extremely successful with it, you know reading, anticipating the tape, good overall market, good buyers in there, the futures moving, knowing full well the buy programs would kick in, who just made a living scalping—trading eighths and quarters—which is a very difficult way to do it. They were very good at it. But you can't do it now that you're able to split the eighth—with the market a teenie spread it is very difficult, and that's not the way that I suggest that one should trade . . .

No, no . . .

But those are the dynamics they are looking at. It's very difficult to do.

There is a daytrading book out there that a hedge fund manager wrote that basically discusses his trading for sixteenths and eighths and things like that. It is a tough way to make a living.

You can't last for too long doing it. If you last for two weeks, you're lucky.

I won't mention the name of the book, but the reviews from the readers of the book on Amazon.com just shredded this guy. I mean people were getting hurt pretty badly by it. It takes a while, but you get chewed up.

You know Larry, my answer to that is that it is very difficult to scalp when you compete with the people on the floor. You trade futures.

Yes and you hear a lot about the guys who were successful floor traders in the futures who can't make a living when they come off the floor or they just don't do as well.

Same thing I think in the equities. There are floor brokers down there and there are registered traders on the floor with open wires and hand-held devices. So if you're a regular daytrader sitting upstairs, utilizing the normal tools—Trac Datas and Signal and everything else—you don't have that flow, you're not looking into the specialists' eyes. You don't know whether it is a double-yellow ticket. A double-yellow ticket on the floor of the stock exchange means the specialist is buying or selling it. You're not looking into the eyes of four or five floor brokers and seeing they are all anxiously waiting to buy or sell stock. Unless you are talking directly to the floor and have that communication line open, you can't make those kinds of trades.

But sitting up top, it's very nice to sit back and be able to look at it and just get on board when something's going through an inflection point with buying pressure if you are buying . . . or vice versa if you are selling and the direction has switched. And you can recognize that and you don't have to be on the floor. Now, that can change dramatically in a second—somebody walks into a crowd with a new order—but you know, that's the game, that's trading. And I try to reserve all the trades for those types of situations. I want to be able to look at it and say, yes, that has changed direction. Or maybe it's made three or four higher lows or a pullback with closes all between the mid-point and the high. Each time I would sit there and say "okay, I don't care what they do, as soon as it trades over the high of the low day, that's it, I'm in, dynamics all being equal."

One of the other things I wanted to talk with you about is program trading. How do you use program numbers and fair value? How does program trading apply to daytrading?

Program trading or fair value numbers are different because a lot of different firms have different costs of money. One good site to look at is, of course, the Chicago Mercantile Exchange, at www.cme.com. They have information there on what program trading is and how it affects the market. The levels that we use are at the mid-point of people that pay commissions and people that don't pay commissions, and are based on the cost of money. So our numbers are right in the middle. And what I do with them is I look at them with NYSE ticks—I'm always looking at the NYSE ticks—and that gives away the program trading. I'm also looking at the up volume/down volume.

There is nothing you can do to apply program trading to your daytrading, specifically. But what I do is, let's say, for instance, a sell program comes in. How do I know? The NYSE tick will all of a sudden go negative or drop dramatically. It will fall real quick by 300, 400, 500 ticks, depending on the size of the program. Now when I see the ticks starting to go negative, relative to what they were, I immediately look at the S&P 500 cash index. Because if it's just a program and the buyers are real strong out there, and the S&P cash doesn't really go down that much and doesn't really move or follow it, I know it's just a program.

If it is a $10 million program or a $15 million program—somewhere between $10 and $20 million—stocks like GE will all drop 3/8, 1/4, 1/2, real quick. If I look at the sectors and see that they're mostly green, I make the determination that the overall market is strong

If I make the determination that the overall market is strong because I'm looking at the sectors, and they're mostly green—in other words, everything else is there, it's just a program—that's when I try to buy stock. I try to *fade the programs*: If it is a sell program I'll buy stock on a pullback. And vice versa, if there is a buy program and a tape that is not so good, I'll try to sell some stock—under the guidelines of what my trading plans looked at and if I was trying to get a short off. And that's how I'll utilize it.

And what will happen is every day the programs will come in at different numbers. Sometimes when the brokerage firms are doing programs, they can do it at much different numbers than what you see posted anywhere or what you will see on TV, because they basically have a very low cost of money. So you can't do anything in advance, you can just react. But what I do is as soon as I see things start to change, I just write down on a piece of paper—hey, the spread was 2 points, and all of a sudden sell programs were coming in. The spread was 4 points or 3 1/2 . . . that's where things picked up. And usually what will happen is those numbers will stay consistent for the rest of the day because program traders will try to outdo each other and everybody is trying to get in and get their program off and they give up a little to do it each time. So each day you kind of watch, and it will happen early in the morning . . . say the first half hour or hour, you'll see the programs start to go.

Kevin, let's talk about this because you said something that is the opposite of what I would have expected. I would have thought that you were going to say, "Okay. I see a buy program is going to hit. I want to come in immediately here and buy General Electric." But that is not what you want to do here. You want to wait for a *sell* program to hit, see if the market holds well and then come in and *buy* GE.

Yes, I do because it's easy to get price. That means I'm buying it on the bid or down because everybody steps aside. I'd rather buy a stock that's pulling back in an up trend. I'm talking about a stock that's above its open, that has rallied up and now it pulls back due to program selling. I'd rather do that because it's a much stronger situation.

Got you. It's almost opposite thinking, but it is obviously the correct way . . . you've got things moving in your favor.

Well, it is. I know one rule that works on the pullbacks and also when you sell short. I don't know if it's a rule, but it's one guideline that works. You buy pullbacks on stocks that are trending above their open and you sell short stocks that are trending down below their open. Very rarely do you make a ton by counter-shorting a stock that's uptrending above its open and trying to catch both moves, the long and the short.

How do you prepare yourself for each trading day? What do you read and what do you look at? Assuming an up trend, how do you pare down the number of stocks to track? How many stocks can you track at any given time? What technical software do you find useful?

I don't use any technical software. I just use a stock scanner that searches for RS (relative strength) value and ADX. I use several Web sites that give you some data on volume and whether the stock finished in the top of the range. The software I use is strictly Trac Data and a couple of Internet sites. I'm just looking at the market in general—at the tape—and just watching things change direction. And that's strictly just bar charts, volume, price, time, and range expansions . . . very simple, basic stuff. But I won't jump in, in the middle of the day and say, "Gee, that looks good," and just start to trade something to get a feel for it. I have a pre-defined entry point based on the charts from the night before. And I have pre-defined patterns that I'll look at on the intraday, five-minute charts.

And then just by utilizing two or three patterns—like pull backs or consolidations off the daily charts—I find I have *too many* stocks. At that point, I try to narrow those down to the ones that finished with the most volume up or the ones that finished the highest in their ranges so that I don't have that far to go. And then I'll couple these with the volatility factor of the stock. I'll look for stocks with high relative strength values combined with high earnings and great momentum. And then I look for stocks that have pulled back—but not below their 10- or 20-day moving averages—two to five days at most before making a go again. Those are the stocks that I'm going to lean toward at all times.

So you want things that are really flying in runaway mode, as I know Mark Boucher likes. But even on a daytrading basis, you want the kind of stocks that can give you range. You want the highest volatility stocks with the best liquidity that have the strongest pattern. That's how I try to eliminate them. If it's a choice between a VISX or a CAT tractor, it's going to be VISX. So you eliminate . . . you go through that process.

And then you also want to stick with those stocks where you have some liquidity. If it's an over-the-counter stock, you really want to see four or five market makers down a good 3/8- to 1/2-point. This is so that if you buy it on the offered side or at the mid-point and you make a mistake and the inside bid disappears, you can approximate where you will get out. On the listed stocks, I stay primarily with the over-the-counter stocks, the NDX 100, and those special Internet stocks that look like they are trading with a little reality . . . and then the highly liquid, big-cap stocks.

Let's jump ahead here. Explain what a Slim Jim is.

The primary Slim Jim that you are going to see is a long, narrow consolidation. It's either near the highs of the day or the lows of the day or it's either below the high or above the low. And you usually see a minimum of six to eight bars, assuming a five-minute bar chart. The longer the consolidation, the tighter it is, the better the move. And you're looking at the Slim Jim in two ways. The first is to go long, if it hasn't had two or three breakouts already. If it is consolidating at the high but it hasn't really got a good run relative to its range, you're looking to take it to the upside.

It sounds pretty straightforward.

It is, but trading isn't just about looking at chart patterns, it's about what's going on around them. This kind of approach works because you've got all the players in the market working for you. There will be institutional buyers and program buyers pushing the market up. Also, the specialist might be long, and if he is, you can bet the stock will accelerate to the upside. Hedge funds will be trying to front-run the institutions, and so on. And there will also be the normal technical

Slim Jim: Calpine (CPN), 5-minute

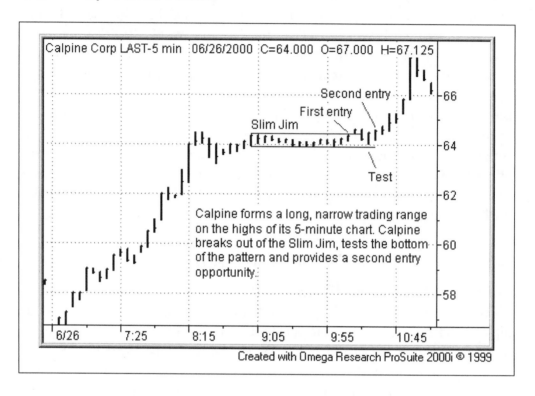

Calpine Corp LAST-5 min 06/26/2000 C=64.000 O=67.000 H=67.125

Second entry
First entry
Slim Jim
Test

Calpine forms a long, narrow trading range
on the highs of its 5-minute chart. Calpine
breaks out of the Slim Jim, tests the bottom
of the pattern and provides a second entry
opportunity.

Created with Omega Research ProSuite 2000i © 1999

buying by retail investors. It's a pile-on effect that can make these turn out to be
"moon shot"-type trades . . . 1 1/2 to 2 points in a day.

The other way to trade it is if it's at the high of its day and it's still in a
Slim Jim after two or three consolidating-breakouts to the upside. If momentum
swings in the marketplace, you may very well be able to short that for a quick
daytrade on the downside, even though it's been a strong stock. You can do this
because it might be up 3 or 4 points and beyond the move of its normal range.

And the other type of Slim Jim that you'll see is with a stock that is down 4
or 5 points and has consolidated at the bottom of the range. This stock could go
either way. But it was already down beyond a standard deviation, down 3 or 4
points. Then the market turns and just explodes to the upside. So you can catch

them at the bottom of the day for a rally back if they are down big and they go the other way.

One thing about Slim Jims is that you can load up 75 to 100 stocks on five-minute charts and put them on a list. And what I do is I just have a little down arrow button and I go through the whole works from A to Z. And I just keep hitting it all day long to see what's setting up.

So that's the primary Slim Jim: a long, horizontal, narrow consolidation. The narrower it is, the more compression you have. And you want to know what? The best trade you can ever get long-term is a five-year-or-more, horizontal trading range that's been down for a long, long while and get an explosion out of that. Take a look at Dell or any other stock . . . that's how they all exploded. So the same thing works on five-minute charts as it does on long-term charts. And, Larry, you can certainly attest to that with the commodities.

Yes, very true. In a sense, low volatility precedes the move.

For sure. But Slim Jims also take the form of dynamite-triangles. These are little consolidations that you see during the day that you relate to the prior day's consolidation. So the whole process is relating something to something else, whether it be today's bar with yesterday's bar, today's bar with five bars ago, daily to weekly or weekly to monthly. You can get some explosive moves with the Slim Jims. Slim Jims work because institutions get new money in and have to put it to work. The market might be running a little bit, and they don't want to run in and pay up for the stocks. So what they do is they go buy futures. They give an order to a major firm like Morgan Stanley or Goldman Sachs or some big futures players to buy futures at fair value, if they can. And these are S&P 500 stocks. So in the meantime throughout the course of the day, the firm buys the S&P futures at fair value. Somewhere around 2:00 p.m., 2:30 p.m., they can't buy any more futures at fair value since the market is a little too strong. They have to come to market and give those orders to buy the underlying stock, the underlying cash. And what will happen is you will see these explosions at 3:00 p.m., 2:30 p.m., and 3:30 p.m. on the S&P stocks. And the S&P average explodes.

Multi-Year Slim Jim: Dell (DELL), Monthly

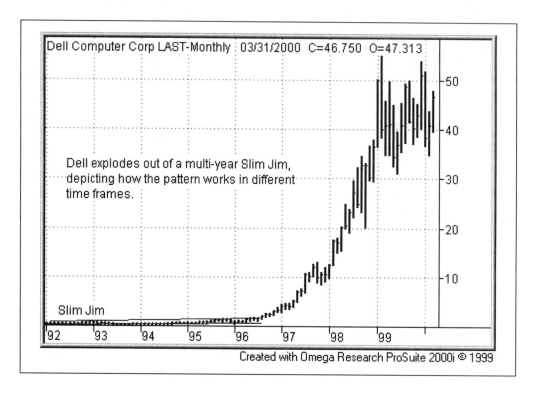

Dell Computer Corp LAST-Monthly 03/31/2000 C=46.750 O=47.313

Dell explodes out of a multi-year Slim Jim, depicting how the pattern works in different time frames.

Slim Jim

Created with Omega Research ProSuite 2000i © 1999

You will get orders coming down to the floor—for instance on Chevron, a $95 stock, to buy 400,000, with a half-hour to go—that must be done. I used to see them all the time when I had 94 brokers. And they'll say, "Can you help? I've got to buy in size, I have to get done." Well, what happens is no one is going to sell that. Now as that stock starts to move up and up, the specialist is probably going to short most of it, but he's going to darn well short it at much higher prices. Those are the explosions that come out of the Slim Jims. So I'm always conscious of that, knowing that that can happen.

If the market is pretty strong and you see those consolidations, especially when they haven't had three or four of them during the day, the first breakout is always the best. And then it kind of diminishes as it goes because you run out of range in price of the stock. But that's what happens and that's why you see those explosions that make such powerful moves: they come right out of Slim Jims.

Let me ask another Slim Jim question. Is it better to enter when it passes that day's high or just play it when it breaks out of its Slim Jim even though it is below the day's high? It always seems intimidating to play the low . . . there's a high looming over you.

Again, if it's the first intraday high that pulls back and forms a consolidation, then I'd play it going back to the upside. If it's a stock that's already run up a couple of levels and it's up there and it's made a high, it's like a spike and ledge and then you play it to the short side.

A strong stock may retrace one-half or one-third of the move. But it will form something as it consolidates to decide whether it's going to make a run to new highs or not. It will do something there. It will form a reversal pattern or it will go into a little trading range such as a little triangle. If it's above the opening, the market dynamics are good, I don't see any real sellers or anything showing up on the offer side, and it's just moving back and forth in a consolidation, I'd play it breaking out again. I would do this even though it's below the high and even though it's probably not sitting the same way as it was sitting at the high in the consolidation.

What would you say is enough volume to indicate that institutions are most likely accumulating stock?

Well, you can look at it a couple ways. I have 50-day average daily volume and 30-day average daily volume indicators, and I also like to look at volume relative to the day before and to the prior five days. There are two other things that you can use. One is to have a service such as Bloomberg's that lets you see how much volume traded on the bid side, how much volume traded on the offered side, and how much volume traded on the mid-point. And you can go back "x" number of days. That to me is the best way to determine what volume is doing. If a big-cap stock doesn't trade lots of volume, but it all traded on the bid side and it was 20 to

30 percent less than its 50-day average daily volume, and all of a sudden I see all that volume on one side or the other or a bias with a midpoint down or a midpoint up, that also tells me something. You also can look at the volume-weighted, average price.

The volume-weighed average price is just an average at each price the stock traded at relative to volume during the day. This is an interesting number because if institutions are competing to buy stock, what will usually happen is the stock will close above the volume-weighted average price. And that's very, very positive.

If the institutions are having their way and they can scale down, the *selling pressure* is greater, and the stock will keep closing below the average—they usually close below the volume-weighted-average-price because the institution is able to scale down. That's very, very helpful in conjunction with the absolute volume that you're talking about.

Kevin, do you advocate that stock traders just starting out keep a very small position of 100 to 200 shares even though flat commissions are eating into any gains? Or is it better for them to paper trade and then jump right into 500-share lots?

I think there are two things you should do. Paper trading with no money is not going to help you from the standpoint of managing the trade from a profit standpoint, reading the dynamics, and also pushing the button to get out of a trade that goes against you. You have to trade real-time to do that.

Having said that, I think paper trading is great, and we shouldn't call it paper trading. You should select stocks to see how your selection of stocks does, to see whether those stocks gain anything the next day. You should look to see what the profit range was above the high, what the range about your entry point was on the stocks traded. Was it a second entry? Was it a first entry? And you should start to get a feel of that part of the trader's equation and not sit down and say, "I've made this much money or whatever," but look at the dynamics of what those stocks did. And then say, "look, I'm running 50 to 60 percent." Well, in the real world, if you're running 60 percent on paper, when emotions get involved and it's real money and you can do 40 to 50 percent, you're probably going to be okay in a reasonable amount of time when you get some experience. That's the only reason I advocate paper trading. It's very good in the beginning for stock selection and for getting the feel and idea of trading.

But the other thing about trading small size and a small amount of shares gets back to money management. And you say, "Well, gee, the most I can lose is $100." Obviously, that's the point on 100 shares. So you're not going to get hurt and your capital is not going to get hit. But if you lose too many trades and you're approaching that number—whatever number you give yourself, 50 trades in a row or whatever—you're not going to let yourself get there. You're going to see that your stock selection is not good at this point in time and after six or seven straight losses, you're going to bail out and say, "What am I doing wrong?" And I think that's the way to go about it.

During the break-in period you should also go to a firm and say, "I want to be in this business. Can I do 100 shares and get a reasonable amount or rate for some break-in period?" Most firms will work something out with you where you can do that. And I strongly advocate that.

Yes. Paper trading is good to a point and you should certainly do it. But it will never replicate the psychology of trading, which is when you've got a position moving against you and you've got to react to that. Because you're on paper and there's no money on the line, the reality is you're not going to react the same way if you're all of a sudden getting hit real hard.

No question about it.

If you're in a position and it's running in your favor, either in your favor or against you, you still have to pull the trigger. You have to get used to the type of stress that's involved. And you just can't know how your mind is going to react when you are just doing it on paper.

Another thing in line with what you are just saying is that it's very hard to get a feel for the kind of noise that you can get on your entries. Many times, you get what looks like a good entry, but you get stopped out really quickly and then the stock runs back up again. You may even get stopped again, if that's the case. But it's very hard to know how you will react unless you are trading real money.

It's better to do it with 100 shares than to do it on paper.

Absolutely, with 100, 200 shares, depending on the stock involved.

What's the best advice you have for aspiring short-term traders?

Other than risk control, I'd tell traders to ignore most inane market news and opinions. They should look at relationships between price bars, highs and lows, opens and closes, and volume from day to day. These are what tip you off to market dynamics. Are the buyers more aggressive than the sellers or vice versa? A series of higher closes and higher highs coming out of a pullback situation on increasing volume tells me a story—I don't need to listen to the news. When you combine this with the institutional side of the story, it gives you a pretty good perspective on the market.

When someone asks me, "Why are you buying that stock?" I tell them, "Because it's going up, and the stocks in the group and the larger market are up, too." I don't try to pick bottoms or tops; I pick my points—if they turn out to be tops or bottoms, so be it. If you're picking your points based on market dynamics, you'll pick a lot of tops and bottoms anyway.

A pattern is a pattern—it's where it occurs that's important. What are the players doing that will push the market one way or the other? Look for trading ranges, triangles, and other congestion areas that get you into the market with little risk, and let the institutions do the work. I get on board when pieces are in place and the market is going in the direction I want it to go. If the institutions are interested, I'm interested.

Thank you, Kevin.

Good to be here!

CEDD MOSES

By Kevin N. Marder

The name Cedd Moses has a certain ring to it. Surely, it's not a name that one stumbles across very often in life. I first came across it in the early '90s when I saw performance rankings for the U.S. Investing Championship. Moses finished first in one of the USIC's equity divisions in 1991. Right around the same time, I noticed that Moses regularly finished among the top performers of Money Manager's Verified Ratings, a service designed to track portfolio performance. I'd see the same handful of names consistently dominate the MMVR rankings, and Moses seemed to always be near the top. It's one thing for a trader to have a good year, but something entirely different to consistently shoot out the lights as Moses had done.

And then it was in 1992, I believe, that I again came across Moses, this time in an interview in *Barron's*. A few years prior to that, I had begun adopting Bill O'Neil's philosophy of buying aggressive growth stocks sporting high relative price strength. As I learned in the *Barron's* piece, Moses' big influence was none other than Bill O'Neil. Here was a guy not only putting up big numbers, but running big money as a hedge fund manager to boot.

Whereas some of the biggest hedge fund managers have called it quits over the past couple of years, Moses has been able to achieve returns of 137 percent in 1998 and 81 percent in 1999 (this is net of all fees). Managed Account Reports ranked Moses' hedge fund in the top 1 percent of all hedge funds for the three-year period ended May 2000. In addition, Nelson's *World's Best Money Managers* ranked his fund in the top 1 percent of all U.S. equity products for the three-year period ended March 2000.

Kevin N. Marder: Did you have a love of the market from a young age, like so many other top traders?

Cedd L. Moses: Yes. When I was 12 years old, my grandmother set up a custodial account and gave me a few shares of stock. Right away I went to the library to see whether or not I should hold the stock or sell it. At that time it was just pretty generic, fundamental information, but at least it piqued my interest. Then later, as a teenager, I started getting O'Neil's *Daily Graphs* and following those. I also started going to his bookstore in West L.A. and began getting to know him and getting a feel for his CANSLIM strategy of investing. He did a back test of about a 37-year time period and he looked at every stock that doubled within a year, as well as the characteristics that a lot of those had before they doubled.

This was even before he called it "CANSLIM"?

Exactly.

So this was what, 1980-ish?

Yeah. Way back then. And I started looking for those factors, flipping through chart books myself, looking for the ideal cup-and-handle patterns and companies with accelerating earnings and sales growth, etc. But I would do it manually.

With the help of *Daily Graphs*?

Right. Exactly.

Since O'Neil had not written *How To Make Money In Stocks* at that time, how did you learn his approach? Were there other books that you read?

Oh yeah. I read a lot of them. I was basically reading everything I could. Another influence was a book by Nicolas Darvas . . .

How I Made Two Million Dollars in the Stock Market?

Yes.

That's one of my five favorite books.

That and things like Gerald Loeb's *Battle For Investment Survival.* I mean I basically read everything that I could get my hands on. *Market Logic* had an impact on me. That was written by Norman Fosback, who had an approach where he would look at a series of indicators and back tested them to see if they had any kind of accuracy. That was the beginning of my building an econometric model to give me a feeling for market risk. What other books did I read? There was a ton that I read. *Reminiscences of a Stock Operator* influenced me.

And now again, this was when you were in high school?

High school and college. I did a lot of trading in college. I studied mechanical engineering—computer science—and by the time I graduated school I had offers to go to work for defense companies and so forth. But I wasn't really interested in that. I wanted to go directly into the stock market, so I started working in the brokerage industry right out of college.

What company was that?

It was a small firm. Baraban Securities. I don't know if you remember them, Kevin.

Oh yeah, sure. Are they still around?

They are, but they got swallowed up by another company.

I think I remember reading about that. And were you a broker there, then?

Yeah. I was a broker and I was also heading up their trading desk. I learned a lot sitting on the trading desk.

Were you trading just for the firm's account or . . .

No, I was entering trades for the other brokers.

What would you say the big learning lesson was when you sat on that trading desk at Baraban? Was there one big thing that you learned that made the thing—

—because I dealt a lot with the other brokers' orders and orders they were getting from the public, I got to realize that the public, a lot of times, was wrong at key turning points in the market. I would see the sell orders pouring in at the market bottoms and I would see the buy orders pouring in at the market tops. I would see people making typical mistakes, psychological mistakes, like trying to buy beaten-down stocks, broken stocks, and selling their winners after a small gain and holding onto the losers, and buying losing stocks and falling into that trap, losing money.

That's interesting.

When I was a teenager, I learned the hard way one time when I rode a stock way, way down. It just kept going down every day. I didn't know anything about using benchmarks at the time, so I learned the hard way. When O'Neil's approach came to me, it made a lot of sense. You've got to know where to get out and cut your losses. And that's still a key part of everything I do. I define my risk on every trade before I enter it.

Do you do that based on a straight percentage basis? Or do you look at a chart and say, okay, here's some support, so if it breaks that support level, I'll have to sell?

It depends on which security it is. If it's a futures trade to hedge my portfolio, I have a specific benchmark and use a momentum oscillator to get me out. But I'll have a maximum risk that I'll take on a trade. And then on each individual stock, my decision depends on how much upside I feel the stock's got based on my screens. If a stock has the potential to double, based on my main quantitative screen—which consists of 22 different screens—I tend to give those a little more room. My benchmark is then based on an absolute bench off the stock's high since I've owned it, as well as a relative bench.

Okay. We'll come back to the when-to-sell criteria a little bit later. You were at Baraban for a number of years. You went straight from there into your own money management company?

Basically, yeah. After a few years, I turned into the top broker at Baraban even though I'd never made a cold call. This was because I had already developed my stock selection process to a point where everybody recognized that I knew how to make money trading. So the firm actually changed their whole scope toward something called co-brokering, which I developed, where I was basically managing money. The other brokers would raise money for me and we'd basically split the commission. They would have the contact with the clients. And then eventually I broke off on my own and for a little while tried to start up my own brokerage firm.

I was already trading for clients as if I was a money manager, so I decided to move on and start up my own money management firm. That was back in 1989. And it's been successful ever since. I was basically trying to do it in another form within the brokerage industry from 1983 to 1988. I couldn't advertise a track record because I was in the brokerage industry and they were sensitive to the fact that your clients can call up and sell their stock at any price they want, affecting your track record.

I'd heard that you'd started off as a daytrader. Is that correct?

I used to do a lot more trading intraday based on sentiment indicators, momentum indicators, and relative strength.

Were you holding positions for less than a day or taking them home overnight?

I traded options and I would trade positions in stocks on margin and I took on large positions that were a large percentage of my portfolio. I'd only hold them overnight if the trade was working. I would not hold a losing position overnight.

So you would maybe sell the winners within three, four, five days or so?

If they were still working, I would stick with them. The whole philosophy was to let your winners run. As soon as the market would start to turn against me or a stock would lose momentum on the upside, then I would get out. I had indicators to track the momentum. Sometimes I would hold stocks that had powerful upside momentum for a long time. Like in the '80s I held Wal-Mart for a long time . . . and also Home Depot.

Was it in 1991 that you won the U.S. Investing Championship?

Yes, 1991.

What was your return for that?

I'm trying to remember. Actually, it was such a huge number that we decided not to talk to clients about it because we didn't want their expectations to be too high. We could just talk about triple-digit performance. It beat the previous records that were out there at that time. By the time I started my own money management firm, I had my technique refined in terms of using more diversification. When you manage a pool of money, you have to widen up your benchmarks a little bit and use a little more diversification to help control volatility and try for longer-term gains for your clients.

Let's get into your basic strategy, then. What are the things that you look for in your buy candidates?

I have three specific screens. Two of them bring out my buy candidates. Instead of flipping through chart books, I went back a few years quantifying the factors that I would look for when I would flip through the chart books. That allowed my system to become much more objective, instead of having to look through a chart book and say "oh, this one looks good, this one looks bad."

I can sure relate to that.

I was able to quantify the things that I would look for and I was able to back-test them to see what kind of results they would have generated in past periods. I kept refining it and adding more and more characteristics that I would look for and did more back-testing of other new factors and new ideas that I had. I continue to do that, but right now I am up to 22 characteristics that I screen for in my primary fundamental screen.

Do you still use your Five Market Principles model?

Yes, that's incorporated into how I control risk. They are incorporated into my three layers of risk control.

Can you go into some of the specific things you screen for on the buy candidates?

Yeah. There are two screens that bring up my candidates. One is the fundamental screen. That's where 70 percent of my names come through on the buy side. There are fundamental characteristics, liquidity characteristics, and technical characteristics that I look for. On the fundamental side, companies have to be exhibiting strong current earnings-per-share and sales growth, and have a history of at least four quarters of strong sales and earnings growth. I also have a valuation

The Five Market Principles Model

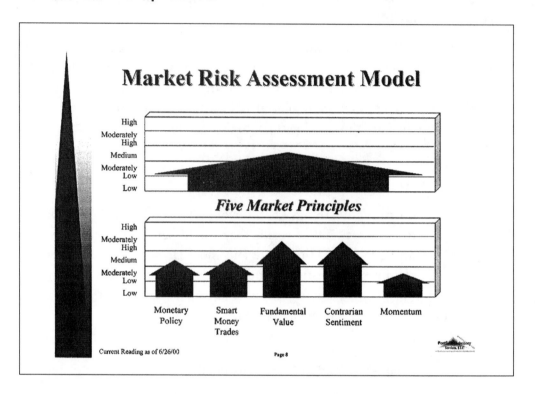

screen where I look at P/E relative to the growth rate of the company. There's a screen based on that. The actual numbers are kind of proprietary . . .

Sure.

I use this to make sure I'm not paying too much for a stock relative to its growth rate.

Is this like a forward P/E-to-growth ratio, then?

Yes.

Again, this could be proprietary, but you would take today's price and divide it by the forward four quarters earnings forecast by the Street—or the next fiscal year earnings forecast—and divide that by the expected growth rate in the next fiscal year. Is that the way you do it?

That's kind of a simplified version. Actually, it's the weighted moving average of the forecast for the next year, two years out, and the past year. The heaviest weighting is on this coming year.

The first year.

Exactly. It's a weighting of those. Again, in testing, I've been able to find a factor that works the best by quantifying it. It's something that's hard to do yourself, mentally, by just looking at a chart. And the amount that I'm willing to pay in terms of valuation is also a factor of a couple of other fundamental factors: earnings surprise consistency is one.

For example, a company that consistently has beaten earnings estimates by a certain percentage . . . those are companies that are much more well-managed in terms of Street expectations . . . managing their own company's growth. For those companies, I'm willing to pay a larger premium for the growth there, if there's a lot of consistency and visibility going forward. Also, companies have to be exhibiting positive earnings drift in order to make it through the screens. That's the other fundamental factor which is something I developed internally, too. That's a factor that's only been available in the last five years or so. At the time, O'Neil didn't have it. A lot of people didn't have it, because companies like First Call and Zacks, for example, didn't have their earnings estimate data available on a real-time basis like they do now where you can screen for it on a real-time basis.

Again, this could be proprietary, but do you look at drift over the last 30 days or 45 days?

It's the 45 days going into the earnings number. I've found a high correlation between positive earnings drift and positive earnings surprises. To sum it up, the fundamental factors I'm looking for are companies that 1) are growing strongly, 2) are still selling at a reasonable price relative to their growth, 3) consistently beat their numbers, and 4) have a high probability of beating the number that quarter.

The whole screen is broken into three different categories: fundamental, liquidity, and technical. The liquidity factors that I look for make sure that I can get in and out of a stock in one day. I tend to trade between small- and large-cap. But because of the size of my fund, they have to be at least $250 million in market capitalization. They have to be exhibiting a certain amount of average daily dollar volume. They also have to have a tight, bid-ask spread. And all that's done through the screen, so that eliminates names that aren't liquid enough for me.

And then I have the technical factors that I screen for. First, our stocks have to be above major moving averages that the market's above. For example, if the market's above its 200-day, then the stocks have to be above their 200-day. If the market's above its 50-day, the stocks have to be above their 50-day. They have to be outperforming 80 percent of all stocks, and I measure this through relative strength. I have two different relative strength measures: short term and long term. The long-term measure is very similar to O'Neil's measure of relative strength. And last, they have to be exhibiting positive up-to-down volume. They have to exhibit all these technical factors in order to come through the screen.

Oh, okay, so special situations is—

—a whole different, separate screen. It brings up all different buy candidates.

Right.

The fundamental screen brings up a couple of names a day, usually, except in a weak market when there are a lot of stocks breaking down with poor technicals. Then no new names tend to come through.

And what about the special situations screen?

Moses' Investment Process

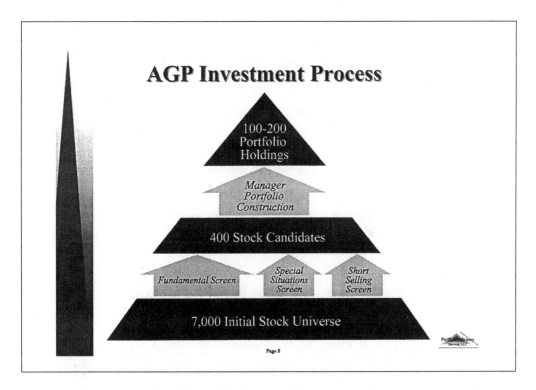

The special situations screen isn't as tight in terms of fundamental factors as the fundamental screen. The most important fundamental factor that I am screening for there is just a positive earnings drift, so that there is a high probability that the company is going to beat earnings expectations that quarter.

Okay.

So the company can still be losing money. Like the Internet names came through this screen in the mid- to late-'90s. Even though they were losing money, they were beating earnings expectations and the earnings estimates were rising, especially going into the numbers. They were coming through that screen. Then they have to be exhibiting the same liquidity and technical factors as my fundamental screen, so it's a larger pool. Then they're ranked, based on their relative strength.

Now, as far as looking at a chart goes, how do you integrate that with the screens that you've just spoken about?

Well, once they've come through the screens, that tends to bring up a couple of new names a day. Then I look at the chart pattern. Assuming the stock's in a basing pattern, I wait for either the relative strength or the price to break out of that basing pattern before initiating a position in the stock.

Do you build a position before the actual breakout occurs?

If the relative strength is breaking out.

Otherwise, you'll actually be buying on the day of the breakout, then?

Right.

And do you insist on the volume being pretty big on that breakout day? For example, O'Neil likes to see volume increase 40 to 50 percent above the average on that breakout day.

I like to see that, too. And if it increases more than that, then I take a bigger position. The size of the position is dependent on how much strength is in that breakout as well as the liquidity of the stock.

Do you have any set amount or set percentage that would be your opening position?

About 1 percent.

And this is, did you say, with a $350 million fund?

Base Breakout: Qualcomm (QCOM), Daily

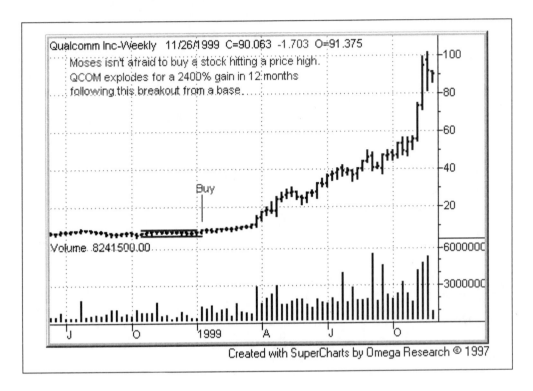

Qualcomm Inc-Weekly 11/26/1999 C=90.063 -1.703 O=91.375
Moses isn't afraid to buy a stock hitting a price high.
QCOM explodes for a 2400% gain in 12 months
following this breakout from a base.

Buy

Volume 8241500.00

Created with SuperCharts by Omega Research © 1997

The fund's about $300 million now.

And then how do you add on to positions when you're right? Do you like to pyramid up as the thing moves higher?

Yeah. With about 10 percent of my positions, I feel comfortable taking a larger position in a good market. In that situation, I pyramid up, if the stock is very powerful coming out of a base, to between 1.5 and 2.0 percent. I'll go up to 3 percent on a stock that bases again and breaks out real powerfully again. That's rare.

Base Breakout: Cisco Systems (CSCO), Daily

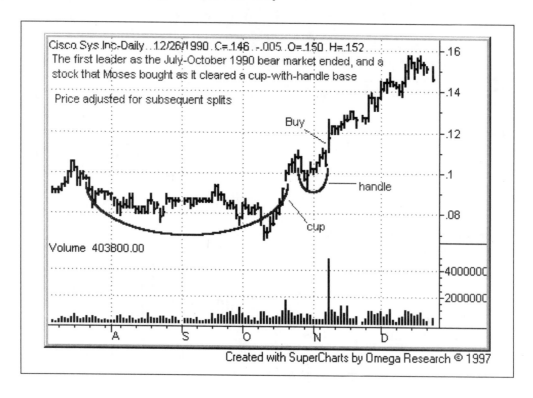

Cisco Sys.Inc-Daily 12/26/1990 C=.146 -.005 O=.150 H=.152

The first leader as the July-October 1990 bear market ended, and a stock that Moses bought as it cleared a cup-with-handle base

Price adjusted for subsequent splits

Buy

handle

cup

Volume 403800.00

Created with SuperCharts by Omega Research © 1997

Moving it up from 1.5 to 3 percent, would that be all one buy or would you make successive buys?

I would go from 2.0 to 2.5 percent if it breaks out again, but if it breaks out really powerfully, then it would go to 3 percent. Usually there would be some appreciation between then, too, if it's a really powerful stock and it naturally just becomes a larger percentage of the fund. So it might already be up over 2 percent by the time I start adding to it, moving it to 2.5 percent or to 3 percent.

I don't take larger than a 3 percent initial position on a stock right now because of the size of my fund and diversification. But I'll let them appreciate.

When your fund was, say, $20 million, $30 million, $40 million in size, was the size of your positions larger at that point?

Yeah. I would go up to 5 percent on a stock.

With the opening position, you mean?

No, the opening position was between 1.5 and 2.5 percent.

And then you would go up as much as 5 percent if it was one of those add-on types.

Real leaders.

Does that pretty much cover what you look for in buys, then?

Pretty much, yeah. The important thing is the screen that's got more fundamental factors in it. Those are the ones we think have more upside. We have tighter benchmarks on the special situations than we do on the fundamental screen. Special situations help us get more diversification because it brings up names that might be companies that aren't making money yet, companies that are turning around . . . like it brought up the oil service names . . . it brought up a lot of Internet names early on. It gives us more diversification and allows us to get into some companies early on.

Otherwise, though, apart from your special situations screen, are you trying to pick stocks in the best-acting groups?

Yes. That's basically it. With the fundamental screen, we'll basically buy any name that comes through there that's acting good in terms of the chart. So it will naturally get us over-weighted in the sectors and groups that are leading the market. That does tend to happen . . . like during the '80s, a lot of healthcare and retail, and during the '90s, a lot of technology. But the special situations screen brings us more diversification and gets us into other groups that might be starting to emerge . . . like Internet stocks and biotechs. These groups started moving before they had earnings.

And what about shorting?

A lot of people that focus on the buy side have trouble on the short side. Since I've been able to quantify a lot of my stock selection process and back-test it, I can keep my head clear enough so that I can also focus on short-selling candidates as long as they're coming through screens. I don't believe in shorting stocks just because they're overvalued. That's a mistake that a lot of people have made.

Yeah, hordes of folks got killed shorting Internet stocks.

Yes. Our goal is shorting stocks before the company misses the number that quarter . . . because we all know what happens to those stocks when they miss numbers. So the best factor that we've found is negative earnings drift because it has a high correlation with negative earnings surprises.

That makes sense.

If there's a dropping of earnings drift by a certain percentage in the 45 days before their number, there's a high probability that they're going to miss their number. They also have to be liquid and exhibiting negative technicals, such as breaking moving averages that the market's above.

Would you also want to see a stock break some support on a chart?

Exactly. That's part of the short screen. We've quantified breakdowns in charts through weak relative strength and breaking moving averages, and a high amount of down volume relative to up volume. There's new names that come through the screen every day and I'll look at the chart patterns and double-check it and then put the position on. In certain market environments, if there's a lot of risk in the market or if the market's acting poor, I'll offset long positions that we have with short positions so that it cuts our overall risk in the market. It allows us to hold onto some of our big winners as long as they're acting good, but at the same time offset them with short positions in a lot of losing stocks.

So those are our three screens.

Moving over to your sell decision, can you give me the factors that you look at? I guess we should split this up. If you're wrong on a stock and it drops right after you buy it, where would you consider cutting the loss and moving on?

Well, on special situations I set a benchmark based on the price action and a support level. I try and buy the stock just coming out of a basing pattern, and I put a price benchmark just below that base.

Below the top of the base or the bottom of the base?

It really depends on the relative strength. If the stock breaks the top end of the base independently of the market—let's say in a strong stock market—then that's a really bad sign. But if it breaks the top end of that base, and at the same time the market's in a major correction, then the stock still might be okay. So then I bench it off the bottom of the base. That's how we handle special situations.

Then on every stock that goes in, we put on an absolute bench off the high since we owned it, and a relative bench, relative to the market. So for example, with a fairly liquid stock, the maximum bench we take is 20 percent relative to the market. So if the market goes up 10 percent and that stock drops 10 percent off its high, then it would be sold. The maximum risk on a volatile stock we'll take is 30 percent.

That's something we went back and back-tested. I don't hear many people talking about relative benches.

I've never heard anybody talk about it. Your research reminds me of the research that Mark Boucher does . . . very painstaking, thorough, nothing-but-the-facts-ma'am type of stuff.

Yes, the relative bench is something that's been incredibly useful. I mean if you think about it, one thing that it does is get you out of stocks just before the market goes into a major correction. So it takes you out if they start dropping relative to the market. Ahead of a big correction, you're just taken out of the most vulnerable stocks through that relative bench. It helps protect you. For example, going into the 1998 correction we were actually only 30 percent long and we had a big short position on before the correction really began in the third quarter. The same with the March-May 2000 correction. We were out of a lot of stocks before the market correction began, especially the weakest groups that were starting to really break down. That relative benchmark has been really useful.

And then the other thing that we bench off of is related to earnings estimates, which we monitor real-time. We have a fundamental benchmark, so if estimates drop by a certain percentage in the 45 days going into the number, that would also take us out of a name because there's a possibility of a negative earnings surprise.

Those are our sell disciplines.

That includes selling to cut a loss as well as selling to nail down a profit, then?

Yes. Sometimes a stock will go up 300 or 400 percent and then it will drop a certain percentage relative to the market and that takes us out of it. As long as the stock keeps outperforming the market and making new highs, then we tend to stay with the position.

Do you ever take a specific set percentage and say, "Okay, the stock just dropped, say, 20 percent off its high, I'm going to sell the stock here"?

Oh yeah, we have a set relative bench and an absolute. We have an absolute bench as a protection, too. It helps us in real bear market conditions or corrections. But the relative bench has protected us before those corrections and bear markets have begun and keeps us in the leading stocks.

As far as the absolute bench goes, does that vary from stock to stock, then?

Yes, it's dependent on the stock's volatility.

How much does this amount to?

It's between 20 and 30 percent off the stock's high, maximum.

How do you handle a climax blow-off, where a stock runs, say, 80 percent, something ridiculous, in a week or two? Do you sell into that or do you want to see the stock put in some kind of peak and then come down 10 or 20 percent?

If a stock's running up big, selling it can be kind of a subjective decision. Some of the Internet stocks did that in a short period of time and then they double and triple again in a short period of time. I'm sure you've seen that, too, Kevin. It's kind of a subjective decision when a stock's going straight up, whether or not that's a blow-off or that's the beginning of another huge explosion in the stock. So I try not to make that decision myself. I let the stock's action after that dictate what's going on. But if the stock appreciates that much—like doubles quickly—a lot of times it will become too large a percentage of my portfolio. So then the stock would be cut back. We would trim the position at least. And if the stock started dramatically underperforming the market from that point forward, then the stock would be sold.

As far as your general market indicators go, I know you used to have 15 different ones. How many do you have now?

Twenty-five.

Could you talk about some of your more important ones?

Sure. The 25 break into five categories: momentum, sentiment, smart money, valuation, and monetary. It gives risk ratings on the market from a short-, intermediate-, and long-term perspective. In the short term, the best predictive tools on the market are sentiment and momentum indicators. For sentiment indicators, very valuable ones are the VIX, which I know you guys use over at your shop, and the put-to-call ratios on both the CBOE and OEX. The good thing is now you can follow those intraday through the CBOE's Web site.

Yes. In the old days, I used to call them up every 60 minutes or so, but—

—yeah, we would do the same thing! But now it comes up live on the Web site so you can just keep that on your computer screen.

And besides sentiment, you also said market momentum?

Yes, market momentum. The best situation for a short-term market top is when sentiment is extremely positive on put-to-call ratios among speculators and then market momentum turns down. Often that's a sign of a short-term top when momentum has confirmed that a short-term top is in place at the same time as there's excess optimism.

What are some of the momentum indicators that you use?

I use the MACD, which I use for different time periods.

Different time periods?

Yeah, different time periods depending on the index that I'm looking at. And also the McClellan Oscillator and Summation Index . . . we've used those pretty successfully. Those are some of the best tools. And then price action in the market is something I also watch. For example, accumulation and distribution days in the major averages . . . if they're breaking on higher volume or lower volume than the previous day.

That's a favorite of mine as well.

If you see the MACD confirming a top at the same time you see the market volume picking up on the downside and too much optimism, you've got to be real concerned, at least in the short run.

With the MACD, if you were looking at the histogram, would you use more of a move from positive to negative territory? Do you think that's more important, or for example when the thing peaks and the histogram bars get, you know, shorter and shorter?

The perfect situation for a top is when you have a non-confirmation. The market makes a higher high but the histogram makes a lower high. And then the histogram moves from positive to negative . . . so a non-confirmation in terms of the level of momentum on the histogram. Those are the best sell signals—using the MACD—when you have a lower high break from positive to negative. That's when you have the sharpest short-term sell-offs.

So those are the most important factors in the very short-term. But on the intermediate- and longer-term basis, monetary policy is the highest weighting in my model. I use indicators on monetary policy that I've developed. Ned Davis has developed some that are good, too. Indicators of smart money trades have nailed the market tops and bottoms in the last two decades really well. One measures what the members of the NYSE off the floor of the exchange are doing versus the members that are on the floor.

I actually first learned that from you in your *Barron's* article of '92 or so.

Oh yeah?

Yeah. I never knew anything about that and started following it after that. Back then, I think you had pointed out something like when the long positions are in excess of 20 million or 25 million shares a week . . . when we start seeing a few weeks of that, that's very bullish. Am I correct in saying that?

The numbers relate to buying relative to selling. Right.

Is that still the case today?

Yes. Over a 10-week period of time, if you see it averaging over 10 million shares a week, that's pretty significant. But it can get up to as high as 20 million shares. And conversely, on the sell side, when you see more than 10 million a week being sold. For example, ahead of the 1998 correction and ahead of the March-May 2000 correction, we saw heavy member selling and you also saw a pick-up in specialist shorting vs. the public. You also saw a pick-up in corporate insider selling. Typically, there's about a 2-to-1 ratio of corporate insider selling relative to buying. But when it gets up to 3-to-1, that's a warning signal. And when it gets down to 1-to-1, that's a positive signal.

And then another thing that called this correction really well at the beginning of this year was the smart money flow, which is the change in action between the first hour and last hour of trading accumulated over time. I'm sure you're probably aware of it that the smart money is known for trading more in the last hour of the day and the more emotional money invests during the first hour. So if you see a day when the market's up big in the first hour but down big in the last hour, that's a sign of distribution in the market. And if you take the price change in the market in the last hour minus the first hour, and accumulate that over time, you can see divergences between that and the chart of the market itself.

I've also looked at this, once again courtesy of your *Barron's* article.

It called the '87 crash . . . like nailed it . . . the '90 correction, the '98 correction, and the March–May 2000 correction. The smart money flow was collapsing at the beginning of this year, so you could see a lot of distribution going on. So that's a pretty good tool, too. I kind of mix all five of the areas in intermediate- and long-term signals. But I use a little bit different indicators for momentum and contrary sentiment for long-term confirmations. And then I also use funda- mental valuation tools that aren't strictly based on P/E, but factors that are based more on valuations relative to interest rates and also the supply and demand of stock in the marketplace. Say, if there's a period of a lot of stock offerings, that's a negative in terms of valuation of that principle versus a lot of stock being taken off the market—that would be a positive for supply and demand.

So all those tools go into the five market principles and give me an overall assessment of market risk on a short-to-long-term basis. And when long-term risk and intermediate-term risk are high, and there's potential for a correction or a bear market, and it starts to be confirmed based on the price action, then I take my risk off the table and have an equal percentage of longs in my portfolio as shorts.

It's worked out that my longs tend to outperform my shorts, so I can make money in that environment and that's why I've been able to be non-correlated in significant down markets. In a tough market environment like 1998 or early 2000, I can make money.

What will be the highest cash position you raise during the course of a year as a percent of your total portfolio?

Hypothetically, it could go to 100 percent if I don't have any long positions and there are no attractive short positions coming in. But that's extremely rare. Usually, looking more at the net exposure—I try to go to about a 0 percent net exposure unless I have confirmation of a bear market which has to come through those five different principles, too. In that situation, I would take a net short po- sition. That's rare . . . the last time I had a signal for that was before the '87 crash.

Otherwise, I don't really believe in being net short the market . . . pretty tough.

Right. I haven't really been a short-seller myself. You know, O'Neil said in that book of his that he'd only made money in something like two of the prior nine bear markets. When I read that I thought, well, you know if it's not good enough for him, maybe it's not good enough for me. So I've only rarely shorted. And that was about it.

If they're small enough bears, you can just get out of all your long positions and wait out the bear market.

Exactly.

We try and get out of our long positions, but sometimes there's some stocks that are still working up in bear markets and we try and stick with those and try and offset the risk of those positions with short positions. That's kind of the philosophy.

Obviously your strategy has changed over the years because you're running much more money now. If you were running a smaller account, say, $500,000 or $1 million or so, would you be trading the way you did in the beginning days when you relied more on chart patterns and momentum?

No, I don't think so. One thing the quantitative screens have allowed me to do is to select stocks that dramatically outperform the market. And I don't have to thumb through chart patterns every day.

Right, right.

My current strategy also is able to give me stocks that have a lot more upside potential. Sometimes I'd be buying stocks just based on their chart patterns and they'd do pretty well for me. But in the meantime I'd maybe miss another one that exploded. Looking at the screens . . . it helps me find the stocks that have the biggest upside potential and focus directly on those just before they break out. Otherwise, you're looking at a 7,000-stock universe. This way, I can focus on just about 400 stocks and watch those much more closely. If I was just handling that small amount of money, I probably would be taking larger positions as a percentage of the portfolio. But that's only if the client was willing to take a little more volatility.

I mean if it was your own account, let's just say, would you take position sizes of 10 percent or something like that?

No. I don't think so. Now I feel pretty comfortable being more diversified and not having to put up with that much volatility. Five percent, potentially.

Interesting.

But that's just where I am.

What have we left out here?

We've been able to achieve our objective of being a high alpha fund. Our average alpha is 4 percent a month. This means we add 4 percent on average to the S&P per month. At the same time, we haven't had to sacrifice in terms of diversification. You know, we've been able to be extremely diversified and have low volatility in down markets and actually make money in significant down markets. Four percent alpha is considered big enough in the business that we're in. We're adding 4 percent a month.

That's while you own the stock, you're adding 4 percent? Or before you buy the stock, you're buying stocks with . . .

No, no, just our average monthly performance versus the S&P. We add 4.06 percent per month. That's been the average on our portfolio. Our objective is outperformance and not having to sweat down periods in the market.

You've been most generous, Cedd, in sharing so many of the specifics associated with your strategy.

It's been my pleasure, Kevin.

MARK BOUCHER

THE MIDAS TOUCH

By Kevin N. Marder

Few people must know as much about the ups and downs of being a trader than Mark Boucher. Before he was ranked the top hedge fund manager in the world over a couple of five-year periods in the 1990s, he experienced the harsh reality of watching his account collapse by 90 percent during the 1973–1974 bear market.

This latter experience impressed upon Boucher the absolute necessity of devising a rigid money management plan. Boucher took the task to heart, emerging from this near-calamitous event to log a well-deserved reputation as "the man with the Midas touch," a reference not only to his hedge fund of the same name, but also to his record of consistently potent returns with one of the lowest levels of volatility of any hedge fund manager in the world.

Much of Boucher's thinking is detailed in his book, *The Hedge Fund Edge.* I always have a lot of respect for a trader who decides to start from scratch and figure out "what works" in the market. Boucher took this approach to the nth degree early in his career, spending years and thousands of hours doing the painstaking research needed to cull the wheat from the chaff among the heap of indicators and data available. What he emerged with, and how he got there, is the subject of our interview.

Kevin N. Marder: Mark, when did you first get interested in the stock market?

Mark Boucher: I started trading when I was in high school. My father died of cancer when I was nine years old. In 1972, he started a trust fund for me for my college education because he knew he was sick. He put $100,000 into it, which was pretty much most of his savings that wasn't depleted by his illness. By the time I got to college in the early-1980s, that account was worth about $10,000. What had happened was that the bank in charge of the trust had put it in high-flying Nifty Fifty stock mutual funds and kept it there the entire time. So it lost 90 percent of its value. In between the time that he died and the time that I needed it for college, we went through a major secular bear market and we pretty much caught it near the bottom by the time I needed the money.

That experience had a major impact on me because it was my first real exposure to investments. It taught me the importance of not buying and holding, particularly with the high-flyers, and the risk involved in investing money. Like in any bull market, when you get to have a number of years—five or 10 years—where the market's done very well, people start saying, well, you know, all you really need to do to make money on a long-term basis for any type of college planning or anything like that, is to just have a disciplined plan to stay invested in the market. And I learned that that really wasn't necessarily the truth.

So your first exposure to the market was a rude awakening.

Yes. When I was in high school, I knew that that account was down somewhere between 70 and 90 percent and that it wasn't enough to pay for my college education. So in addition to trying very hard to get a water polo scholarship, which I did, I also saved up all of my money from working in the summers and I started investing it. When I started in the late-'70s—it was quite a different environment than in 2000—gold stocks were particularly strong at the time. Through some recommendations and some research I had done, I invested most of my life's savings in some long, nine-month options on gold stocks. I ended up turning $3,000 I had saved up into about $50,000. And that was still when I was in high school. Then I went ahead and lost about half of it before I figured out I'd been very fortunate to have gotten involved in that big, secular move and that I really didn't know what I was doing and wasn't the genius that I'd thought I was.

And so I began to change my investment strategy and I dove into every book and everything I could to try and learn. This is because after I'd lost half of that, I still barely had enough to go to school with my scholarship. I knew I was going to have to make that money last quite well.

Where did you go to college?

I went to University of California, Berkeley.

Did you continue to invest and trade in college?

Yes, I traded my way through school with the trust fund money and the money that I had made.

What was your initial strategy in those early college days?

I was much less risk-averse than I finally became. So I had some very, very wild swings. Because of my experience in gold after I made all of that money in gold stocks, I began to delve more into commodities. I went through a period in January 1980—just before gold went limit down—when I was a millionaire on paper for a couple of days in a row. When the limit down period stopped after Fed Chairman Paul Volcker made margin requirements retroactively higher in the gold market, I ended up with something like a $20,000 profit. I was throwing a millionaire's party and then a few days later I wasn't even a hundred-thousandaire!

Another trade that was similar happened within a year. I had a very strong pyramid move shorting orange juice futures. I promptly had a profit of over

$100,000. Over the weekend there was a freeze and the contract went limit up each day for over a week. That just about wiped me out.

Whoa.

So after going through some pretty extreme ups and downs, I began to understand risk more and also learn that some of the best money managers weren't the ones that had the highest returns. They were the ones that had the most consistent returns and had very low drawdowns. The real trick to managing money effectively is to make the most money on the least drawdown, not necessarily to make the most money, period.

Can you define drawdown?

Drawdown is basically the maximum drop in your equity value. It's the worst percentage drop from any equity high. If you hold a stock, and it goes from 10 to 100 and it makes up half of your portfolio, and then it drops down to 80, that's going to be at least a 10 percent drop in your whole portfolio from the equity high. Even though it's all profit, that's part of drawdown. And especially for a money manager that has new money coming in all of the time, it becomes much more important what your drops from equity peaks are. That's the risk that people really are measuring.

So you traded your way through college. Was your degree in business?

It was in economics.

When you got out of college, where did you end up?

I didn't end up anywhere. I basically traded on my own for about a year and a half. I had a couple hundred thousand dollars in the bank, and at that time that seemed like a lot of money. However, I began to get sort of lonely and bored with just trading on my own, just sitting there with a screen and no employees.

Not having people to have contact with was a lot more psychologically difficult than I had imagined. So I began to write some papers and do some things to try and get involved with different groups that were giving seminars. I got involved with CompuTrac software, which at the time was the premier technical analysis software package . . . probably the only one. And actually CompuTrac software got me involved in using computers to do analysis. That's how long ago that was.

I remember CompuTrac. They were early.

Right. They were early and they just didn't keep their lead, unfortunately. When they were bought out by Teletrac, they were still in the lead and they just let it die. Tim Slater, who originally started CompuTrac, invited me to speak at one of the conferences. I was doing quite a lot of stock trading and also a lot of seasonal commodity spread trading, which was fairly low risk but offered decent returns. I did a talk on that at the CompuTrac conference. After my speech, Tom Johnson, a Stanford Ph.D. and professor, and a graduate student named Paul Sutin, came up and talked with me. I was trying to find something to disprove the Efficient Market hypothesis. It seemed like the returns that I was talking about with these seasonal commodity spreads were way out of line with the risk that was being taken and so he thought that might be a way of disproving it.

We got together and I helped Paul do research and I also assisted him in writing a thesis on that. In the process, I got involved with Tom and decided we would spend about three years doing a major research project. We had about six different graduate students and Tom and myself, and we had all of the research facilities from Stanford, Berkeley, and the University of Chicago at our disposal. We did this huge project looking at the common criteria of the stocks that did well versus those that didn't. We looked at currencies, interest rates, different commodity futures, different foreign exchange movements, a lot of macroeconomic variables, a lot of advanced statistical analysis to do correlations, and other things. And we came up with a very large group of models that we used as a background to guide us in the different markets.

After we had gotten done with a big phase of the research, Paul got his Ph.D. and went to Switzerland to begin working for Chemical Bank as a trader. We had written up some of our work in various trade magazines and for the Stanford Research Institute and had some papers out on pattern recognition and some other things. At the time, these were very popular issues. So we got invited to speak at Chemical Bank and do some consulting there. In addition, we were invited to speak and do seminars at several places in the U.S. and Europe. At the end of those seminars, we ended up in Switzerland and had several offers for us to use what we had been talking about in our talks for a hedge fund. And so Paul and I decided to branch out and do that and Tom decided that he wanted to continue to do research. And so we gave him a research grant and some of our salary and that's how we started off.

What was the name of the hedge fund?

Our first hedge fund was Manning Hedge Fund. A lot of the stuff we used came from our research as well as some follow-up research we'd done. We had decent years in the 20 percent range of gains. We had done a lot of research that showed different patterns and their long-term historical behavior. But one of the things that we found was that, on an annual basis at turning points, a lot of those highly reliable patterns went through phases where they were 20 to 30 percent reliable instead of the 70 to 80 percent that was the norm. And so you could have fairly substantial drawdowns in rough periods during turning points in the market.

That led us to do some research that ultimately showed us that it wasn't nearly as important what patterns you were using to enter and exit as it was that you were in the vehicles that were moving. At the time, Tom was doing a lot of research whereby some money manager or trader would come to him with a system and say "look, here's the system, here's my track record for it, here's how it's done, here's exactly what it is, and how can we improve on that?" One of the projects he had that was really influential involved three people. Two of them had very elaborate patterns that they were using exclusively to get into positions. The third had a system in which 90 percent of his criteria was involved in selecting a vehicle that was really moving. And he was just using a simple moving average on it . . . a moving average that didn't make money if you tested it on any vehicle. But that trader was making twice as much as the other two traders.

That led us to look into our own work and realize that vehicle selection was much more important than picking a correct pattern. And we really wanted to get into runaway patterns and runaway moves. And if you could do that, that would certainly give you an edge in terms of reliability and would allow you to reduce your risk. That was actually much more important than anything else.

When you say "vehicle," you're talking about a high relative strength issue, then?

We have what we call "runaway criteria," which are things like gaps and thrusts. Bill O'Neil talks about things like follow-through days; that's really very much what I call "thrust." Generally we have a whole set of runaway market criteria, and we want to get at least five in the last 21 bars. It's just a set of individual day patterns that indicates very strong buying or selling. The patterns give us an idea as to the strength of the trend. So the idea, really, is that you go where the oil is. The oil in the markets is wherever there are runaway trends. This is because most markets and most stocks spend more than half the time in trading ranges or consolidations where they're not trending strongly. And about 25 percent of the time they are really running rapidly. If you have some way of catching just some of that runaway movement, that's the time to really risk your capital. The rest of the time it's not worth the risk. That's the concept.

As far as the variables go, did you initially come up with them way back when you started this hedge fund, the Manning Hedge Fund?

Yes. We contacted O'Neil and found a lot of his research and re-did a lot of it and came up with our conclusions. We tried to find anybody who had research. Frank Cappiello had a lot of research, particularly on institutional holdings. We did a lot of work with Martin Zweig's stuff, in terms of monetary variables. We just tried to find anybody that had some very good stuff. We didn't want to reinvent the wheel, but we wanted to find stuff that worked. One of the things that we found concerning a lot of O'Neil's stuff is that a lot of the CANSLIM stocks that he looks for are very, very volatile. Over the long run, they tend to make it hard to produce a very smooth equity curve. You tend to have bigger ups and downs. A lot of the people that do that can have incredible years. But then you can also have some tough years and your drops from some of the good periods can be pretty big. If you happen to get in at the wrong time, your drawdowns are a little bigger.

We did a lot of research on that and found that there were a number of ways to cut both return and risk from doing it, but you got a better risk/reward ratio. We mostly focused on stocks that were undervalued for their growth rate. Basically, the ones whose P/E is relatively low compared to their earnings growth rate. And so they've got a little bit of a value component to them even though they're growth stocks. They tend to have a little bit less volatility on the downside and they tend to move up a little bit more slowly, but that allows you to move up your trailing stops a little more consistently and—

—so that you don't get stopped out quite as much.

That's right.

How do you measure P/E? Is it on trailing earnings?

Yes, it's on trailing earnings. If you've got estimates that look like the earnings are going through the roof, or for some reason to expect that, you want to take that somewhat into consideration. But basically, if it's a consistently growing stock that has three years of higher annual earnings, a long-term earnings growth rate of at least 25 percent, quarterly earnings that are 25 percent or more, and some good earnings momentum, we would want a P/E that is 70 percent of the lesser of the long-term growth rate or the last two quarters' earnings growth rate. And if it was a turnaround situation, where you had 70 percent or higher earnings growth in the last two quarters, then we would want the P/E to be 70 percent of whichever was the lowest of the last two quarters' earnings growth rate. So it gives you some flexibility.

Stepping back a little, was the Manning Fund your own fund?

I did it with Paul Sutin and we had a partner, who was a financial backer. We did okay with that, but we had a lot of problems with the financial backer. He was very eccentric, and the three of us didn't get along. Paul ended up inheriting quite a bit of money at the end of the 18-month period that we had pegged as an initial trial period. And so I went off on my own at the end of that period and started Midas Trust and Midas High Yield Trust, which initially were trusts in the British Virgin Islands. Then in 1995, we had loaded up the number of people in those trusts and the main investor had actually died. So I couldn't convert those trusts into a hedge fund, but I basically took the profits that I had from my share of that and started Midas Funds in the Cayman Islands. Those two are essentially the same, but one allowed for new investors to get in while the other didn't.

This is when you started running your own ship, then?

Yes.

And you still have both of those funds?

Yes. And then I've got probably 80 percent of the money I manage in private accounts. I trade a lot of different methodologies and a lot of different asset classes. "Long/short" is one of the categories and I have a couple of strategies for that. And I usually have a couple of different managers that I farm out half of it to. And I do the same thing for commodities. I've got four or five of my own systems for commodities that make up half of our commodity exposure. And then I'll farm out to Trout and Tudor and some of the very top global futures traders, and I do the same thing with real estate. We cover a whole host of different asset classes in the fund to try and really produce gains in every year and have a very low drawdown. While we don't have the best total returns—I think our compound annual return is just barely under 30 percent—we've done that on less than an 8 percent maximum drawdown over the last seven years.

I think 30 percent is pretty sensational.

We have volatility in our annual returns. What happens is we have a year like the beginning of 2000 or a year like '92 or '93 and if we have a decent allocation to our long and short strategies and our global equity strategies, we tend to do extremely well. We started in '92 and we were fortunate to have a year that was over 80 percent.

That's great.

That helped out a lot. We've had a lot of years where we're up in the 10 to 20 percent range. Over the long run, that's been our average and we've always had positive double-digit returns, but there's a lot of volatility in those figures. We keep the risk down in what we're doing. If it's a good environment for something and it looks safe, we're pretty aggressive into it. But as soon as it starts to look like it might not even be safe, we're pulling out of it and we've got other asset classes that we're allocated to all of the time. Our fund basically is designed for a typical Swiss bank client, because most of our clients are really from Swiss banks and that's where 80 percent of the money we have comes from. That money tends to be even more risk-averse than I would be alone.

It's more risk-averse because you're dealing with high net worth individuals?

You're dealing with high net worth individuals that are not trying to get rich; they're trying to make a decent return and not lose any money. To a certain extent, the difference between European hedge fund investors and U.S. ones is that the Europeans tend to be a lot more risk averse, and particularly the ones that go through Swiss banks. I'm sort of trying to do a mix between Trout and Zweig DiMenna, two of my big heroes. Trout has had some phenomenal, almost T-bill like consistency of producing a 12 to 20 percent return. Zweig DiMenna has higher returns on a very long-term basis but has a little bit more swings in equity than I would like to have. If I had a 20 percent drawdown, I think I would lose a substantial portion of my clients. So I really can't afford to be that aggressive.

I'm trying to make decent returns, but I'm trying to play it very close to the vest. The only way to do that is to have a lot of different strategies and lot of different asset classes that are totally uncorrelated to each other going at the same time.

How does your fund's performance compare with the performance of other hedge funds?

I think Nelson's ranked us in the top 10 for five-year returns for the last four or five years for the particular type of style that we are. I think Nelson's put us in the global asset allocation strategy type. I know that in that group, we are the lowest drawdown of any fund in there. What really bugs me about all those rating services is that they're only looking at one number, which is total return. That really doesn't give you a very clear picture of what a really good manager is, in my opinion. It's someone who produces returns on drawdown that are substantially higher.

Weren't you ranked No. 1 by Nelson's?

Two of the last five years I was ranked No. 1 for the last five-year period.

Which years were they?

I believe it was 1997 and 1998.

Can you tell us a little about your long/short strategy in the U.S. market? How would you enter a position with that strategy?

We have a set of criteria that we call up fuel criteria for stocks. Basically, it's quite similar to O'Neil's stuff. We focus on the growth-at-a-reasonable-price version of those stocks. We tend to focus on ones that are a little bit lower on the mutual fund holdings and where institutional sponsorship is going from practically nothing to where it's starting to pick up sharply. And the stock has a P/E that is 70 percent of either its long-term earnings growth rate or the last two quarters' earn-

Breakout of cup-with-handle base: Keithley Instruments (KEI), Daily

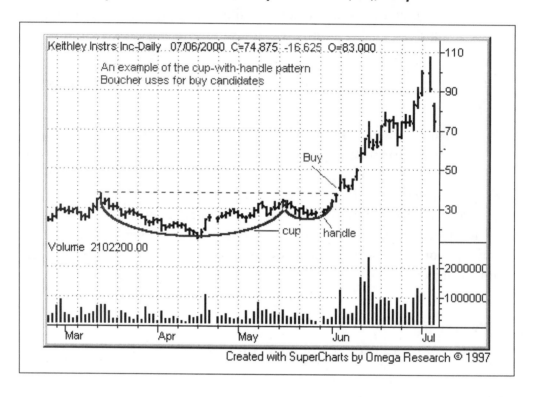

ings growth rate, depending on whether it's a turnaround or a consistent-growth stock. Then our criteria are very similar to O'Neil's. We tend to look for flag patterns. We use cup-with-handles as well. But my favorite pattern is a flag pattern, which is something where you've had a very strong run-up of at least 50 percent or more in the stock and you have four-plus weeks of it going sideways and not retracing 38 percent of the last major up move. And then you get some volume accumulation indicators that break out before price. It breaks out with strong volume and usually with what we call TBBLBG, which means either a thrust, a gap, or a lap. A thrust is a large-range day with volume higher than the previous day that closes in the top third of the range and a lap is sort of like a gap from the closing price level. And you want to have good volume.

We look for a stock that meets all of our up fuel criteria and also breaks out of a flag pattern or a cup-with-handle that has a handle in the top half of the range. We want to see at least three or more accumulation days, which are up days on higher volume, before the breakout. And the breakout should be on strong volume and either a gap, lap, or thrust. Those are the two real entry methods that we use consistently to buy stocks. And we put a protective stop below the last pivot point. Using a percentage stop, we've never really had a lot of success. I know O'Neil uses an 8 percent stop. What we've found is that tends to reduce the reliability of the trade over the long run, or at least when using our methodology. So we use a stop below the last pivot point and try to use the distance between entry and open protective stop as one of the parameters that tells us how much to allocate to a particular stock. It's a little bit different, but it's very similar. We do the same thing on the short side. We look for stocks that have our down fuel criteria and are breaking down from flag patterns on the down side, down side cup-with-handles, descending triangles, or four-week-or-longer consolidations that are relatively tight. Again, we want the breakout to be on higher volume than the prior day at least, and we want it to be on a thrust, gap, or lap down if possible.

The long and short setups are basically just a mirror image of themselves. We run the top relative strength, earnings-per-share, new high list and the bottom relative strength, earnings-per-share, new low list. We do this because basically we found out that when we tried to go the other way and just find all the stocks that met our criteria, we would often miss stocks. We would see them at the end of the week and we'd go back and say "damn it, that stock met our criteria and we missed it." And there aren't a lot of these stocks that meet all our criteria in the first place. So we ended up saying "you know what? Those are our criteria, but we're going to watch every damned new high and every damned new low and make sure we don't miss any." Because there just aren't enough of these to be able to afford to miss them. So we started doing that. And when we started to do that, we found out that that was actually an extremely valuable list. If you look at the concentration of groups and subgroups in that list, anytime you've got a lot of members of a particular group that are breaking out of valid bases at about the same time, that's valuable information. Because if you buy any member

Breakdown of flag pattern: Rhythms Netconnections (RTHM), Daily

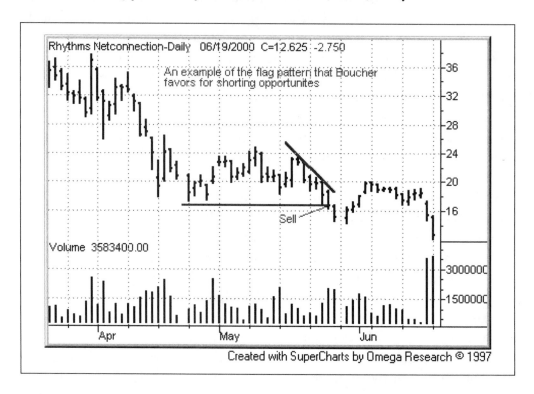

of that group, it's likely to be a leading group and that move is likely to be more reliable than if just one or two stocks are breaking out.

So we found that by doing something that just helped us not screw up and miss a trade, we ended up finding a lot of valuable information from it. And it's become a core part of that methodology. Now we really are trying quite a bit more than we ever did before. Not just to position in the stocks that meet those criteria, but if we have a choice, to position in the ones that are in the leading groups as indicated by those lists.

You said your stop loss point would not be based on a percentage off your entry, but when you undercut a pivot point.

Right. We have an indicator that's pretty complex for determining that. But basically anytime you get a low that has six higher lows around it, that's a pretty good rule of thumb for the pivot point that we'd be using. Once you get a certain size move, then of course we have trailing stop techniques that move up pretty quickly. Really, it's very rare that you go a month or more without us having to move stops to breakeven. So we try to play with the house's money as soon as we can. But we want to make sure the market has made a low that's a decent pivot point and then made a new high off of it before we move our stop.

Do you use any general market indicators in this particular strategy?

I've got 20 different market timing systems that I use in the market timing part of our allocation. We look at those and they give us a little bit of background as to how risky or safe the market environment is. But the honest truth is that, over the years, we've pretty much grown to respect the new high list and the new low list. The number of stocks that meet our criteria that are breaking out is probably the best evidence of the health of the market of anything we've got. Early in 2000, we had the wonderful environment which you get occasionally, where you had a very huge amount of opportunities on both the short and the long side at the same time. That allows you, with very low risk, to leverage your portfolio and get some pretty spectacular returns. Whenever that happens, and it usually runs for a significant amount of time with significant percentage moves in both directions, it's generally a turning point in the market one way or the other. You have to be careful because you can get some very fast gains that turn around on you very quickly. So as soon as we saw that start to come unglued in early-March 2000, we advised people to take half profits and took at least that much profit in our own managed accounts. We had a similar environment in '92–'93 and really hadn't had anything like it since then.

You're referring to the early-2000 advance in the Nasdaq at the same time that the Dow and S&P were declining?

It goes beyond that. Since 1998, you had a two-tiered market. You had a stealth bear market in the majority of the stocks while a smaller and narrowing group of stocks dominated by the Nasdaq 100 kept going higher, particularly at the end of the move. That type of environment can be frustrating for a lot of different strategies. For ours, it's ideal.

Do you look at sentiment indicators?

Sure. We have a whole host of sentiment indicators that we use in our market timing approach. That just gives us a background for how risky or how reliable the environment is.

Would they be anything that you would take trades based on? Or do you just use them as background information?

We have around 20 different timing models. And we take 1/20 of the capital that we allocate to timing-model trading and trade each one independently. A lot of those have a component of sentiment in them.

What is the percentage of a portfolio that you allocate to one position? Do you like having a lot of different positions that are smaller in size?

We try to be concentrated but diversified at the same time. An ideal number of positions is somewhere between five and eight.

That's with no leverage.

Right. When we go to leverage, we often get repeat buys and we may have as many as 20 positions at one point in time. But that's very rare. Usually, even if we're fully leveraged, it's more like 14 or 15 positions. A lot of those, if they're not repeats of the same stock, are breakouts in others that are in the same industry. So they're really more concentrated in that respect. Basically, we're trying to play somewhere between six and 10 areas.

Is your initial buy a certain percentage of the account?

We'll never risk more than 2 percent on any one trade—that's the first money management rule. That often is the policing as to how much allocation. Generally, we're looking to put something like 7 or 8 percent in a stock initially. Basically, we're using risk to determine what our allocation is. Sometimes you can get a situation where you have a very tight flag pattern that's been there for months. And one blink and the stock breaks out nicely and you can allocate significantly more to that and still have your portfolio risk be only 2 percent versus a stock that has a very wide path. We'd never put more than 20 percent initially into one position and we wouldn't allow a position to get up to more than 25 percent of our portfolio.

But if you started with an 8 percent position, you might add on to it in a pyramid fashion.

Absolutely.

What books would you recommend to traders?

Cappiello has a good book. I think it's called *Finding the Next Superstock*. All of O'Neil's books I love, and I think his new one, *24 Essential Lessons for Investment Success*, is particularly better than the first one. It's probably better-suited for someone that's had some experience using his stuff. It's got a lot more useful information. His first book was fantastic, but it was designed to take someone from not investing in stocks to being able to use CANSLIM stuff. I think the second book is more geared toward refining those things even better. So I like it better. I like all of Zweig's books. I like to read the books on money managers, so *Money Masters* and all of the Schwager books are good for that kind of thing.

I think what you try and do in any field is to figure out who's very successful at it and then try to figure out what they're doing. And then you try and take as much of that as you can and put it into your own stuff. Kroll wrote a book on futures trading that discusses money management in a way that a lot of stock traders would benefit from. It's not directly related to stock trading, but I think the idea of how to manage risk that futures traders have to do to survive is something that stock traders can really benefit from.

It's been my experience that many traders give short shrift to money management principles. You're known as a player who places the importance of money management on a pedestal. Do you think money management is more important than an actual strategy—

—yeah, I think that I would rather have good money management and a mediocre strategy than have it be the other way around. That's your defense and tells you how much you're going to make.

That's a profound point to end on, Mark.

LEWIS BORSELLINO

BIG ITALY

By Marc Dupée

Patience, graciousness, and gentility in social situations veil a ferocity that has made him one of the most famed traders in the world trading arena. Giving away his vocation is his slightly raspy voice, an occupational hazard common among pit traders required to scream buy and sell orders in the frenzied and deafening environment of the open outcry trading pits.

Lewis J. Borsellino took an instant liking to this harried environment, once commenting, "The moment I walked out onto the trading floor, I thought it was the greatest thing I ever saw in my life." He has survived, prospered, and made millions in his 19-year tenure in the S&P 500 futures pit and has brought many people along with him, opening doors and showing the ropes to family, friends, and acquaintances.

At one point during the epoch when trading for both institutional and personal accounts was still permitted, Borsellino was the largest trader in the S&Ps, transacting contracts with an annual notional value in the billions. While he still trades on the floor every day, Borsellino is following the times, expanding his trading activity and operations into the electronic age.

A tough competitor and sportsman from Chicago's West Side, Borsellino credits his success and trading longevity to discipline, a quality he thanks his father for, and one that he ranks in his 10 Commandments of Trading. A man of intense focus, Borsellino claims that when the markets become crazy, he becomes more sane: "The wilder the market gets, the more disciplined I become." Borsellino wrote a book, *The Day Trader*, which not only covers his trading experiences, but also depicts his colorful life.

As one of the longest standing veterans in the S&P pit, Borsellino has seen it all. While an expert in the technicals of trading, he stresses how practice and discipline have imbued in him a "sixth sense" about trading, a sense that he underscores is critical to his success.

Emphasizing that discipline and practice are required to excel, Borsellino tells aspiring traders to "perfect their methodology to the point where it becomes robotic. Once you reach that point where reflexive actions take the place of thought, you then become a great trader."

Marc Dupée: Why have you succeeded at this game when so many others have failed?

Lewis Borsellino: Well, I think the No. 1 thing that any trader has to have to succeed is discipline. I have The 10 Commandments of Trading that I follow (see end of interview). You have to be a disciplined trader through all kinds of trading . . . through good times and bad times. It's the good times that I see that end up destroying people. They think that they're invincible . . . they think they can't make a wrong decision, that they can't do anything wrong. And they end up taking more risk than they're accustomed to. Then all of a sudden, the market does what it usually does. It surprises people and moves the other way . . . and you're carrying the guy away because he got too big for his britches. I think that this is the No. 1 reason why I've succeeded. I've always been grounded, and have always been a disciplined person when it comes to trading.

The other thing is, as I often say to people, I don't really trade for money. I trade for success, meaning I want my plan to be successful. The product is money. When Bill Gates formed Microsoft, he wanted the best product and it just happened to make him one of the richest men out there. I think that is true of any trader. If you're successful, you have a good plan, good buys, know where to stop out, know how to control your losses, and know how to learn from your losses.

Learning from your losses is probably the biggest key to success, because the losses actually tell you what you're doing wrong, what kind of market you're in. If you're in a trend-following market, a reversal market, whatever . . . the losses will tell you what's going on.

You mention that, similar to a lot of veteran traders, you have learned to rely on an ability that is like a sixth sense when it comes to reading the market. What is that sixth sense? Is it something you think you can garner or detect in screen trading?

Well, Marc, what a lot of people say I do is use gut and instinct. But what they don't see is what I've done behind the scenes. Like 10 years ago, we bought all the rights to Gann.

All the Gann charts, right?

Right. We've always been technicians, we always do our homework and prepare ourselves for the market. So after 20 years, there is not much that I haven't seen. And what happens is my brain is like a mini-computer: It's able to process very quickly. So it looks like I'm acting instinctively, but there is a fine line. If you're an expert at pattern recognition—and that's what the art of charting and technical analysis is all about—you're able to recognize patterns very quickly and see scenarios. Then, is it instinct, or is it learned behavior over 20 years? I think it's a little of both. I certainly have more gut instinct—I have probably forgotten more about trading than some guys that are just starting.

I love that story in your book about the time back in October 1987, on the Thursday following Black Monday, when you stepped into the S&P pit. And

having been an order filler yourself for four years, you could sense the nervousness of brokers who had big customer orders to fill.

Just before the opening, a Shearson broker offered 1,000 points lower. You tested how low they would be willing to go by yelling "2,000 lower." The Shearson broker came back, "3,000 lower." You returned, "4,000 lower" and then the Shearson broker went 5,000 lower. When the market opened, the S&Ps were down about 5,600 and you bought 150 contracts, only to turn around and sell them seconds later to some trader across the pit—2,000 points higher than what you bought them for—pocketing something like $1.3 million.

That move seemed like part bluff in a poker game and partly the indulgence of participants' fear of the downside.

Oh, definitely. I mean in '87 it was like a ghost town around here . . . not only the fear of the traders, but the exchange officials, everybody. It's no secret that (Fed Chairman) Alan Greenspan saved Wall Street and La Salle Street. Margin calls were not being met, firms were on the brink of going bankrupt, and there is no doubt in my mind that he saved Wall Street and La Salle Street at the same time back then. And you've got to understand that 5,600 points, when our biggest day ever since the inception of the contract was like a 1,000-point move, was huge.

What a windfall. Have you had any other trades like that?

I've had other days when I've made high six figures. I just did an article for CNBC.com that says daytraders don't swing for the fences, and I talk about that trade. But when I look back at my career for the last 20 years, it's all the singles and the doubles that have made me all the money, and not the home runs.

A lot of traders say that. And if they are hitting singles and sticking to their plan, then once in a while they swing and get that homer.

Right. Once in a while you get that homer. So if I can get one every two to three years, I'm real happy.

No doubt. Was it the FBI that was investigating that trade? Anyway, you came to learn that George Soros was on the other side of that Shearson trade.

Actually that had nothing to do with the FBI. What happened then was the Shearson broker made a mistake and entered the order twice. And when they liquidated the error, it was like a $50 million or $60 million error. Soros sued Shearson and sued all the participants in the S&P pit.

It was funny when I went there. Their theory was the Shearson broker disclosed the order to me, and being the biggest local at the time, that there was some kind of conspiracy. I said he didn't have to disclose the order to me, I saw him shitting in his pants and I offered them lower and he offered them lower. I had every right to do what I did: I was a member [of the Chicago Mercantile Exchange]. As long as I was willing to take everything I offered at that price, there was nothing they could do about it.

Then, someone hadn't done their homework, because when I bought the 150 contracts, I tried to buy them from the Shearson broker. But the broker behind me, a Salomon broker, hit me on the 150. So you know, it was a clear understanding of how the market *doesn't* work.

There are a lot of people out there who don't understand how the market works. You think about it. How did the Merc end up with the S&P contract when they started the Russell, I believe, at the NY Merc at the time? And here we are in Chicago, Wall Street's there, yet we end up with the S&P contract. You know everybody was vying for the S&P contract and the Chicago Mercantile ends up with it. They gave it to us and now all the portfolio managers use it to hedge their activities.

How did they end up with it?

It is the simple fact that, you know, New York does stocks and Chicago does commodities. Nobody does it better than Chicago. You've got the Board of Trade, you've got the Merc; you've got the oldest futures industries in the world.

When you're in the pit, do you find bluffing a useful strategy?

The one thing you have to be careful about when you start bluffing and push-ing the market around, is that you're gonna get hit. I often tell people, "When you're wrong, you'll get as many as you want." Right? You've got to be careful. There are times where, when I'm long, I'll give my orders to order fillers and I'll bid the market up, and other locals and other people may try to bid it up in front of me.

The one thing about being around as long as I have, being a large trader, being known for having a pretty good sense of the market, is that a lot of traders do like to follow me. So it's a way for me to get out that's, you know, sort of bluffing. You've got to be careful. Like I said, when you're wrong, you'll get as many as you want.

In your book *The Day Trader*, you point out that you will always trade but that you are making a transition, as the subtitle implies, *From The Pit To The PC*, and that you are increasing your focus on your fund, Borsellino Capital Management. I'm interested in how this transition is going, and if the formidable skills you've developed in the pit are transferring to the PC.

Well, first of all, we're reorganizing Borsellino Capital Management. The focus switched after the book came out.

The book was published in mid-1999?

Right, May 1999 is when it came out and that's what got us to TeachTrade.com. It's the role of an educator. And besides that, I got involved in a SOES room about two or three years ago. I watched people who had no idea of what to do when it comes to trading. They were just seeking information. And then I looked out there and saw what people were charging them and what they were getting for what they were paying. It made me sort of sick.

So that's how I started TeachTrade.com, and actually it has taken over the focus. What we're allowing people to do on TeachTrade.com is institutional qual-ity research. We're not charging for it now, but it will be at retail prices. Goldman, Merrill . . . all of them have research centers. Over the last 19 years, we've developed trading systems, we have over 20 years of experience, and we've invested millions of dollars in research. We're going to let people access that.

And access is by imitation, meaning they'll be able to watch us. We let you know when we're long, when we're short, and our thought process behind buying which stocks. We watch the underlying stocks that support the S&P 500 and the Nasdaq 100. We've met with a lot of success.

As far as the screen trading and making the transition from the pit to the PC, the difference is you have to be more patient on the screen. You can't scalp. It's still the same gut-wrenching sort of mentality and you go through the same things when you have your trades on. But on the floor you can go to a trade, where on the screen you've got to wait for a trade to come to you.

For example, if I want to buy S&Ps at 1500 and I've got a mental stop at 1497.50, if I'm on the screen, I'll buy the 1500s and I'll put my stops in. That's the end of the story. When I'm on the floor, I might buy the 1500s, I might buy nine-halfs (1499.50), I might scale down into it and add more to it. If I'm correct, I'll sell those nine-halfs and scalp in and out from the long side all the way up to my upside objective, where on the screen you can't do that. You've got to pick your entry point—you may scale into your entry point—but you've got to pick it and you've got to have your stop and then that's the end of the story.

In your book you say you're one of the best when it comes to reading support and resistance and order flow and reading how the market will react to events such as the Fed's tightening today (March 21, 2000). Could you explain how you read support and resistance in the pit and whether it's different in your screen-based trading?

Well, it's no different. There's no difference in reading support and resistance. What happens on the floor, though, is you're able to see it acted out. On the screen, you don't have the noise and the emotion and the drama of the other individuals acting on those resistance points. If you've ever been on the floor and a key area of resistance has been penetrated or there has been a big up move, the emotion of that move looks like a big wave when everybody is buying and everybody is selling. It's a nice feeling of euphoria if you're long and everybody's buying, and it's the feel of terror when you're long and everybody is selling. But technical support and resistance is the same on the screen as it is being in the pit.

Same question for order flow. Now that the Merc has made rules that require locals to stand down in the pit, reserving the outer ring for filling brokers, how do you maintain an edge for interpreting order flow?

That hasn't really changed the idea of seeing order flow. We're able to stand on the step below them. When Merrill Lynch is bidding on 500 contracts or 300 contracts, we're still seeing that.

Do you feel you can maintain this edge for interpreting order flow off the floor? If so, how do you do that?

You have to understand that it's two different types of trading. You remember I said I don't really care about the order flow when I'm trading on the screen.

If you're just scalping in and out on the floor, you are looking at order flow. Hopefully, if you've got a big order-filler who is 1500-even bid on 200 contracts, you might be 15 1/2 bid on 50 contracts, leaning on him. That's how people take advantage of order flow. And, you know, it's the same as when you look at the Nasdaq market makers that are bidding, say, 150 for 20,000 shares and someone bids 150 1/8 for 10,000 shares. It's the same sort of premise.

You've mentioned that one of the things that has made you successful is your ability to read how the market will react to the next "twitch or itch" of the Fed. What signs do you see on the floor that will help you know what the Fed's move might be? Were you on the floor today?

I was on the floor. I went down there at 1:15 p.m. when the numbers did go out.

Did you see anything today that gave away what the Fed's move might be, even though everybody was expecting the 1/4-point interest rate rise?

Three Fake-Outs After A Fed Rate Move: September 2000 S&P 500 Futures (SPU0), 3-minute

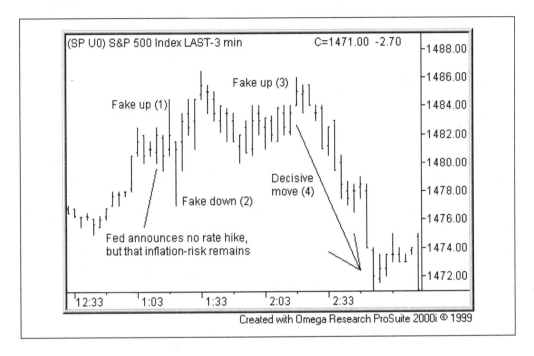

Following the Fed's June 28, 2000 FOMC meeting on interest rates, in an event occurring three months after the interview, the S&Ps exhibit the same pattern Borsellino describes, *only to the downside*. The contract initially rallies, breaks, rallies and then breaks, making its fourth and decisive move to the downside.

Well, one of the things that I've been looking at over the last couple of months is the disconnect where the Dow and the S&Ps are lagging behind the Nasdaq. And today you had the same thing. The Dow was up, the Nasdaq was down, the S&Ps were down on the opening, and what I looked for today, after that number came out, was the consolidation. When I saw the Nasdaq, the Dow and the Spoos all going up, then I laid it in. Then I got long and stayed with them. Because once we started going, we started going.

But typically when we have a Fed number, we tell people to look for the fake-out. What we were looking for was a break, rally, break and then a rally. And that's what happened. We got a little bit of a break, it rallied, then a little bit of a break and then the rally took off.

Why were you looking for that pattern?

Over the years, that's what we've seen. That's one of those things that is a gut thing that we've always seemed to notice.

Is this a familiar pattern that you've seen in the Spoos pit, a fake-out pattern?

We look for that fake-out. Because in the past, I've noticed this is bullish. I'm looking and looking and I'd buy it as soon as the number came out and it would go down against me and then I'd get out and get chopped up. So what I'll do is try to stay pretty neutral for the first 10, 15 minutes and then when the rally starts we look for a good area to get in. Actually, we had 1500 as a big buy-point area. And then as it got up there, I saw that the Nasdaq and everything had turned around and I just stayed with my longs.

Are there signs you can see down in the pit besides price action that will let you know what the next "twitch or itch" of the Fed is going to be?

Well, not of the Fed. But now that we can have wireless connection with my technical research people, I have a clerk who does nothing but stand right next to me with a headset on, and talks to our tech guy. And he's watching news, he's watching support and resistance areas and he's telling my clerk to "tell Lewis to watch 1505, tell him to watch 1500, if it goes through there we'll be looking for 1497." One of my techs we call the "human search engine." He has 25 monitors in front of him. And that's all he does. He's a human search engine.

How can you tell when a program trade comes into the market? Can you key off of that to make money?

In the past, years ago, it was a little easier to identify, especially when I was filling orders. I'd get an order from Salomon Brothers to buy 1,000 S&Ps and I'd get them done in about four ticks. And I'm like "wow, how does that happen?" And then I'd watch the cash start ticking down and then I knew they were buying Spoos and selling cash. There are a lot of different methodologies . . . people hedging options and doing program trading. Now they're actually arbing the S&P with the E-Mini and they're doing an S&P/Nasdaq spread. So the participants all have something different . . . everybody's looking for that Holy Grail edge. All I've ever found out is buy low and sell high. That's the key to success.

Or buy high, sell higher?

Yes.

Off the floor, what specific patterns and parameters do you look for in your technical analysis to determine when to enter the market?

We like to do a lot of momentum buying. We're also contrarian. My philosophy over the years has always been to look for what everybody's *not* doing because when everybody's short and you're long and that thing turns around, you're going to be in pretty good shape. And we look for very low-risk trades, especially when we are on the screen.

When we're trading from upstairs, what we look for basically are trades that have a $2 or $3 stop. And if you're risking $3, you've got to make at least $6. We look for a lot of support points and a lot of momentum. And like before, when you're talking about your losers, your losers actually identify what kind of market you're in. You know, sometimes you're buying new highs and selling new lows, then all of a sudden the market stops, turns around, stops you out and then continues to go that way.

Or you buy a high and you stop, it turns around and goes the other way, it goes down to the lows, you get short, put your stop in and you get stopped out on that. That will tell you if you're in a range-bound market. So should you be fading new highs at that point? Sure, if you're in a range-bound market, now you want to start fading the highs. And if you're in a momentum market, that's when you'll buy new highs. So you have to identify those things, and we're pretty good at doing that.

Are there specific patterns that you look for in defining momentum or is it just a break of a certain level?

It doesn't just hit you in one day. Patterns take weeks and sometimes months to form. For example, why did we think 1500 to 1502 was a big area today? Because last week on the run-up, it went up and pulled back and we've made a triple top at 1500. So we knew that once it got through and the news was there and positive and we had everything moving together, 1500 would be a good buy because there would be a lot of stops up above it. So you definitely look for chart formations that show triple tops, triple bottoms; those are the kinds of things that really jump in. Moving averages . . . the 60-day moving average is a big moving average for us.

The 60-day moving average works well in the Spoos pit?

Right.

Are there specific patterns you look for to get out of the market? Or again, like you said, do you get out when it hits a level or hits your target?

We definitely have objectives. We look at the objectives, but then again the old saying comes, "we never argue with profits either." One of the things I've learned over the years is that when you turn your profit and you hit your price objective, take it. Sometimes the market keeps going and you could have made another $10,000 and I see people moan about that. I look at them and say, "you never moan about profits." Profits will never take you out of the business, losses will.

I've heard other world class traders like yourself say that one of the most difficult things to do is to perfect the exiting of their trade.

Breakout of Critical 1500 Level: September 2000 S&P 500 Futures (SPU0), 3-minute

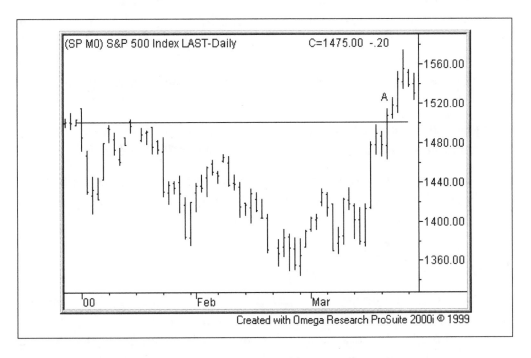

June S&Ps break through 1500 at (A) on March 21, 2000, the day the Fed raised interest rates 25-basis points, triggering stops in a move through a triple top pattern.

Oh, definitely. And you think about it, especially with all these newbie stocks. Everybody's hoping they can catch the next Qualcomm. Who knows where that's coming from. The people who caught Qualcomm, caught it . . . it was lucky. The insiders knew it . . . the guys who spun the company and so on. But if you got on it, you got on it. You don't cry over spilled milk. If you made a profit, you just applaud yourself for having a successful plan, and that's it.

How or when will you pyramid your trades while screen trading?

Do you mean how will I add to a position? Well, one of the things we never do is add to a loser. We never average. We'll pyramid the trade as we see different areas of support and resistance being tested and firming up and we look for consensus of all three of the indices moving in the same direction . . . definitely when we're trading Spoos (S&P 500 futures) and Nasdaq. If we get all three moving the same way, that's when we like to jump on and add to our positions.

I suppose that makes it a little clearer now, particularly since we've seen such bifurcation between tech and the blue-chips in 1999 and 2000.

That has made for very difficult trading. I think the period from October 1999 to February 2000 has been one of the most difficult times of trading that I've seen in a long time.

Really?

Yes, and it's because of the disconnect. Here you are watching Nasdaq making all-time highs, and you want to buy the Spoos but they keep beating them up. Every time the Nasdaq makes a new high and you go to buy them, the S&Ps get a little rally. Then the Dow sells off and the S&Ps sell off and you get chopped up.

Do you have a clerk near the Nasdaq pit?

Actually the Nasdaq's right in front of me. So I can see it and I can see the board. And I don't flash orders up there. If I want to place an order, I tell my clerk on the phone. He'll call the desk and put in the order for me.

You said you like to do low-risk trades; two to three bucks a stop.

Especially trading upstairs. Definitely upstairs.

Is that what you use as a stop loss rule?

My stop loss rule is, whatever your stop loss is, I want a 2 1/2-to-1 ratio. If I'm willing to risk $2 on a trade, then I have to make $5 in profit, a 2 1/2-to-1 ratio. For every dollar I risk, I want to make 2 1/2.

And will an upper channel be what you'll be looking for to determine what that upside potential will be?

Exactly.

How do you keep yourself balanced when you're on a run?

(Laughs). You know what, it's just 19 years. In 1987, I made $4.4 million. In 1988, I made $90,000. Okay? So I'm the ultimate doom-and-gloom guy, and that's what I look at. You know most professional traders like to trade from the short side. Me, I've been a bull since I've walked into the pit. I love to buy them. I keep telling guys, you want this thing to crash? You remember 1988 when business dried up and brokerages laid off 30 percent of the people? If you want a healthy market, let's keep going up.

Look, I've seen up and I've seen down and I understand that you've got to stay calm. The minute you start to believe in all the accolades that they throw at you, then that's when the market is going to show you. I've seen it happen to the biggest guys. I've seen Richard Dennis take $600 million and lose 300 of it in six months. And Victor Niederhoffer, too.

Those two were both trading off the floor.

Right, but I've seen guys on the floor who've had tremendous runs and then all of a sudden the next thing you know they're trying to borrow money from you.

Did their egos have something to do with why they crashed? Did they believe everybody that told them they're so great?

I think they had a temporary loss. They're very good traders, both of them. But what I think happened is they had a temporary loss of discipline. And they had too much pressure on them from their customers to perform. And when that happens, your plan and your logic sometimes get thrown out the window. I see it with my new traders. The worst thing that can happen for my new trader is he comes in and his first five trades are all winners. And I've got a cocky kid on my hand, and the next thing I know he's in my office the next day telling me he lost everything that he made in five days, plus double that. And, you know, he's got my foot up his ass and I'm telling him, "all right, now you don't have a job anymore." I preach that to them. I'm unusual. When I have a bad day, or a couple bad days in a row, or I've overtraded and I've lost a lot of money, I go out and I buy something.

Retail therapy?

I go out and I buy something. Not to make myself feel good. But to remind myself what a dollar is and what it gets me. And to remind myself that I've been fortunate to be earning the living that I have over the past 20 years, and have been fortunate to have been good at what I do.

In dealing with losses, you've said that you view losses as loans made to somebody else in the market, to somebody else in a zero-sum game. Can you expand on that a bit and on how that view helps your trading?

Well, that's my psychological edge. That's that competitive nature coming out of me. When I've had a bad day . . . in futures, for every winner there's a loser. It is a zero-sum game, where with stocks it's not. It definitely gets my adrenaline flowing when I've had a bad day. Especially when I've made stupid mistakes, rookie mistakes. I go home and I work out and I try to exhaust myself because I know I'm going to be up all night waiting for the market to open and the bell to ring so I can get back in there and get my money back.

That's what you write about in your book, that losses are loans to somebody else. But that doesn't really calm you. You still want to go get that money back. It's a temporary loan.

It's a temporary loan. Hopefully! That's the way I've viewed it over the last 19 years. And that's part of my competitive nature and the idea of trading for success. I've said it a million times to people around me: It's not the money. The money has been very good and it has been a product of being good at what I do. But it is the respect and admiration of your peers. It's the ability of me to be able to compete against the other person . . . it's me against the institution and me against the market. Trading has the highest highs and the lowest lows, Marc, and hopefully throughout your trading life you experience them both and there are more highs than lows and you know how to deal with them both.

I understand that dual trading is when you handle both orders from customers as well as trade your own account. You mentioned that back in the days when they allowed dual trading, the system worked to your advantage because you were already handling 30-, 50-, 100-lot sizes and bigger, and it gave you the confidence to pull the trigger on your own trades. That led you to become the biggest trader in the S&P pit at one point, transacting up to one-quarter million contracts annually with a notional value in excess of $62 billion. Could you describe what it is like to be, as you say in your book, "in the market flow" or "in the zone," trading that 100-lot size?

It's a two-edged sword. It's like being Michael Jordan, going out there every day and every day people wanting you to score 50 points. And you've got that pressure and you've got your own pressure on yourself and the ability to do it. And guess what? When you are in the zone and you've got everything going for you, you can't do anything wrong. You can throw 50-lots and 100-lots around and you're exiting them and turning profits with them and so on. And when you're out of that zone, just like Michael Jordan, all of a sudden you're only hitting 15 percent of your shots. It's the same thing that happens with trading.

I compare trading to professional athletics. There is the emotional side and the psychological side. When everything is clicking, you can do no wrong. And then when you've had a few losing days in a row, then you're out of sync. And when you're out of sync, everything you do is wrong, even if it's a five-lot.

But the one thing that I've learned is that you can't read your own press. You don't always have to be the biggest guy; you don't always have to be the biggest trader. You have to be the most *consistent* trader. And yeah, to this day I'll still take a 100-lot, I'll take a 200-lot. But more on my terms and not on the terms that I'm trying to prove to somebody that "hey, I'm Lewis Borsellino, I'm the biggest trader." When you're 25 to 30 years old, you're a little more cocky than when you're 43. I don't have anything to prove to anybody anymore at this point.

Do you think it would be possible for a trader without the dual-trading pit experience to develop that kind of sense that you have, in terms of trading size and being in the zone like that?

Oh definitely. I've been around some young, new stocks traders that have had seven-figure years already.

The SOES guys you were working with?

Some SOES guys and some people that have got enough capital behind them. You've got to understand that some of those Nasdaq stocks, they have more volatility and more swings than the S&Ps themselves. So if you jumped on Rambus and caught a $180 move, or if you caught Qualcomm in 1999, then you caught some of the opportunity that is out there. We are actually doing a lot more stock trading than we ever did.

Yes, with the volatility there in some tech stocks, it makes sense.

Not only volatility, the trading programs that we have for commodities are working better with the equities than they are with the commodities, because of the volatility in the equities.

I read in an interview that you did with a European journalist that you mentioned that your "biggest weakness stems from the fact that I've been

successful as a trader with a propensity for making profitable trades." What does that mean?

I said that? My biggest weakness?

Yes, does that ring a bell? The interview was with an Italian journalist.

Oh, all right. I think I was talking about other business decisions that I've made outside of the trading realm or even in the trading realm. I've never been the type of person to get involved in other businesses, because of the independence that I have as a trader. I think because of the independence that you get as a trader and the ability to say to somebody, "look I don't need your business idea, I don't need your investments," I've passed on some very good ideas that were very profitable. And it makes you sometimes too independent, and maybe sometimes closed-minded in your business decisions.

Here I am explaining to people why I'd be a good money manager—"I've survived for 20 years, guys"—and I still have people questioning me. Not that I'm egotistical, but when I look at other money managers, I'll ask them a series of questions and I'll find out they haven't had one-tenth of the trading experience that I've had. So that is where I think he quoted me from.

It's hard for me sometimes to explain why I would be good. Not that I'm the best trader who ever lived, but I've lasted 20 years, and this has been my formula of success.

I often make the analogy to that of the golf swing. You look at all the different golfers out there and they all have different body types. And they all have different swings . . . except at the moment of impact, they all look the same. So there are a lot of different traders out there, different personalities, different make-ups. But when you get down and you do that interview with them, Marc, you'll find out they all have the same qualities when it comes to discipline, structure, and so on.

In January 2000, you wrote for CNBC.com, "One thing never changes: If you want to know what the setup for the market is today, study where it's been

for the past several days—or longer." You mentioned earlier in the interview about price points and about your analysis. I'm curious how you use volatility. How do you put volatility into your analysis of technical support and resistance?

Let's say you're trading in a real volatile market, you buy the 1500s and you're willing to risk 400 points because that's what your research is telling you. Well, in real volatile markets, it may go down and stop you out at 1496, turn around on a dime and rally through your 1500, and go another 1,000 or 1,500 points. Here you've missed the move because you got stopped out. And what happened was, because the markets are volatile and because of the volume that's being traded, it has a bigger whipsaw. So when we see those, when we see that sort of volatility, what we'll do is cut our size back and then expand our stops so that we ultimately have the same risk . . . but we're adjusting for the volatility.

Or if you have a strong directional bias, you could benefit by doubling up on your order.

Yes, but when you're talking about volatility, what will happen is that the bounces will be bigger. With extreme volatility you're better off cutting the size back and expanding the stops so you don't get stopped out of the move. Normally, if you're getting a trending market, that's when you can sell' em, sell some more, sell some more, and it trends very orderly to your exit point. It's the same thing with buying in an upward trending market.

Is there a standard, or most common method, of calculating pivots in the S&P pit?

No. Everybody does different pivots. And the terminology that they use is different. One of the good pivots that people like to use is when you've gotten the opening range, and we've traded below the opening range and then we come back and go through the opening range. And then you have your moving averages that people use. We use a combination of a lot of different things, a combination of a lot of different research. I mean we use stochastics, we use Fibonacci, we use Gann. We use a combination of things together that I don't think other people do.

And the thing about technical analysis is that you can think of it as being an auto mechanic. You've got your engine, but they're always tweaking it to try to get it to go faster and try to run smoother. That's the same thing that we do with our technical analysis. Sometimes the bonds are the leaders and you're watching the bonds and they're going to give you an indication of what the market's doing. And sometimes there are different underlying stocks or a group of underlying stocks that will tell you what the market is doing. So that's why we have our analyst with 25 different screens.

So in the S&P pit, what a lot of people look at is the opening range. What time frame is that? The first half-hour?

No, the first five minutes, I mean the first minute that the market opens up and the opening range is established. That's a big one. Old highs, old lows, intraday highs, intraday lows; those end up becoming pivots.

I spent a day in the S&P pit on Veterans Day in November 1999. One of the clerks pointed out that the E-Mini volume was exceeding the volume of the S&Ps, and apparently that was unprecedented. How do you think electronic trading will affect open outcry, or have your opinions on this subject changed since you wrote the book?

As the public becomes more educated in the trading of futures, I think eventually open outcry may fall by the wayside, depending on how big and if the volume comes. But you have to remember what the role of the local is: He's there to provide liquidity. And until there is enough retail and institutional participation to absorb that liquidity, then the open outcry will exist.

If you were starting out now, what would you do differently?

I don't think I'd do anything differently. (*Laughs*). I think that I may have expanded more within my field.

What does that mean?

I would have branched out and done other ventures and would have been more open-minded about other things, other markets.

But then I'm a firm believer that you can trade Eskimo futures . . . ice futures. As long as you're a trader and it moves, you can trade it. But I think I would have gotten into the equities more. Like I said three years ago, we started doing equities. I think I would have been into the equities more than I have, because I've always watched them. We have 65-70 stocks we watch every day to give us an indication. And I've watched some big moves go and didn't participate in them because I was participating in the S&Ps.

It's hard to have your attention focused everywhere.

Right. But here we're watching these and we've seen some big moves made in them and that's why two years ago we started trading more equities. We're actually getting more involved with equities.

For someone starting off now, how would you advise them to proceed?

First thing I would advise them to do is to get as much education as they can about the markets. Try to get a job at an exchange or at a brokerage firm or find a reputable person who has been trading for at least a couple of years so they can align themselves with them. I'd also tell them to go to Teachtrade.com and get some very good lessons on what they're going to experience as a trader.

And I would ask them to attempt some simulated trading. It's a good idea, even if my experience with simulated traders is that there are always eight out of 10 winners, and then when they get to the real thing, they are lucky if they have one winner out of 10.

So what I do with my new guys is I make them simulate. I make them work on the floor and I make them do all of our research. Right now we have three of our stocks guys doing all of the charting updates and so on. And I make them do from three to five hours of research a night. And independently of one another, I make them give me the research on the 60 stocks and their opinion of how it has been formulated. That is what a lot of trading is. It's consensus building. I have three different analysts who work analyzing S&Ps and so on and they're not allowed to talk with one another.

It sounds like you bring others along with you—people whom you sponsor.

At first I brought my brother and my cousins. When I became successful, I got so many relatives that found me! And I sponsored them because they were my relatives and friends. And then about four years ago I started sponsoring other people. We have four guys on the floor trading and we've got six guys up here trading. And I have another four people in training right now doing research who are wannabe traders. And then we have three more people on staff that do nothing but technical research. We have a team concept and we include the people that are doing the research in the profits with the traders. This is good because what I've found over the years is that a lot of people who are good at research are terrible traders. They just don't know how to pull the trigger.

That's a good way to pool different people's talents. How or where does the average trader go wrong?

That's another thing about trading. There have been so many guys over the years, where I've said, "This guy will definitely make it," and he doesn't make it. And there are guys I go, "This guy doesn't have a chance," and he ends up being my best trader. It all comes down to one thing: I call it the emotional side of trading.

People who are good at discipline and controlling their emotions and knowing how to pull the trigger and not worrying about the losses and are able to

handle the winners without getting a big head . . . those are the ones that succeed.

You have to worry about the losses, but you can't become like a
deer-in-the-headlights sort of trader after you've had some losses. But I never
know until I throw them into the battle. You know, we get them pretty well pre-
pared. However, when we throw them into the battle, that's when we see.

ENDNOTE

Borsellino's 10 Commandments of Trading

1. **Trade for success, not money.** Sure, we all want to do well and reap the financial rewards. But the real goal is the success itself. In trading, this means
   doing research and technical analysis, devising a plan of action, executing a
   trade with a pre-determined profit target and a "stop" to limit losses, and
   following the plan to the ultimate conclusion of a successful trade. Money is
   only a byproduct of that success, not the goal.

2. **Discipline.** If there were one quality that traders must possess above all others, it would be discipline. This ability to master your mind, your body, and
   your emotions is the key to trading. You can have the best technical analysis
   available, but without discipline it will be difficult, if not impossible, to execute trades consistently and profitably.

3. **Know yourself.** Are you the kind of person who can handle a lot of risk?
   Or do you break out in a cold sweat at the mere thought of risking something, such as your own capital? Your risk tolerance, coupled with the
   amount of capital you have, will determine the kind of trader you will be
   (long-term position trader or five-minute scalper). Do you trade based on
   systems alone or are you a discretionary trader?

4. **Lose your ego.** The quickest way to end your career is to allow your ego to
   influence your decision-making. You need to silence your ego in order to
   listen to the market, to follow what your technical analysis is indicating and
   not what you think should happen. When you can put yourself aside and

bow to the whims of the market, you will have a greater chance of success. But believing that you are successful because you possess a certain skill—or, more dangerously, to believe that you have mastered the market—is a path to almost certain ruin. At the same time, you can't be so emotionally fragile that unprofitable trades shatter your confidence.

5. **Hoping, Wishing, Praying.** When it comes to trading, there's no hoping, wishing or praying, only the cold, hard reality of the market. You can't put on a trade and then hope that the market goes your way. And while you may get a break now and then, you can't wish and pray for one. The only way to trade is with a plan based on technical analysis of the market.

6. **Let your profits run, cut your losses quickly.** When you're in a profitable trade, let your profits run to your target and then exit the trade. Don't kick yourself if the market continues to go up or down and you lose out on additional profits. You'll never go broke taking a profit. And don't get greedy and hang onto a profitable trade so long that it becomes a loser. When you're in a losing position, get out quickly. Always trade with stops based upon a pre-determined loss that you can tolerate. Don't hang onto a loser in hopes that the market will turn around.

7. **Know when to trade, when to wait.** Being a good trader doesn't mean you're in the market every minute and perhaps not even every day. You trade when your system and your strategy say you have a buy or sell to execute. If the market doesn't have a clear direction, then wait on the sidelines until it does. Keep your mind on the market during those uncertain times, but keep your money out of it.

8. **Love your losers like you love your winners.** If you have a bad trade, it's not because your broker doesn't like you, somebody gave you wrong advice, or you weren't loved enough as a child. You made a bad trade because of some flaw in your analysis or your judgment. Or perhaps the market simply didn't do what you thought it would. Remember, the more you trade, the higher percentage of losing trades that you will have. The key is to keep your risk and reward in balance so that your net profits will more than

compensate for your losses. Above all, take responsibility for your losers, analyze them and learn from your mistakes. In trading, you have to love your losers as much as you love your winners.

9. **Three losing trades?** Take a break. If you have three losing trades in a row, you need to take a break. This is not the time to take on more risk, but rather to become extremely disciplined. Sit on the sidelines for a while. Watch the market. Clear your head. Re-evaluate your strategy, and then put on another trade.

10. **The unbreakable rule.** Every once in a while you can break a rule and get away with it. But one of these days, the rules will break you. If you continually violate any of these Commandments of Trading, you will eventually pay for it with your profits. That's the unbreakable rule. If you have trouble with any of the Commandments listed above, come back and read this one. Then read it again.

Source: TeachTrade.com

DAVID RYAN

THE TRAIL BLAZER

By Kevin N. Marder

Like many other traders and investors in the 1980s, I was first exposed to David Ryan through his appearances in *Investor's Daily* commercials that aired on the Financial News Network. In the 1990s, *Investor's Daily* became *Investor's Business Daily* and FNN was swallowed up by CNBC, but Ryan continued to prosper and grow as a trader and money manager. As an employee of William O'Neil + Co. for 16 years, he benefited from working closely with Bill O'Neil himself, eventually being promoted to an in-house money manager responsible for investing the company's money.

The markets are littered with traders that have had one great, "trophy" year. Ryan not only won one of the equity divisions of the U.S. Investing Championship in 1985, but duplicated the feat in 1986 and 1987. The latter year was a particularly difficult one for many traders, given the extreme emotions of euphoria and depression that prevailed. As an early proponent of the O'Neil style of buying stocks with fast earnings growth and high relative price strength, Ryan served as a role model and trailblazer for many aspiring traders.

Like those of other traders influenced by O'Neil, Ryan's approach to the market is unlike that of 99 percent of all other market participants. Buying a stock as it makes a new high in price, a scary prospect for most investors, is business as usual for Ryan. Moreover, buying a stock with a rich P/E multiple is also not apt to make his palms sweat.

On July 1, 1998, Ryan left the O'Neil organization to pursue a dream: running his own money management firm, Ryan Capital Management.

Kevin N. Marder: How did you initially get interested in the stock market?

David Ryan: In 1974, when I was 15, I had a trial subscription to *Daily Graphs,* the O'Neil chart book product. That's how long ago I started. Although I don't know if I ever had a full subscription to *Daily Graphs,* I would pick them up occasionally. I started reading them and then I think my Dad gave me a subscription to *Value Line.* During the summer, I remember we'd go swimming in the pool we had at our house. And then at 1:30 we'd all come in and watch "Gene Morgan Charting The Market," a show on a Los Angeles PBS station. (*Chuckles.*) So I got fascinated by that whole thing. I think I even went to a Gene Morgan seminar once a long time ago.

I remember watching his show a few times and seeing him draw those trend lines.

Oh, he was a classic! He was so good at calling the market after the fact. And that's how I started watching the McClellan Oscillator and the Summation Index.

Where did you go to college?

University of California at Los Angeles.

Did you immediately start working for Bill O'Neil upon graduating from UCLA?

No, I actually had a job on the floor of the Pacific Coast Stock Exchange as a runner for about a month. I quit that job a week before they would have laid me off, since they were automating their systems. I don't know if you know where the old O'Neil building was . . . it used to be near Olympic and Bundy.

I used to go there on Saturday afternoons and pick up my *Daily Graphs*. That was a ritual, seeing all the other stock junkies doing the same thing.

It used to consist of a full bookstore as well as a discount brokerage firm. But then when IBD came along, they took out the bookstore. I used to go pick up the charts there and read the books. I found myself saying, "why don't I just go up and see what goes on in the rest of this building?" And so one day I just walked up the stairs and went to the receptionist and asked who I could talk to about a part-time job or an internship. She sent me to O'Neil's assistant, with whom I talked for about half an hour. Even before I got home that day, there was a message from Kathy Sherman, *Investor's Business Daily's* head of communications, who said that O'Neil wanted to talk with me the next day. So I said okay, sure.

I'd never been on an interview in my life. And he's asking me questions. What do you want to do in the next five years? Do you want to go to business school? Etcetera, etcetera. So then I started part-time at O'Neil + Co., just working half a day, just doing basic stuff. And then it evolved into a full-time job and it went from there.

In terms of fundamentals and technicals, what do you look at when you search for a stock to buy?

I'm looking for two things: a company that has strong earnings in combination with a strong stock price. If the two aren't confirming each other—if the earnings are there but the stock is not performing well—then I'll just continue to track it until the earnings and price performance do confirm. Especially in 2000, what with the big focus on technology stocks, it's amazing how there are a number of companies trading at very low multiples with great growth records that people are not even paying attention to.

And what if a company has no earnings but is still in a dynamic growth phase?

The only time we'll buy a company that doesn't have earnings but has very, very strong price action—and that includes just about every Internet stock—is if you have an entire group move occurring. And this has happened at times in the past. It happened in the biotechs; it happened in cellular stocks in years past. So there are times where we're just playing the price performance and the relative strength because the group is so strong.

Why don't you want to buy a stock that's been beaten down?

First of all, you've got a lot of overhead supply. You've got a lot of people who bought at higher prices who are going to say, "Well, if I can only get back to where I bought the stock before," . . . then they would sell out. It constitutes a lot of supply as the stock moves higher. If you're buying a stock that's already gone through that and is trading close to or into new high ground, then there are only happy shareholders and the only people who are selling the stock are people who are taking a profit. The stock has a free range above it to continue to run.

Getting back to the Internet stocks you mentioned, do you have any screens that you sift through if they don't have earnings? Obviously, companies like eBay or AOL are profitable, but what about something else in the Internet world that's losing money now? Is there another fundamental characteristic that would help you in screening out the stock?

If it doesn't have earnings, we pretty much rely on the market and try to do some research into what specific area of the Internet it's in and what kind of revenue estimates it might have. And we also look at the market cap versus the other stocks in that similar space because sometimes there is a catch-up in terms of market cap. But with some of those Internet stocks, you're almost winging it in terms of which one's really going to make it and which one isn't. You just don't know which one is going to sign a deal with another company and see its stock jump 20 or 30 percent in a day.

When you look for earnings growth, is there a minimum figure you're looking for, like 20 percent?

Yes, at least 20 to 25 percent. But the bigger the growth, the better off.

Do you find yourself buying many stocks where the earnings are growing in excess of 100 percent?

Yes.

What sort of size constraints do you put on something you're looking to buy? Is there a minimum number of shares that trade per day on average, or market cap, or float, or anything else that you look at?

Our size constraint is usually based on average daily volume of the stock and I think we really don't go any lower than something that trades 20,000 shares a day. We'll go that low if we really like the company, but in most cases a stock will be trading hundreds of thousands of shares a day.

When you look at entry points on charts, technically, do you have a few favorite chart patterns that you like to favor?

The cup-and-handle is one of the better ones, but it does not show up nearly as often as people might think. A cup-and-handle really has to occur in a general market correction. That's when a lot of them show up. So if you get a market that corrects 10 percent, you'll have a lot of the good growth stocks that will pull back twice that, maybe 20 percent, maybe even 25 percent. And also it would take maybe about six weeks down and six weeks up and then it should drift off a little bit. The other one I look for a lot is just a flat base, the stock breaking into new highs off of a fairly long consolidation.

What's interesting about Internet stocks is that they trade in dog time. It's said that one year for a dog is the equivalent of seven years for a human. It's the same with an Internet stock. If an Internet stock is based out for one week, that's the equivalent of seven weeks on any normal stock. Everything is compressed on those Internet stocks. So the time they take to base out, the time they take to correct, the time they take to move—it's all in much, much shorter time frames. With these, it's hard to get used to buying off short bases. If you've been disciplined for so long to be buying a certain way and then things make a 50 percent move, sit there for three weeks, and then break out and go another 50 percent, it's just very hard to change your methods when that is occurring.

I take it you've changed things.

It's still very, very tough. We do it, but we do it smaller . . . we take smaller-size positions for those types of stocks. We also vary the size of the position based on the volatility because I just will not have one of my top positions in a 10-point trading range every day. It's very easy to get shaken out of some of those things. So we tend to buy a basket of them and spread the risk out among a number of stocks rather than concentrating all in one stock. This is especially important as you get bigger and bigger size money to handle. You can do that when you're very small and can get in and out very quickly, but the execution and the price movement on these things are so big in such a short period of time that it's hard to even get out sometimes when you've got 5,000 shares. This is because by the time you place the order, especially if it's moving, your execution can be 4 or 5 points lower than the point at which you picked up the phone. So it just makes it a little bit harder to go through the volatility of these stocks, particularly when you get up in terms of size.

As far as getting out of a position, what sort of general parameters do you look for when you're ready to sell a stock?

A lot of it—I would say a majority—will be technical in terms of how the stock is acting. We look at price-and-volume correlations on the stock. We also look at relative strength. Has its relative strength line gone into new high ground on maybe its last move into new high ground? We look at moving averages and trend lines to help us stay in a stock or come out of a stock when it's time to sell. And we're also constantly moving up and down the size of the position based on how the stock is acting. If we feel a stock has had a good run and has gotten very extended, we might just cut the position size. We can cut it in half, maybe to a quarter of what we had before, and then just mark time with the stock as it goes through a correction and then look for another entry point as the stock starts moving back up again.

Do any of your losing trades stand out in your mind as something that was a real learning experience for you?

I don't know exactly what the stock was right now, but I just remember—I think it was in 1988—where after winning that U.S. Investing Championship three years in a row, I started looking at the results more than executing each individual stock and position. I was taking position sizes that were much too large and giving myself such a small leeway and room for error. I would take a big position size, but then if I lost a point or two it would really start adding up. I took a lot of small losses, but they were on bigger positions. I was trying to get big, huge gains again, but I was doing it in the wrong way . . . I was breaking some of the rules and taking positions that were much too big, too quickly. I think I was flat for 1988.

When you say big-size positions, do you mean 25 to 30 percent?

Oh yeah, I would start off initially and go with a 15 percent position. And then within that first day or two if it started working out I would add another 5 percent. But then if the stock started turning down, I would have this 20 percent position in a stock that's starting to fall.

Do you use the 50-day average for anything at all? A lot of people seem to think that's a spot where institutions like to come in and provide some support.

Yes, it's something we look at very closely. We also look at the 10-day and also the 150-day moving average. I really no longer use the 200-day because the 200-day is a full year of trading and the way stocks are moving these days, they don't really even pay too much attention to the 200-day moving average.

What do you use the 10-day for?

The 10-day is used for shorter-term moves and also for Internet stocks a lot more than stocks outside the technology area. I look at things like what side of the stock the 10-day moving average is on, or whether the stock has been above the average for a long period of time and is now coming through, or whether the stock is breaking a downtrend and going through it. So we use that fairly often on the Internets.

Would you buy a stock if it comes down and touches the 10-day moving average?

It would have to depend on what kind of volume it's come down on. Is there another support point close by? It depends on exactly where that 10-day moving average is.

As far as sell parameters, when you're looking at technicals, is there any basic rule or two that you use? For instance, if a stock comes down 20 percent off its high, does that concern you?

If it's come down 20 percent, we're probably out of a majority of that position because we're watching it fairly closely. Again, we're looking at other trend lines and moving averages that it's probably broken before it's gotten down to that 20 percent decline point. It all depends, on a stock-by-stock basis, how much we have sold by that point. In most cases, we will have at least trimmed a quarter to a half of the position by the time it's already off 20 percent.

As far as general market analysis, what do you look at?

I try not to get too complicated. I look at the daily Dow and that works, but it's not foolproof. You can get whipsawed and you have to be careful in using it. It's like anything else—nothing is foolproof. I look at some of the McClellan oscillators and summation indexes for general trends, but a lot of it is based on "Can we find enough stocks to buy?" and "Are the patterns showing up that we like to be buying off of?"

Let's say the averages looked a little shaky, maybe after a big run-up or something. If there were still some stocks out there that were setting up technically, would you be buying some on the breakout?

As time goes on, you just have to be a little bit more careful, and if they do not work out, then quickly cut the loss, especially as you get later into a move. It seems like the last stocks you buy right before the market starts correcting are the ones you sometimes get hurt the most on. This is because you're buying the breakout and they can come off very quickly for the sale.

When it comes to money management, how do you add to a position? Do you purchase, say, one-half of your normal-size position on the breakout and then add another half as it goes up a few percent?

We try to take at least a 1 percent position in a stock as it's starting out. If it starts making a nice move on the first breakout then we can quickly move it up to 2 percent or so, or even more if we like the company. It all depends on how liquid it is, too. Sometimes it's hard to buy that much of a stock that quickly if it's a smaller-cap stock. Then we'll add to the position as the move continues. Because we've got a larger-size portfolio now and it's a lot of other people's money, we're not taking huge positions in stocks, especially with the volatility. We probably have a little over 30 positions and only one of them is over 5 percent. And that's also because it's up between 75 and 100 percent since we bought it, moving that position to a weighting farther out. But we try to start out with 1 percent and then we move it up from there, based on the stock and where it is technically.

Can you give an example of a stock with an interesting chart that you recently bought?

You could probably use Home Depot as a good example coming out of that base at about 45–46 at the end of September. What's good is that it pulled back down on top of the base on lighter volume. Then it started moving out and as it went through 50, we added more. It got up to the mid-50s and spent a few weeks there. We probably added a little bit more there and then got a nice 56-to-almost-70 run out of it. Then, when it broke down on big volume on the first day of the year, I think we cut the position almost in half . . . because it *had* a nice, long run.

And then it got hit with that type of volume. That's where we feel, "Hey, it's time to lighten up and take some of the profits." Because when you see that much volume on a stock getting hit that hard going through the 10-day, then you can say it's probably time it takes a rest, so you can cut back on the position. We still have a position in the stock and will be ready to add to it if we start seeing the volume increase and the stock starting to come back up through probably 64 or so.

If things break down in this stock and, say, the whole market, will you retain any core positions or are you going to be all in cash at some point?

Well, if the whole market starts breaking down, then I'll just keep on selling stocks down. And if I get to a 100 percent cash position, that will just tell me there's nothing out there to buy. But I'll also be looking for stocks on the short side to add to and I'll also hedge some of my positions as the market starts coming off.

Any other charts of interest?

People may laugh at this, but something like Citigroup just broke out. Good volume. And I like to have some big-caps in my portfolio for stability because if you've got all high-relative-strength stocks in your portfolio . . . I've seen it hap-

Series of Buys: Home Depot (HD), Daily

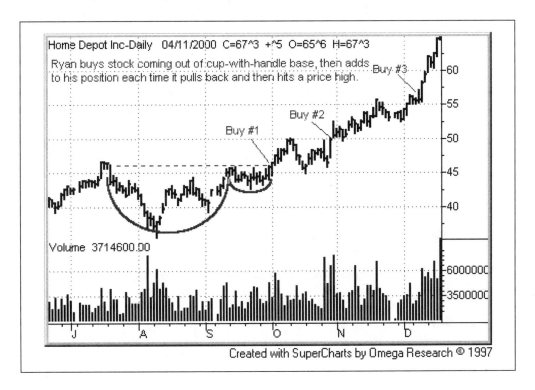

Home Depot Inc-Daily 04/11/2000 C=67^3 +^5 O=65^6 H=67^3

Ryan buys stock coming out of cup-with-handle base, then adds to his position each time it pulls back and then hits a price high.

Buy #1

Buy #2

Buy #3

Volume 3714600.00

Created with SuperCharts by Omega Research © 1997

pen where all of a sudden you've got all these positions in high-relative-strength stocks and suddenly the market doesn't want those any more. And it's like a light going out. You can really suffer quickly. So you put a few of these lower-risk stocks in there and it helps the volatility so you don't have huge swings. It all depends how risk-averse you are and how you structure your portfolio.

A lot of people are under the assumption that shorting is as easy as the long side of the market. Would you agree with that?

No, especially when the majority of the time the market's going up. You've also had corrections in 1998 and 1999 that have been swift. These corrections don't last long. Also, some of the rules have changed since Internet stocks have come along—a stock corrects 50 percent and then comes back and doubles back to its old highs and then it goes again. Some of those things I had just never seen in all the years I'd been watching the market—the explosiveness and the moves.

I would say the No. 1 piece of advice I'd give on shorting is "do not short too soon." You have to wait until its top has been completed. And that usually takes two to three months. Too many people are trying to short on that. I even try to do it because we all want to get that top tick. We all want to say, "I shorted it right up here." It's an ego thing. The best shorts are the ones where the top has been put in for a number of months and then you've got some overhead resistance. To try to pick off the top in a stock is very, very hard and sometimes you can get extremely lucky and get within those top few days, but it is tough. I would say your odds are much, much better if you've let the stock base out, come down, try a few different rallies over a few months' period of time, and then see it start rolling down. That's the best time to short.

Thanks, David.

JEFF COOPER

HIT AND RUN

By Kevin N. Marder

I first learned of Jeff Cooper through his first book, *Hit and Run Trading*. I had read Larry Connors' first two books, *Investment Secrets of a Hedge Fund Manager* and *Street Smarts*, and was impressed with his no-nonsense style. Cooper's book, published by the same company, was written in the same 100 percent meat, fat-free manner. Although I had already staked out the intermediate-term time frame as my chosen turf, I couldn't help but be curious about Cooper's strategy of pulling profits out of the market on an intraday basis.

Whereas daytrading became a fad in the late '90s, Cooper had already had a decade of experience under his belt. An ocean view home in Malibu attests to his trading success.

Cooper's greatest legacy, perhaps, is that he serves as a role model for many aspiring daytraders. This was accomplished through his books, *Hit and Run Trading, Hit and Run Trading II*, and *The Five-Day Momentum Method*, whose strategies quickly became the prototype used by many daytraders and swing traders.

Kevin N. Marder: How did you first become interested in the stock market, Jeff?

Jeff Cooper: My initial experience was in 1962. My Dad had one of the first private hedge funds in the country, and a lot of his business was initial public offerings. In the early-'60s, he retired from the textile business and moved the family from the East Coast to California. He wasn't really a golfer or a sportsman, and he just gravitated to the stock market as a hobby. Before you knew it, brokers had him buying stocks on margin.

One day in May 1962, my Mom was in a hospital having an operation and Europe woke up that morning and decided it wanted to sell stocks because of Kennedy's fight with the steel companies. The market tanked and my father was on margin. Instead of his brokers doing what they said they were going to do, which was to sell stock A to protect stocks B and C, they waited for a margin call on stock A, waited for a margin call on stock B, and waited for a margin call on stock C, and just sold them out accordingly. One of the reasons they did this was because my father couldn't be found, since, unfortunately, he was in the hospital with my mother.

My father went broke and we had to move back East to where his base was so he could start working again. That was my first real experience with the stock market.

Did your father stay away from stocks after that?

Eventually he built up another company and sold it. He always had an axe to grind with the market and wanted to get back what he had lost. Some of the brokers that he had done business with had some compunctions and guided him into the new issue market in the late '60s. It was a hot go-go market then. He ended up being a real factor in the business at that time. To this day, I remember being in high school and hearing him, when I would walk by his desk, say "hit and run." That's what he was doing. He became very risk-averse because of his first experience, and just started turning money over. And he was able to take back from the market about threefold what he had lost. So I was always enticed when I saw what he did.

I got into the sporting goods business in the mid-'70s. When I got out of that business, I didn't have anything to do. I looked for something to do and my father basically handed me the Red Book of securities dealers and said "get on the phone and I'll tell you what I'm looking to buy, and start calling them." That was my initial experience with the stock market. And then I went to work with Drexel Burnham for a time and decided I really didn't like the sell side.

Was this the infamous Drexel office on Rodeo Drive in Beverly Hills?

Right. After Drexel, I went back to work with my father for a couple of years. During the time I worked with him doing new issues, I wanted to understand what made the markets work. My father couldn't really help me in that way since he was a great tape reader more than anything else. So I began reading everything I could come across and started matriculating and learning the markets by trading stocks that were other than new issues . . . and to a large extent, I got killed. The new issues were a way for me to pay my way over the hump. They were a cushion for me at the time.

They paid for your education, then.

Precisely.

What was your initial strategy in those early days? Were you short- term oriented like you are today?

No, I wasn't. I was taking positions for weeks at a time. My equity curve was extremely jagged. I didn't really have a strategy. I didn't know anything about market tone, the overall market. A lot of it had to do with listening to brokers and their opinions about what earnings would be. That's how a lot of people get their initial exposure to the market . . . looking at fundamentals.

So you worked a few more years with your Dad?

I went out on my own in 1985, and started making money on my own. I was still doing new issues and I also traded, because trading helped create commissions and made me a more-favored client to get bigger pieces of the new issues from brokers. That's the name of the game. When '87 came, I didn't go broke like my Dad did in '62, but I took a big hickey. It wasn't until the decline in the summer of 1990 that I became fed up with my equity curve looking like a roller coaster.

And I decided that if I was to continue to play the market, I wanted to do it on an extremely risk-averse basis. I became much more concerned about my return *of* capital than my return *on* capital. I figured that the only way to do that was to become very short-term oriented, with the notion that momentum begets momentum. When it occurs, it usually lasts for a period of time, meaning at least one to three hours or one to three days. That's when I started taking bites out of stocks, staying in them very short-term, as in one to three hours or one to three days.

When you began trading the short-term time frame, was your initial strategy similar to what you use today or was it totally different? Were you looking at the same things that you look at today?

It took time to develop them. That was the impetus. They developed slowly, and over the years. It really wasn't a raging market until the end of 1994, early 1995, when we started going vertical. I was still doing some new issues, but that was the base for where the ideas were created. It just came slowly, one by one, you know.

In your *Hit and Run Trading* books, you speak of various setups. Did you start developing them in that period?

Yes.

Do you have a basic set of criteria that you use for entering a position?

Expansion Breakout Setup: Globespan (GSPN), Daily

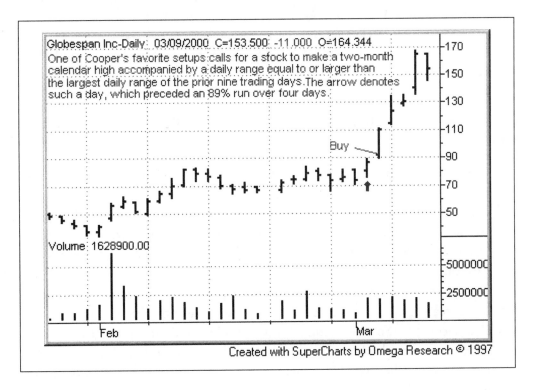

Globespan Inc-Daily: 03/09/2000 C=153.500 -11.000 O=164.344

One of Cooper's favorite setups calls for a stock to make a two-month calendar high accompanied by a daily range equal to or larger than the largest daily range of the prior nine trading days. The arrow denotes such a day, which preceded an 89% run over four days.

Volume: 1628900.00

Buy

Feb   Mar

Created with SuperCharts by Omega Research © 1997

Basically, in order to make money short-term, you've got to be where the action is. So I'm looking for stocks that have a lot of volatility and have shown a propensity for volatility intraday, and on the daily charts as well. The strategies revolve around price action and the notion that a stock in motion will remain in motion, at least in the short-term. One of the things I started looking at was an expansion of range on breakouts of consolidations, whether they be to new 30-day or 60-day highs. And also I came up with the idea that the nature of stocks was to thrust, pause, and if they were legitimate thrusts, they should start to pivot back in the direction of the underlying thrust. I saw that stocks in fast moves typically would only pull back for two to three days before continuing. So I would look for stocks with real strong momentum, and assume that institutions, mutual funds, and money managers, having all the time and money in the world, would look to buy on pullbacks. My initial strategies were breakout strategies that looked for a larger-than-normal range. I also focused on an expansion of range to identify strongly-trending stocks that were pivoting out of multiday pullbacks.

So you were looking for the expansion of range on both price and volume and—

—not so much volume, at the time. Basically, price. I didn't have enough knowledge about volume studies. One of the things I used to do was take an index card and hold it over the chart and start moving it forward. I would ask myself what would I have done here, what would I have done there, and I'd see how many times I would have been wrong. I found that to be a real good acid test of trying to learn price behavior.

One of the things I found early about volume was that I saw many breakouts on increasing volume that failed. And I saw many breakouts on light volume that succeeded. So I really didn't know how to interpret it and I ended up using price as the final arbiter. To this day, I do continue to use volume for the big picture . . . in other words, for looking at a sequence of distribution days and accumulation days. But as for a day-to-day basis, I still believe anything can happen at a given time.

When you say "big picture," are you referring to the general market?

I'm referring to the big picture of an individual stock and the general market.

Was O'Neil an influence on what you were doing?

O'Neil was a very big influence, Kevin, as I know he was with you, especially because he was becoming a big influence on so many money managers. *Investor's Business Daily* was also becoming a big influence. So many things in the market, be it a head-and-shoulders pattern or a cup-with-handle pattern, become self-fulfilling if you have a lot of people looking at the same thing. I felt it was important to know what he was looking at and found that a lot of what he was talking about was conceptually correct. It made a lot of sense.

In my early days, until I read William O'Neil, I was nervous about buying stocks as they went higher and higher. I thought that the higher it was, the more vulnerable it must be. But when I started reading O'Neil and I saw the power and the five- and 10-baggers these stocks would rack up, I started seeing that the institutions were not as nervous as I was, and would hang on. That's when I started realizing that, as a momentum player, you want to buy new highs. In order for a stock to go higher, it's got to take out prior highs.

This is just pure common sense, yet most investors remain locked in a strategy that shuns buying a new high.

A lot of times prior to that, I'd faded breakouts and gotten killed. I'd just figured there was a lot of juice in the stock, and somebody will come and try to take advantage of that. And it took a while to realize that that didn't work. The higher things were, the higher they tended to go, and vice versa.

What is your criteria for exiting a position? Is it based on a percentage drop or a point drop?

I generally never want to let a position go 1 point against me. My feeling is that my commissions are 3 cents and 4 cents a share. I would rather re-enter when a stock revalidates. My belief is that large losses must start with small losses. So I'm extremely risk-averse. Most of my positions now are trading positions, intraday positions. Though sometimes I take positions home overnight, I do this less and less frequently, especially in a choppy market. Having done this for a number of years, I've been able to accumulate some net worth. The daytrader's dream is to be able to make money both ways—not only through intraday trading, but also through letting money work in Treasury bills at the same time.

So before that you were only holding positions overnight?

Yes. Now I'll take the isolated one or two positions home if they're in a very strong trend and if they've closed well and if the underlying market is in the same direction as the position I own.

You say that you risk a point. Does that change as the price of the stock moves up? A lot of stocks here in the last couple of years—

—no, I always deal in points. A stock like Juniper Networks that's above $150 and into the $200 range, I may give a little more leeway. And that may be a point and a half. But I'm not using percentage stops. I don't change my position size, typically. I'm usually trading 1,000 to 2,000 shares. Sometimes if the stock is over $200, I'll start with 500 shares and work my way up. But I'm trading in round lots of positions and using points to exit.

Are there any general market indicators that you particularly favor in terms of giving you a feel for the overall market? Or does your work, which includes long and short positions, sort of obviate the need for any kind of general market analysis?

When all the pieces come together, you have an edge. I say I don't pay attention to fundamentals, but I certainly pay attention to what the money supply may be doing and what the Fed may be doing . . . and if there's an economic number that's coming up . . . and the behavior and the psychology of the market is very important. Although I key off price and patterns, I'm looking at other market indicators such as the advance-decline line. I'm looking at the put/call ratios for sentiment and I'm looking at new 52-week highs and new 52-week lows. I also look at the number of stocks above or below their 200-day moving averages, those types of things.

We know how you cut a loss short. How do you nail down a winner on the way up? How do you book that profit when you do have one?

As you know, Kevin, the Nasdaq market has become so hypersensitive to trading volume and order flows lately. I find that ever since the electronic communication networks, the ECNs, started dominating the market and squeezing the bid/ask spreads to sixteenths and thirty-seconds, there is very little inventory in Nasdaq stocks available. The market makers just don't want to make markets. They don't want to keep inventory. That's created a lot more volatility, which can be good or bad. Volatility can be the trader's friend. It will depend on market tone for the day and what I think the overall trend is.

In January, February, and March of 2000, I was hanging onto positions, and there were a lot of trend days. A trend day is when a stock opens at or near its low, takes out the morning range, and closes at or near its high. I tend to try to hang onto a position at least until the end of the day. And if something was just pivoting back out of a pullback—a strongly trending stock that had come off for a couple of days and done a retracement—and if it was like the first or second day out of a pullback and closed well, I'd probably continue on until it tests its prior swing high. But in a choppy market, as a stock starts to move up I'll let out maybe a third of the position as the ducks are quacking . . . because you find these spurts of momentum. And then I'll try to target shoot at resistance points—intraday or daily resistance levels.

Do you ever pyramid up into a winner?

In a bull market, yes. During the day, I will.

How do you typically do that? Do you double up as the stock moves higher?

That's exactly what I'll do. If I'm not sure about what the stock is doing, I may start off with 500 shares. And then I look for confirmation of the action—most of the time I'm using the S&P futures to key off of. If I find that everything gets in gear, sometimes I'll anticipate the breakout and I'll put on an initial position and use a very tight stop and even much less than a point . . . maybe just a quarter or three-eighths of a point. I'll try to anticipate the behavior of the stock.

For instance, if the market has been down during the morning and the stock has shown real good intraday relative strength, and I see the futures start to turn around, I'm anticipating the stock may come on again and break out. So I'll open a position as the stock takes out the prior day's high or breaks out of an intraday consolidation, then I'll add on.

So it really sounds as though you're using daily charts to get the overall pattern setups, the bigger picture, and then you'll drill down and use the intraday charts.

That's exactly right.

Do you use five-minute bar charts like a lot of traders?

I use 10-minute charts. I don't know why I gravitate to the 10-minute. It filters out a little bit of the noise that you get from a five-minute. Basically, what I'm looking for is volatility and structure. So I'm looking for the structure that a daily bar chart provides and then I'm looking at the intraday patterns to key off that.

As far as timing your entry?

Right.

And exit.

Yes.

Do you tend to go with pullbacks more than breakouts?

I would think so. One of the reasons is that, O'Neil might have said this—and I forget what the exact numbers are—but 60 percent of most all breakouts pull back for one day and I think another 30 percent pull back for two days. I may be wrong about the total being 90 percent, but O'Neil found that a lot of break-outs pull back. So I'm definitely interested in breakouts and I'm always looking at new 30- and 60-day highs. And then I want to watch their behavior . . . I want to stalk them over the next couple of days. That's how I use breakouts. And then I'll buy if I see them come on again.

Is the 1-2-3-4 pattern one of your favorites?

Yes. One of the ways I determine trend is by using the ADX indicator. If you have an ADX over 30, whether a stock is trending up or down, it's in a strong trend. Although it's an arbitrary number, I've found in my research that once the ADX of a stock gets to 30, it can often go to 40 and 50. Once a stock has

1-2-3-4 Buy, Sell Setups: Nasdaq Composite, Daily

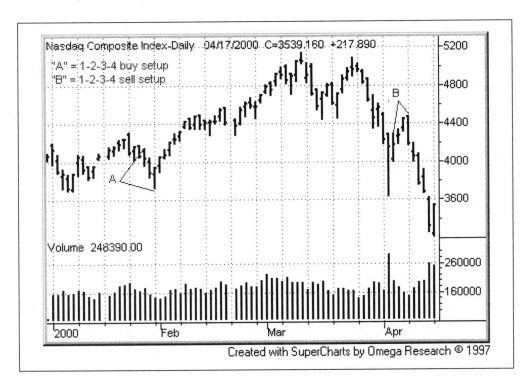

shown it's in a strong trend, I put it on my hit list. Once I see the stock walk off an overbought condition by a two-to-three day pullback, then I'm looking for any kind of sign of resumption of the underlying trend. Larry Connors and I created this strategy together and it's stood the test of time.

Where will you look to enter?

Typically, I will consider entering if I see three days of pullback, which could be an inside day and two lower lows. Once I see the stock take out the high of day three, that's the trigger.

If a stock comes down more than three days, say, four, five, six, or seven days, is there still enough potential thrust back on the upside?

I think so. There are normal trends and then there are runaway trends. Larry and I first created the 1-2-3-4 concept from runaway trends. Over time, I've come to find that there is a natural tendency of things in the market to play out in threes. For instance, even stocks that aren't in strong trends that are breaking out from low-level bases may show three days of pause or pullback to consolidate and then continue, too. To answer your question, a 1-2-3 pullback, an initial simple pull-back on a strongly trending stock, is how it was developed. Often you'll find that pullbacks come in complex, or two-step, pullbacks. That's where you may see three or four days down, then an initial move up, and then another move down of a few days, and then the overall trend begins again. I think a two-step pull-back like that is very valid as well, conceptually.

Do you have any favorite books that you've read over the years that have influenced you more than other books?

Definitely. The first book that influenced me to a great degree was *Technical Analysis of Stock Trends*, by Edwards & Magee. I became very interested in patterns. O'Neil's book, *How To Make Money In Stocks*, certainly influenced me, as I said before. I also like a book called *Profits In The Stock Market*, by Gartley. And all of Gann's stuff influenced me a lot because I came to view the market as an entity that backed and filled and breathed on its own. I was greatly influenced by Gann's concepts about the presence of symmetry in the market in terms of time and price. Although I've never seen anybody really make any money consistently with cycles, I think there's something to them. I became very interested in that view of the market. I came to take the view that everything that was in a stock that's known about a stock should show up in the price action.

I would never be able to know as much as the next guy regarding the fundamentals of a stock. There are a lot of fundamentals that sneak up on the analysts, too, so how was I going to get a better handle on it than they ever could? That's why I decided just to watch the track of what the big money and the smart money were doing. That's why I believe in technical analysis.

So you don't look at the fundamentals at all, then?

Only in the sense of the big picture, the overall market. Some of the companies I buy, I have no idea what they do, just maybe what industry group they're in. But I may not even know what their niche is.

Do you prefer to see a stock belong to a certain industry group? Or does it really matter?

Yes. I think there's a much greater edge if I see a whole group having a move. I want to focus on the leaders in that group. Definitely. I'd rather do that than try to find a stock doing a solo run while the group is still dogging it.

What percentage of your trades turn out to be winners?

As I said, I used to be a trading junkie. Even as recently as three or four or five years ago, I made maybe 25 trades a day. And at that time, I'd say my winning percentage was 50 to 60 percent. But now that I'm taking much fewer trades and really trying to wait for the best setups, my winning percentage is higher, just because I'm willing to wait. In the last year they've been up near 70 to 80 percent.

When assessing the risk/reward ratio of a potential trade, are you willing to risk a point for a gain of 1 to 2 points, or is it more like 1 to 5 points?

Sometimes I'll enter a trade and I'll buy near support if I think the market tone is turning and I may only risk 1/4 to 3/8 of a point. In those cases, I may only be looking for 1 point, 1 1/2 points, 2 points. If I'm risking a point, though, I'm looking to make two to three. I'll look to sell a piece of a position as the ducks start quacking and as the stock moves up. And then I'll hold onto the balance of it, using trailing stops.

I know your books have served as a blueprint for many short-term traders, particularly your first book, *Hit and Run Trading*. Do you have any advice for the aspiring daytrader or short-term trader?

The market is an irrational creature that feeds off the emotions of fear and greed. To say that the market has bouts of irrational exuberance is missing the point. It always goes to extremes. Supply and demand don't really apply when you're talking about emotions. Everyone wants to get rich quickly, and that's why a show like "Who Wants To Be A Millionaire" is so popular. Unfortunately, it doesn't work that way. You need a plan. My plan is to put numbers on the board and make them grow every day. The other thing that I think is important is knowing how to take a loss. For me, knowing how to take a loss is probably the most important ingredient for a successful trader, especially a short-term trader. We have to embrace risk every day. If you don't know how to manage the difference between your ego and taking a loss, you've got a big problem. Managing expectations is the difference in this business between succeeding and failing. I learned a long time ago not to let my own personal issues of self-worth or approval have anything to do with it. It's a business like any other.

There's one analogy that I think is very appropriate. Society instills in us the quest to be correct, to be right all the time. We're wired to win, to be right in our jobs all the time. We're wired to win—that can be a deadly trait for a trader. I like to compare the idea of being a trader to that of being a baseball hitter. A top hitter connects maybe three out of 10 times and makes millions of dollars. If he lets the other seven "failures" discourage him, he's not going to be able to get up there and pull the trigger again.

I find trading a lot like baseball. I think there are two reasons why most people get chewed up in trading. First, they're in the wrong stocks. You need to be in the stocks that are strongly trending and that have some volatility. A more important reason is that most new traders let small losses turn into large losses because they live in hope. You've got to know how to take a loss. This paralyzes them, both emotionally and financially. I can't tell you how many faxes and letters I've received from people who've read my books and still don't use protective stops. You can't use a mental stop if you're not going to honor it. You've got to give your broker a stop. And if you're going to use a mental stop, you've got to trust yourself enough to honor it.

Let me say something more about taking losses because I feel it's so important. You can't get your self-worth wrapped up in the idea of taking losses. There's a certain psychology that's required to take a loss. Unfortunately, this mind frame is totally against the norm for most people. And let me give an example. A surgeon is trained to be as close to perfect as possible. Most surgeons will be successful 90 percent of the time, if not higher, in the surgeries they perform. They don't know how to lose. This is wonderful. It's a wonderful trait. Now the same surgeon retires and decides he wants to spend his retirement trading. He will trade the same way he practices his earlier profession, absolutely trying to win every time. Taking a loss is not in his psychological makeup. He'll work a losing position as hard as he works a surgery that's gone bad. He'll do everything he can to save the trade, just as he's done everything in surgery every day to save patients for the past 35 years.

Most successful individuals are the same. They personalize losses and apply an I'm-going-to-will-this-thing-to-succeed approach, just as they do to succeed in other parts of life. In trading, though, this can be the kiss of death. To be profitable at the trading game, you've got to learn how to take a loss. You must be willing to take small losses 40 percent of the time, maybe even 50 percent. The profits take care of themselves.

When I get into a trade, I'm always approaching it from the standpoint of not how great it looks, but how's it going to get me, what's wrong about this.

What's wrong about the way I'm seeing this? I've just been humbled too many times by the market. And I find that most of the solid traders I've come in contact with have that common trait. They've been humbled by the market and they have ultimate respect for the market. As soon as I see someone that's cocky entering the trading game I just put on the stopwatch, because it's a matter of time until the market has eaten his lunch.

Baseball has so many things in common with trading. I recently heard a story about legendary baseball hitter Ted Williams. Apparently, he seldom responded to fan mail. But when he got a letter asking him who he modeled his hitting after, either the great Babe Ruth or the powerful Lou Gehrig, Mr. Williams replied: "neither." His idol was Rogers Hornsby, whose strength was the patience to wait for the right ball. Whereas Babe Ruth swung at nearly everything that moved—and though he did hit more home runs than anyone of his era, he also struck out more than anyone—Lou Gehrig was simply able to overpower pitchers with sheer force. But for Ted Williams, Rogers Hornsby was the man. It wasn't so much the stance or the swing, but his willingness to wait for the right pitch that made the difference. When I heard that, it just sent a shiver up my spine, because that in essence is what a good trader is. You must be willing to wait for your pitch, your ball. Otherwise, your performance will be erratic. You can't make the numbers get bigger by trying to overpower the ball.

If you want action, you go to Las Vegas. I take so many fewer trades now than I used to do, even five years ago. Sometimes the hardest thing to do in this business, whether it's trading the short-term as I do, or trading the intermediate-term, is to sit on your hands and do nothing. You've got to have an edge . . . sometimes you have to wait for the whites of their eyes, whatever time frame you're trading on . . . whether you're position trading, short-term trading, whether you're an intermediate-term speculator. I think you need to have the wind at your back and to see the whites of their eyes.

WILLIAM GREENSPAN

PIT MECHANIC

By Marc Dupée

Like many S&P 500 futures traders, Bill Greenspan was a "daytrader" long be-fore daytrading was a household term. He's honed his approach down to a science, dealing with its ups and inevitable downs by sticking to a simple trading approach that he applies patiently, day in and day out.

It's an approach that's worked well for him. After 22 years in the pits of the Chicago Board of Trade (CBOT) and the Chicago Mercantile Exchange (CME), Greenspan (trading badge: "WIG") has established himself as one of the more successful "locals" or pit traders—a fixture in the S&P pit where he trades almost all day.

Greenspan got his start in the embryonic days of the financial futures mar-kets in the late 1970s, when grains were still king and the veteran traders didn't know what to make of the new contracts on bonds, stock indices, and other fi-nancial instruments. He had a moving-and-delivery business at the time. But in 1978, when a friend who had made a lot of money trading soybeans suggested Greenspan try his luck in the fledgling T-bond market at the CBOT, Greenspan made a career change.

Greenspan started to make money regularly after three or four months, and although he admits to some leaner times "during the Reagan years," he has been a profitable trader ever since. Greenspan's approach is the essence of simplicity, honed over roughly a 22-year period of daily trading in the S&Ps.

"In the beginning, I didn't really know what I was doing," he says. "I was scalping, just trying to get in and out."

He freely admits to being something of a risk hawk, favoring stops that may be too tight rather than too loose. His basic approach may seem straightforward, but the fact that he has prospered for such a long period is a testament to its effectiveness.

Greenspan left the CBOT for its cross-town rival, the CME, in April 1987, roughly six months before the infamous stock market crash. It was there that he developed the trading style he uses today, a style based on the philosophy of making "a million dollars on a million trades, not a million dollars on one trade."

Marc Dupée: I've heard there's a high turnover rate for traders in the futures exchanges in Chicago, something on the order of 25 percent.

William Greenspan: Yes. And even higher.

Even higher? The average career of the pit trader lasts somewhere around 23 months. On the other hand, your career in the pit spans something like 23 years?

It's actually been 22 years.

Congratulations. To what do you attribute your longevity and your success?

I'm not a stubborn guy when it comes to taking losses. I do run for cover when I'm wrong. You never go broke taking profits, either. I am a good profit taker. But I know how to milk a trade. When I catch one running, I will milk it and I will trail my stops. I think the key is to be humble enough to take losses. I don't muscle the market or fight the market, as Lewis Borsellino does or even as Don Sliter does.

These, of course, are two other S&P traders.

Yeah. They're both excellent traders. I have tremendous respect for both of them. They trade a completely different style than I do. They do fight the market more than I do.

What does that mean, "fight the market?"

They'll add to positions. They'll fight the market. They'll go head to head against the commercial houses like Goldman Sachs or Morgan Stanley or even Salomon Bros. They think that the market's going down and Goldman Sachs thinks the market's going up, and they'll fight it out.

In speaking with Borsellino, he says he loves to buy them. He has a slight buy bias. Do you have a bias either way?

I've sold the market all the way up. It's the biggest bull market in the history of the world. We sold it all the way. I short intraday corrections. I probably initiate over 70 percent of my trades from the short side.

You're short 70 percent of the time?

I just initiate that side. It's just the easier side for me to play. I tell them in my Commodity Boot Camp classes, the longest I've ever been is short one [contract]. I like the short side. I've probably been hurt more on the short side, considering it's been a bull market. We've had a hell of a run, haven't we?

You said you know how to milk a trade. Do you do that mostly by trailing stops, or is there some other approach?

Intraday Breakdown Failure: September 2000 S&P 500 Futures (SPU0), 5-minute

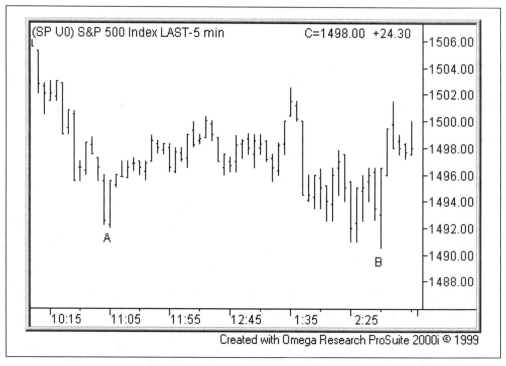

On 6/20/2000 at (A), the June S&Ps establish the lows of the day at 1492. At (B), the S&Ps do not violate the 1492 lows by more than 160 points, triggering a long position in the 1491 area.

Mostly by trailing stops. Like today (June 20, 2000), I have a theory . . . once the high and the low of the day are established, if the market doesn't take out the low of the day by more than 160 S&P points, I think it's a failure and I buy it. The low of the day, early, was 1492-even. The market only went down to 1491. If it had gone down to 1490-30, I would have sold the market. When it went down to 1491-even, I was able to buy two there. I didn't buy a great package or anything.

Then the market responded and immediately went higher, up to 93-even bid. I put my stops in and trailed it all the way up and the market ended up closing higher. I think I sold them out at either 97 1/2 or 99-even. I had several trades at the end of the day, which is a real nice profit on two contracts at the end of the day—in the last half-hour, to take a quick $4,000 out. If you can make $4,000 a day, and I make more when I'm trading well, it transfers to a million dollars a year, or a million-plus a year.

Darned good income. Why do you say 160 points? Why do you select that number as a "failure?"

I don't know why. Just out of observation.

Observation?

Observation and experience of trading. I watch . . . if the market penetrates by more than 150 S&P points (1.50 points)—that's 160 because of the tick—I'll initiate the trade. If it goes from 92-even down to 90.30, that would be 170 points, I would initiate getting short. That just confirms to me that we have follow-through on the penetration of the low.

On the low of the breakout of the morning?

The low of the breakout. I also do that on the penetration of the high of the breakout. You have to expand that when you're doing the E-Mini, because the contract's much less of a tick [value] and it's a little bit more of an emotional market. So on the E-Mini, I use 2 1/4 points.

And does electronic matching affect the E-Mini as well?

Yes. It's not just the matching. It's also that the E-Mini is geared for the small trader. It's geared really for risk-averse traders. They're willing to lose that $50 a handle, where on the S&Ps it's $250. It's much harder to swallow.

That's an excellent point. Are there other traders that have been in the pit as long as you? Lewis Borsellino has been there many years.

I started in the T-bonds in 1978, then I came to the S&P in 1987. Borsellino was already very well established. So was Don Sliter. I knew Don Sliter from the Board of Trade. He went to the wall several times at the Board of Trade before he found his niche. I think he really found his niche in the S&P futures.

By "going to the wall," do you mean going broke?

Yes. And to the wall. It's just hard. You have to find your way.

Besides pit traders having short career spans, with many lasting fewer than 23 months, the job is hazardous. For instance, I've been told it's difficult to get insurance. It's one of the highest-risk jobs, rated just below sky diving and mining.

And air traffic controllers.

Right.

I do have disability insurance. Of course, I have four children and a beautiful wife. I have life insurance. I've carried it for a really long time. Thank God, I've never had to use it. I take care of myself. I kick-box two days a week. I work with a personal trainer three days a week. I play tennis on Wednesdays.

People mostly recognize pit trading as a financial danger rather than as a physical danger.

It's mostly an athletic event. It's pretty vigorous. The athletes seem to do the best. We have a lot of good athletes in there, a lot of guys who played college ball and a lot of guys who wrestled in college. It's very competitive. The athletes seem to know how to psyche out the competition. They're used to competing and competing at a high level. It's not as cerebral as it is physical. It depends what you make of it, though. Everybody has a different style.

It sounds like it's psychological as well as physical. *The Wall Street Journal* **wrote an article where some trader took a trade that you had claimed and then turned around and offered it to you at a higher price. It said you then "went and slapped him right in the mouth and called him a cheat."**

I've had to curb my temper. The exchange is not a place where you really want to fight. The fines can be substantial. Last time I had an altercation was in 1984.

What triggered the altercation?

Well, you know, money is on the line. Especially when you're dealing with such quantities in a fast-moving market.

Is that when altercations leading to fights are more likely to happen, in a fast-moving market?

A guy steals your trade and offers it to you at a higher price. That is pretty insulting.

That's got to piss you off.

Yeah. That's pretty insulting. Now, I have a little bit deeper pockets and I'm a little bit savvier. If somebody does steal my trade, I'll try to force the market against them till it doesn't make it worthwhile for them to steal my trade.

This sounds like one time when you *will* try to muscle the market.

I will try to use my muscle. I would rather lose money than to see him make money on that. But when you're able to, what a great feeling! It doesn't happen that often. Maybe I'm just getting more mature.

Would you call Lewis Borsellino, Don Sliter, and yourself the biggest traders in the S&P pit right now? You three?

No, no. I'm not a big trader. I'm enthusiastic. I never wanted to be a big trader. I was a big trader when I was younger and I didn't have a family and I could come in and swing $60-$80 grand a day. Now, I try to make good money and keep a lower profile. I think the biggest traders in the pit are those two guys . . . Lewis' brother, Joey . . . he's unbelievable . . . also, a guy who goes to the gym every day and boxes. They're unbelievable. Lewis loves to go head-to-head. He'll go head-to-head against Salomon [Smith Barney].

When you see Borsellino doing that, what will you do?

When Lewis is doing that, I generally won't go up against him. Another great trader is Steven Prosniewski. He's one of the best traders I've ever seen, also.

What makes him one of the best?

He's one of the biggest. He'll muscle the market and take a firm position. He's a tremendous earner.

What size will he trade, for instance?

Steven has taken up to 200 contracts at a time. He probably, quietly, has a lot more than that. I don't think he backs away from 50-lot positions at all. Whereas I like to trade in and out of 10-lot positions. You can jam them down my throat all day long.

How did you get into this business?

In 1978, I had a moving-and-delivery business. I was doing very well with it. My friend Marvin Wanger stopped by my apartment and he said, "How you doing this year?" I said, "Great. I'm probably going to make about $35,000, maybe $40,000 this year." He said, "I made that last month trading soy beans." I was a

Opening Range Breakout: September 2000 S&P 500 Futures (SPU0), 2-minute

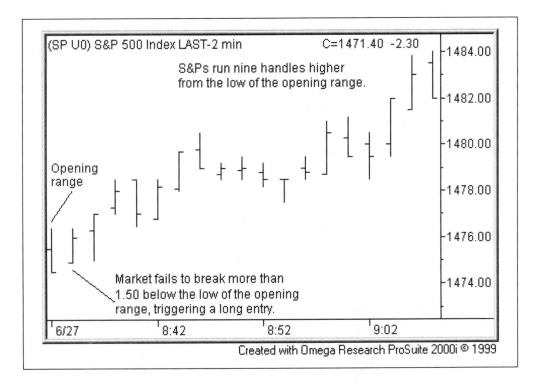

city kid. I didn't know. I said, "Where do you get some?" He laughed and said, "No, no. I'm a member of the Chicago Board of Trade. I want to acquaint you with this deal they have, they're trying to start these new products."

The new products were Treasury bonds, commercial paper and gold. They couldn't get the guys in the agricultural markets to come over and trade the new financial instruments because they had made so much money in the '70s in the grain markets and they liked the hours. The hours were 9:30 a.m. to 1:15 p.m. The Treasury bond hours were like 8:00 a.m. to 2:45 p.m. And at 2:45 p.m., you can't make the Cub games! So anyways, they offered 50 permits to the public. The deal was you had to pay $2,500 a quarter for three years for a total of $30,000. At the end of three years, you paid another $10,000 and they gave you an associate membership at the Board of Trade. And you could expense the

$40,000 off as permit fees. So because of the tax situation, it really only cost you half, if you were successful.

I ended up getting the last T-bond permit available. Jimmy Carter was President. If you recall, he did things to interest rates that nobody thought was possible. We went on to make a lot of money. After my three years were in, I got my associate membership, then I had a membership at the Board of Trade, and I've rolled that into a full membership at the Board of Trade. I also have three more, smaller memberships at the Board of Trade that I rent out for income and a full membership at the Chicago Mercantile Exchange.

What are those seats leasing for right now?

They're not leasing for much now, but they had been leasing very strongly for a while. One of them leases for like $9,200 a month. A couple of the other ones lease for a couple hundred dollars a month.

What's the difference between those two?

One, you can only trade Dow futures and muni bond futures. The other one you can trade anything in the building and anything in the CBOE.

How much is the one for just the Dow futures?

Couple hundred a month.

You've written several articles for *Stocks and Commodities Magazine* and other publications, describing the calculation and use of pivots. How would you characterize your style of trading?

Now I trade the breakouts. Opening range breakouts; breakouts from the high, low, and close; breakouts from the Globex high and low; and also, chart points where there's been a low in the market or a high in the market for several days . . . say a level that the market can't get through . . . it stops at either 1506 or somewhere between 1506 or 1508. I'll trade off those numbers, too. Also, I trade the failures. If the market fails to make a new low by more than 160 points or fails to make a new high by 160 points, I consider those failures and I'll initiate a contrary trade. You'll make a lot of money on those.

Do you incorporate the overnight or the electronic trading activity from Globex?

Yes. You have to do that. There's no sense leaving cash on the table. It is a risk-taking business. I mean, it doesn't work every time. But it works a high enough percentage of times that it provides me with a good income.

Is the formula that you currently trade off of the same formula in your articles?

Oh, absolutely. The pivot formulas work.

Therefore, do you find that these pivot points are just as valid or more valid?

I'm not trading the pivots right now because I'm concentrating on the breakouts. When the market is trading near its all-time high, like it is now, there's less trade. If you take the market, it looks kind of like a bell curve . . . most of the trade occurs in the middle of the range. There's more interest there, where people are buying and selling at that level, thinking it's going to go higher, or think it's going to go lower.

When the market trades up here at the extreme high, like it is right now, it's more emotional and there's less trading. So I'm trying to trade the emotion and the breakouts, the running of the market . . . because it trades very emotionally. So, I'm not using the pivots. There are people who are trading near me that are using my pivot technique. We talk about it during the day. I'm just not using it in the S&Ps right now.

When you use the overnight prices, do you find the levels are more valid than just the previous day's high-low-close calculation?

Yes, but if you use the high-low-close, the overnight high, and the overnight low, and take them together, you have to divide by five. You can't just divide by three. Sometimes, they'll take the closing price, the overnight high, and the overnight low. I would just as soon use all five numbers. You're going to get much more accurate support and resistance levels.

You also mentioned that you never enter a trade without placing a stop-loss.

Particularly, when I'm off the floor. When I'm on the floor, I'll enter a lot of trades. You always have a mental stop.

And scratch them if they are not working out?

I don't really scratch them. You can't make money scratching trades. If I put a trade on, if it goes 150, 200 points against me, I get out.

Tell me a little bit about your Commodity Boot Camp.

It's a great course for trading. It teaches new traders how to get in the market, how to overcome their fear, how to give them the good fundamentals, how to start trading with the right kind of trading parameters, and how to look for a 3-to-1 profit objective to enter your trade . . . in other words, how to risk $500 to make $1500. You can't go one for one. There's no percentage in that. You're going to end up getting washed out.

It shows you how to decide on making a trade, how to calculate where you're going to put your stop-loss and enter the trade, and how to put in your stop-loss order and make your trade's biggest number. Most people have such a fear of trading. Most people are risk-averse.

In that 3-to-1 profit objective, how do you define the profit objective?

A lot of times it's just on money. You just decide how much you're willing to lose. You place a trade . . . maybe you're buying above the previous day's close. You say if it penetrates the previous day's close, I'm going to get out or I'm going to stop and reverse. (He reverses position when stopped out—that is, if long one contract, he will sell two contracts at his stop level, establishing a short position.)

So you just hold on until it achieves the 3-to-1 objective and cover?

I'm not a pig about the market. If you set out to make $1500 on your trade and you make $1500 on your trade, if you stay in that trade you're being a pig. At least you can trail your stop. Maybe the market will give you more than that. Not every long trade's going to the moon. Not every short trade is going into the sewer. You just have regular trades, regular amounts of risk and profitability, and you know you're going to make a lot of trades. I don't ever come in and think I'm going to make one trade. I don't think I've ever done that in my whole career . . . come in and made just one trade. I've come in to trade the market and provide liquidity. That's my job as a member.

I've read that you often do that; you often lose a little just to provide liquidity.

It's just a big, empty concert hall down there if we don't get the orders filled. Not that we want to do it and lose money. Sometimes, we'll facilitate the market and lose a little money just to get the customers' orders filled. It's just part of it. We don't want to have a big, empty concert hall.

You said you make seven figures trading these techniques.

I have for the last four years.

What kind of margin do you need to maintain to pull down that kind of money?

I don't really know. I own so many memberships. I keep up money in my account. I never really worry about that. I never trade too big that they ever give me a margin call.

What would you say is your average annual return on your margin capital?

I don't really have one. My Board of Trade seat is worth about $600,000. My Merc seat's worth about three-quarters of a million. The other seats are worth whatever they're worth. Believe me, if I ever go in the tank and lose money, they will sell my seats. Those act as my—

—collateral?

Right. They will sell my seats. I don't ever doubt that. There are no friends. No prisoners. You're playing for money.

They'll liquidate you.

In God we trust.

You said you wouldn't hesitate to take a 10-lot. But what would you say your average size trade is?

Probably fives. I probably do 5-lots all day long.

How many trades do you make a day? In an average day.

Maybe 150 to 200. Let's say 100 to 150. Around 150 trades.

Other than just breaking through or not breaking through certain levels, are there any other specific technical factors that might get you in on a trade such as specific technical patterns you see setting up?

I don't really use them. I use the basics of technical analysis, which is the high, the low, the close, the Globex high, and the Globex low. My first trades are usually opening range breakout trades. If the market breaks out on one side or the other of the opening range, I initiate my trade.

And your stop-loss is just a set point amount . . . you're out after it's hit?

Yes. Particularly, on my scalp trades and my individual trades. There's no sense marrying a position. You're going to make a lot of trades during the day. You don't really want to get a big hole to dig out of. The main thing is to be able to admit that you're wrong. You're wrong and you can reverse. If every time you buy and they keep going against you, I think it's time to turn around and sell them.

Sell them and go both ways.

You can't be a one-way trader. The market doesn't accept one-way traders.

It can be difficult to admit you're wrong and reverse.

The thing that's really most difficult for people is to short the market. They have a very tough time with that concept: They don't own it, so they can't sell it. People rarely short stocks. They're always long.

Long and wrong.

Most of the money here . . . not most, but plenty of the money is made on the opposite side.

You said 70 percent of your trades are initiated on the short side. Do you ever consider fundamental factors?

Fundamentals are what you use when you're in the pit. I use the technical trades to get me in and out. The fundamentals tend to shake you out of more trades than you can hold on to. Fundamentals are supply and demand. When you see everybody selling, that's supply. When you see everybody buying, that's demand. We're governed by supply and demand. We're governed by the fundamentals.

I was referring to fundamentals in a macro-economic sense or news-driven events.

Of course we use that. God forbid my namesake. For 12 years I've been fighting this guy (Federal Reserve Chairman Alan Greenspan). He rules. He's been winning. It's an unbelievable legacy he has. It's hard for me, when I get on the elevator with a bunch of interest-rate traders . . . "Your uncle's really [screwing] up the economy. He's really [screwing] up the trading! Did you get the call last night?" I say, "No. I'm waiting for him to call me right now." But I'm not related in any way. It just happens to be a very popular name.

Have you noticed any patterns on days surrounding a big number, in front of a Greenspan speech or FOMC meeting?

The only pattern I see is that people are much more nervous. When this guy breaks for lunch, everybody breathes a sigh of relief.

How do you trade off that, when you see that type of psychology in the pits, that nervousness?

First of all, you can watch the way the order flow's going. If the orders come in selling, the locals take the other side of the orders. They're on the long side. If the orders come in buying, the locals will generally sell the market. They're generally short. You can read the pit pretty well to see which way the locals are. If the locals are long, they're going to have to sell it to cover. If they're short, they're going to have to buy it to cover. They get one way or the other in anticipation of what they think the report is going to do.

That's not something your average trader outside the pit can really benefit from or trade off of.

No. It's hard. If it were easy, you wouldn't need them. It's not supposed to be easy. It's never been easy. Maybe when Carter was the President it was a little bit easy.

When you're trading, when or how will you scale up or pyramid the number of contracts that you're trading?

I don't mind adding to winning positions. I never add to losers. That's called cannon-balling. I don't mind if I'm getting long and the market's going up, to buy more. Or I'm getting short and the market's going down, to sell more, up to a certain number of contracts. I don't like to take more than 10, 12, 14 contracts. It's just too many. I'm not recognized as that big of a trader to be able to get them back. I do like to add to winners. I never add to losers.

When it's going a certain way, how will you scale up from five to 10 to 14 or to your maximum?

If I'm long five, I'm bidding . . . it's called wolfing your position. I'm trying to bid the market up to get it to go higher. As I get hit, I add to my position. It's an open outcry. If everybody's bidding 6 1/2 and I'm long at 5 1/2, I bid 7-even for one. I want more bids at 6 1/2. The guy who sells me one at 7-even, he's going to bid 6 1/2 because he wants to make a profit. That adds more fuel to the fire and that means he has to cover his shorts and we try to move the market up that way. It's called high-ticking the market.

Why will you decide to do that?

Because I'm convinced I'm right.

How are you convinced that you're right, so much so that you'll double or triple your position?

First of all, I can see where I can take my loss. The fundamentals are there, all the buyers are there, and I'm already long. So, if I have to sell, there are buyers I can sell to.

How will you recognize them?

The buyers have their palms facing toward them and they're bidding for the market. That's how I know where I can get out. When you look at the market and you see sustained buying coming in, you see one side is stronger than the other. It's not that there isn't an equal number of buyers and sellers, but when the market goes up, the buyers are more aggressive than the sellers. And when the market goes down, the sellers are more aggressive than the buyers. Usually, there's more bid for or more offered. One side of the market is always stronger than the other. At any given time of the day, you look at the market and if there's more people bidding than there are offering, or there's more people offering than there are bidding, you can pick the strong side or you can pick the weak side of the market.

So, when you see it's particularly strong, that's when you might add to a position?

Of course.

Do you have an example, or a story of one of your biggest trades?

I don't know. I've had so many of them. I've gotten carried away a few times. I've made pretty good money. Particularly during the most volatile days. I can take out some pretty good money. I've never had a million-dollar day like Lewis Borsellino has, but I've had my six-figure days. Those are very nice and very sweet. I always stop at the jewelry store and buy something nice for my sweetheart on the way home.

Do you remember the anatomy of any of those trades—how they played out?

They kind of run together. I was here for the '87 and the '89 crashes. I've been here for some tremendous bull markets that we had in the '90s. I was there when the bonds, in the late '70s and early 1980, went from over par—over 102—down to 56 cents on the dollar. When the Hunt Brothers were buying the bonds and they were buying silver and gold. I traded the silver and the gold. I made some pretty good money. It's been a long career.

Do any particular trades come to mind, the anatomy of how one of those trades played out?

It just runs together with all of this time. I probably need some of that gingko biloba stuff to stimulate my brain. They do seem to run together at times.

Understandably. Maybe you have a recollection of a large loss.

Of course you always remember the losses. Do you know why? When you get to a certain point and you get good at what you do, you expect to make money. In the big markets when the trade is big and the market is much more volatile and the tick gets bigger, you expect to go in and make 20 grand a day, make 100 grand a week. When you go in and get careless or stupid, and you lose 40 grand or something, that sticks out . . . it's so out of character. You weren't expecting that.

Has that ever happened to you?

Of course. Everybody's had that.

What was the anatomy of one of those? How did that play out? What got you into the trade? What were you thinking?

Cannon balls. I sold some. It went against me.

Cannon-balling means you added to a loser.

I added to a loser. I ended up short 27 contracts when the market was going down and the market just kept going. I couldn't get them back. Finally, I just gave the order to the broker and said, "Buy me 27 at the market. Do the best you can." I just took my loss. That's just how it went.

It's a fickle place. There are no prisoners. It's money. Money's dumb. Money goes to anybody. Gangsters have money. You just ride it out. When you do careless things, expect the market to be *un*forgiving. It's a very unforgiving place. There's nothing like it. There's no place else you'd rather be. After all these years, I'm never late.

Intensely exciting, eh?

Yes, very exciting. It's a narcotic. It gets you cooking.

In either of those—the big loser or the big gainer—do you feel like you learned more? Do you feel those are valuable lessons?

I certainly learned not to average and not to cannon-ball. It's much better to just take losses and get on to the next trade. If you keep adding to losers . . . you sell four and it goes against you, so you sell four more . . . you've got eight. It continues to go against you. Now you sell eight more. Now you've got 16. And all you ever really wanted was a four-contract position. Now you have a 400-percent larger position than you really wanted and it's all against you. That's a good lesson.

Do you think that has been one of your most valuable lessons in the pit?

Yes, of course. It's not that I'm a good loser. You show me a good loser, and I'll show you a loser. I'm a skillful loser. I know how to take losses. I try to take the best loss that I can.

Do you ever bluff in the pits?

Everybody bluffs in the pits. You close your eyes and offer the market and hope nobody hits you. It's called *wolfing* your position. Try to uptick it. Tick it without getting hit. Maybe you have 10, 12 contracts on, but you still want it to go higher. You bid for it and close your eyes and hope nobody hits you.

Could I ask you to describe that in your own words for somebody who might not quite understand what you're talking about?

You're long the market at 1490 and the market is at 1493 1/2, and you've bought at 1490, 1490 1/2, 1491 1/2, 1492—and you've had it. You got on as many contracts as you really feel comfortable having. You bid for one more and just . . . you bid to the ceiling. You bid 3 1/2 for one, which would be 1493.50 . . .

Hoping to break the market out at 93 1/2, huh?

Hoping to catch the guys who have sold it all the way up from 1490 to 1493. Now, you're trying to buy one at 1493.50. You touch off some buy stops. But you really don't want any more. You have as many on as you want. It doesn't matter when you bid for the market, whether you bid for one or you bid for 10. As long as the print goes up, you're going to touch the buy stops and then the buy stops have to get elected. Once they're elected, they have to be filled.

Why do you use the word "elected"?

It's not a market order until the print goes on the board. I guess it is a common word. The stops are elected at that point and they become market orders.

Oh, because they're standing stops . . . once a print hits the tape . . .

Right. Then they're elected. Now they're active.

That's one way to bluff it—trigger some stops. You're long at 90 and it blows to 93 . . . and then it starts rallying?

That's right. You can sell them at 93 1/2, 94, 94 1/2, 95-even. Sometimes the stops will run into each other and you can catch a real running market and maybe make 300, 400, 500 points . . . 700 points.

What about order flow? You mentioned that already as a way to read the *fundamentals* in the pits: either the hands are facing in—the pit wants to buy—or the hands are facing out and the pit wants to sell. That's one way you read order flow, of course . . .

That's fundamental analysis.

Is there any other way? Do you watch certain major players? Do you watch Goldman?

I watch Goldman Sachs, Morgan Stanley, and Salomon Bros. Those are the key players. Of course, I have a big house that stands right behind me called Chi-Corp . . . Chicago Corporation. They trade actual cash stocks against the futures.

These are program trades?

I think so. They're difficult to trade with. They are a very big player, a very major player. They take big money out of the market doing that. They bid for the market and they have a resting bid on the bid, but as soon as they lose the cash side, they fill the future side. You can't really follow what they're doing very much. I don't watch the cash stocks.

Are there other types of discernable program trades and strategies going on with other players?

All over the place.

It must make the order flow confusing with that?

Yes, of course. Like I said, "It's not easy." If it were easy, they wouldn't need me.

Is there any way that you know that screen-based traders can get a feel for order flow?

Screen-based traders—no. Screen-based traders have to trade technically.

Absolutely no way?

I don't think so. And particularly if they're off the floor.

Is there any other way when you can tell that a program trade is coming into the market or how you can key off that to make money?

Off the premium. I don't really follow it that much. When I see the premium enter into the cash—because the cash S&P leads to the futures—the premium gets to be a certain level, then they'll come in to buy the futures to go and sell the cash stock against it. It's called "The Basket." They're basket traders. They do real well with that.

That's not a method you've ever traded or that you can actually use to key off of?

No. They trade much too big for me to follow.

Do you trade in any other markets?

I like to speculate in the corn-wheat spread. Buy the wheat and sell the corn in the summer, and sell the wheat and buy the corn in the winter. I like to play gold. I don't know why. I don't really make much money at it.

At either one, or just gold?

At gold. The corn-wheat spread has been very good to me.

Why do you select the corn-wheat spread?

Only because I've followed it for years. Sometimes it can break out really wide. I start watching it very closely when it gets around 50 cents. A few weeks ago, it was into 15 cents—that's a tremendous buy. You buy the wheat and sell the corn. Now, it's exploded back out to about 62 cents. You put out 20 contracts like that. You can take some nice money out.

Can you describe that trade in simple terms, for people who may not be aware of how spreads work and why you do it?

I like to buy the wheat and sell the corn . . . same month . . . at a differential. It depends on the time of year. In the summer . . .

And you do this year round and not just for the summer crop?

Yes, in the winter it's reversed. In the summer, you try to buy the wheat and sell the corn because there's much less wheat and much more corn. The corn isn't nearly as volatile as the wheat. The wheat is much more weather-sensitive. I stick away from the soybeans. Soybeans—they got to kill the crop three times a summer before you can make any money on the damn stuff. A soybean'll grow in a crack in a sidewalk because it's such a hardy plant. But the wheat is much more vulnerable and that's what makes it much more volatile. I try to buy the wheat and sell the corn at a differential of about 40 cents or 50 cents and sometimes it gets in there more than that. And then I look for it to snap out, depending on the weather conditions and shortages.

Do you trade gold similarly?

No, I just speculate in gold, usually from the long side. "Be a friend to gold when it's friendless." That's my motto. When everybody hates it, get long in it. When they come for it, they come with both hands.

Both hands. You like to see the big moves.

I like gold. I don't like to be short in it.

Looking back or starting over, is there anything . . .

I'd like to have a chance again. I'd like them to roll back the clock about 21 years. I'd like to have another chance with this much knowledge.

What would you do differently?

I'd trade bigger. Probably wouldn't have so many kids, either. That kind of slows you down. Makes you a little nervous.

Makes you a little more cautious?

I have a beautiful home and all that. I certainly don't want to go back any farther. Kids don't understand that kind of stuff. It really takes a little bit out.

With your current knowledge, what do you think you might do differently, besides trading bigger?

I've learned so much in the last eight, 10 years that I think I would have started differently. I would have been more experienced in trading the markets. I didn't really have anyone to teach me when I came in. I started scalping the market first and then I started doing these T-Bond spreads. It was all self-taught. I didn't know anything about technical analysis or fundamental analysis. I didn't know about opening range breakouts or breakouts from the high of the day or the low of the day. In trading, of course, nobody tells you anything. They don't tell you their secrets. That's their game.

You're sitting here telling us, though.

Yes, because markets are different now. Maybe I'm just more of an open person.

You've written about "value areas" as well. Could you explain what they are and how you use them?

The low of the day and the high of the day are the extreme value areas. By the low of the day, all the people who wanted to sell the market get filled. All the shorts got filled by the low of the day. The same thing goes with the high of the day: Everybody who wanted to get long, everybody who had an idea about buying the market, they got filled by the high of the day. Every guy . . . the last trade out, got filled by the high of the day. That's a very strong value area.

The next day, the high and the low are the basics of technical analysis and are considered very important value areas. When the high of the day gets violated, the pit will tend to get long. There will be buy stops above the high of the day. Again, when the low of the day gets violated there will be shorts or sell orders below the low of the day. All the longs will have to get out because it already violated the low and that was the technical area of support for the market. Those people who want to get in by selling the market . . . those people are proven right because the market has violated the low. And they'll be a bunch of people who got long at that area, who have to get out because it violated the low. It's a technical area, a major area of value.

I guess those are defined by the end of the day. Otherwise, the value areas are very difficult to figure out while you're in the market.

No, they are set intraday. Within the daily trading range, you'll establish a low and establish a high. It may change throughout the day. By the end of the day, there is a high of the day and a low of the day. There will be buy stops above the high of the day, and sell stops below the low of the day.

Where do most people go wrong with their trading and how would you tell them to proceed?

Particularly when they start out, I would tell them to trade small, trade frequently, try to learn from their trades, and don't be too egotistical to think you're right. The market is bigger than everyone. Take your losses. Taking losses is your best friend. If you can be humble enough to take losses when you're wrong, you can last as long as I have. That's the idea. You don't have to make a million dollars on one trade. You can make a dollar on a million trades and still have a million. That's the idea. I'm a daytrader. It's my job. I want to be around for a long time. I don't want this to end. I don't want to go in, make a bunch of money and then not have anything to do. What am I going to do all day?

JON NAJARIAN

MERCURY RISING

By Laurence A. Connors

Whether pounding running backs for the Chicago Bears or puts and calls on the floor of the Chicago Board Options Exchange (CBOE), Jon Najarian plays to win. With operations on every exchange in the U.S., Jon's market making firm, Mercury Trading, is one of the top three option floor-trading firms in the country, placing Najarian at the top of the options game.

But he's paid his dues. Jon started as a clerk on the CBOE floor, where he worked the first six months for free. And during his unpaid apprenticeship, he found that his quick reflexes and competitive nature were well-suited to the demands of floor trading.

Soon thereafter, Najarian bought a limited CBOE seat and began trading his own account in the IBM pit. Within a few years "DRJ"—the letters on his pit badge that would become his well-known nickname—had established himself as one of the exchange's biggest players.

Dr. J's success in the pit led to the founding of Mercury Trading in 1989. The firm currently makes markets in more than 90 high-tech and biotech stocks at the CBOE, trading between 25,000–40,000 options and 3 million shares of stock per day.

Najarian also provides regular market commentary on radio and television for such networks as CNNfn and CNBC. When asked how he finds time for this, Najarian says he wants "to share the experience that I earned by trading millions of options and billions of shares of stock over the past 19 years. I want to show traders how to use options to more effectively build their financial futures."

Laurence Connors: Let's go through your background real quickly. How did you get into trading options? How did it all start for you?

Jon Najarian: I was playing football for the Chicago Bears, Larry. This was in 1981. I had just graduated college. The Bears looked like the best opportunity for me because they were one of the worst teams in the league. And I was a free agent, a linebacker. The Bears starting middle linebacker was holding out on his contract and ultimately never came back to play football. He was trading over at the Chicago Mercantile Exchange during the off-season. And he decided that he was better off physically and financially to stay over there than he was to come back and play football for the Bears.

So the opportunity presented itself to play football for them. I took it. I'm sort of like your partner Kevin Haggerty's sons that play professional hockey, I guess. But unfortunately my career was only four pre-season games. At the end of those four pre-season games, I took the opportunity offered to me by my agent to come down to the floor of the Chicago Board Option Exchange and be a runner. And like many traders before me and since, I took that job for free, for no pay.

In college, did you have any type of financial background or any type of math background to give you a head start in your trading career?

No, I didn't. I was planning on majoring in architecture. That was a five-year degree and I didn't go back to get the fifth year. Instead I got a degree in design, not an architectural degree. My math skills were decent because you have to know a decent amount of math for architecture. But I did not take any business courses. I never took a single business course in college.

After you became a runner, what happened?

Then I came down to the floor. I was very frustrated because no one was really teaching the basics of options. There were books like Larry McMillan's book. But as good of a guy as Larry McMillan is, it was way over my head and it was written more like a textbook. Bottom line: It wasn't very helpful for me. So most of what I learned about trading I had to learn by the school of hard knocks.

Listed put options, Larry, had only been trading on the Chicago Board Option Exchange since 1979, I think. So when I came down in 1981, I'm not even sure if all the stocks that were trading had put options on them. Call option trading dominated and the strategies associated with doing what we can do today with options—you know, play the upside or the downside of the markets with puts or calls—weren't nearly as prevalent as they are today. And experienced floor traders were kind of protecting their turf by *not* teaching people how these various strategies might behave. Because if you discovered it, it was your little kingdom until somebody else figured it out. As a result, it was very frustrating being a young trader because there was really nobody to learn from.

It was about six months before I really figured out what was going on—before I could really start to put it together, to understand that this is why someone would do this kind of spread . . . and this is why they would do a bearish position . . . and this is why they would take advantage of premiums that they perceived were too high. Or when there were too many sellers and the premium levels got too low and they were way too cheap, why you would be a buyer and what type of spreads you would do.

Like I said, it easily took me six months before I got to that point. Then I began trading. I used the money I made from the Bears and I put $19,000, I think, into a Midwest seat, which was the smaller of two seats. You had to have one of the two to be a market maker on our floor—the Chicago Board Option Exchange. I chose the Midwest seat because it was financially more obtainable. I began trading down on the floor. And because I really worked hard on developing my spreading techniques, I began to have pretty good success very quickly. I was always a pretty disciplined person and I began to make money using the strategies and taking advantage of market conditions that were considerably different than they are today.

What year was this?

It was 1981–1982. And back in those times, Larry, they didn't let you have computers on board in the pit like you can today. In fact, there were no computers and they didn't even have direct phone access in the pits because they thought it was an unfair advantage. So everybody in the pit would just stand down there, and it was how fast you could add and subtract fractions . . . and how early you got in that morning so you could print the sheets with the various theoretical values.

In other words, I was trading IBM, and IBM was about a $98 stock back then. So I would run IBM theoretical values with the stock price movement between $94 and $102, 8 points worth, every quarter-point. I'd have sheets and sheets, telling me what the July 95 calls would be worth; what the theoretical value of the July 100 calls would be, what the July 102 calls would be worth, etc. I had sheets that covered a range of prices from $4 above and $4 below the market.

You can imagine the inefficiencies of that marketplace. But it was good for me because I was very quick with fractions, and it was good for the other traders in the pit who were likewise quick with fractions, and bad for people who weren't.

We've moved 180 degrees in the other direction now, because today everybody in the pits has handheld computers. And in fact, there are people in the pit with virtually no knowledge of the markets, who are trading based on how their computers are color-coded to reflect the options' strikes that they should buy or sell. So like I say, you don't need to have nearly the skill-set today that you did back when I started trading. Not that I'm an exceptionally gifted trader in that regard—I think I'm pretty good—but Larry, there were hundreds of traders that were equally good and very fast about figuring fractions and trading very quickly.

It became apparent that some of the factors that would contribute to you being a successful trader were things like counting cards in a game of blackjack.

Because that means you can think in multi-dimensions. If you were a professional chess player or a backgammon player or a poker player, these were skills that were very beneficial. These skills helped you to remember that 10 minutes ago a Schwab broker bid an option just below the market . . . or that on the other side of the pit, two hours ago, the Merrill Lynch broker was trying to sell puts, but he was trying to sell them at a price that was above the market and the market makers were not buyers.

Filing all these little facts away in your mind, you could take advantage of the market when it started to move by reminding the broker, "hey, do you still have those calls, are you still 3 1/2 bid for those calls?" The broker would say, "yeah." And then you'd say, "Sold! I'll sell you 50 of those." Motioning to the other side of the pit you might say, "and I'll buy your puts, Merrill. How many were you offering?" And then the whole pit would get into a big frenzy trying to do the same things because they would remember, too. But many of them were distracted or didn't have the skill-set to remember and do the multi-tasking that enabled good traders to make money even when they didn't have computers to track all these different things. Now you can just basically program your computer to assist you in much of what I just described.

Let's jump ahead. You've been talking about the skills needed to succeed back in the early- and middle-'80s. What skills are needed to succeed today? How has it changed?

I wouldn't say this is a skill, but it is certainly a determining factor in how successful you are going to be. You guys know, Larry, because you use it every day: You've got to be disciplined. The single biggest thing that we look for when we hire traders is their discipline.

Explain what that means.

The kid could have long hair or he could be bald. The kid could be six-foot-seven or the kid could be five-foot-two. The physical and the mental are important, but the most important factor is always going to be discipline.

And explain what discipline means to you. What does that mean?

If you're trading your own money, discipline means to trade within your personal guidelines. This means determining how much money you are willing to risk on any given trade in your portfolio, and then not violating those rules. Good discipline means not saying, "Well, but it's a different situation today. I'm going to let myself go a little crazy." You know, that's obviously a recipe for disaster.

So what we've tried to do when we hire new traders is first explain the guidelines. If they can't trade within the guidelines that we set, we won't keep them as a trader. If I tell a guy, "I want you to buy and sell options in stock all day, but I want you to be delta neutral." That is, as you know, "I want you to not be exposed in the market to the stock if it opens down $3 tomorrow—to losing hundreds of thousands of dollars because you came in massively long. I want you to trade within delta neutral or within 5,000 shares of neutral on this particular stock."

If we have a trader who doesn't seem to be able to hang within those guidelines, we'll cut them loose immediately. And if you're an individual investor, I think the same rules apply. Perhaps it's even tougher for the individual investor, because you don't have a boss. You are your own boss, and you have to set, and adhere to, your own guidelines.

We think this is vital, Larry, and when we speak at seminars we also tell investors, "You have to set a goal for your trade." Whether you are just buying stock or whether you're putting on an option spread, what was the goal when you put the trade on? Is it that I'm buying Harmonic because I think Harmonic could go up to $50 over the next three months and it's a $25 stock?

The more that you shorten your time horizon, the more you become a competitor with other daytraders—which include professional traders down on the floor—and the more you have to know everything we know about the industry events that are going on. Events such as, is there an analyst conference, is there a new product introduction, is there pending litigation, or is there an expected earnings report? The more short term you become, the more you have to care about those factors. The more long term you are, the less you have to care about it.

Yes, it matters if Unisys—as it did today, June 29, 2000—warned about its profits going forward and the stock falls from 23 down to 15. That matters and it hurts. But that is an exceptional event that could hurt any trader or any investor. If you're just trading for the short term, that's a killer. If you're a long-term investor, it hurts. But now you regroup and you decide, do I want to still hold Unisys, or am I getting out? Is it time to exit this thing altogether?

I think the biggest problem investors have is if they don't set a goal and then they don't *reassess* where they are in that trade on a regular basis. Like I said, the shorter term you are, the more you have to care about short-term events. For instance, my traders and I do this every morning: We sit down and we go through all 90 stocks that we are trading. For Sun Microsystems we ask, "are we bullish, bearish or indifferent?" For Micron we ask, "are we bullish, bearish, or indifferent?" Then we ask, "What is our outlook and when are the next big events on the horizon that we know of?" There are always exceptional events that we don't know about, but what are the known events that we can plan for, like earnings and so forth? We do this every day. Most investors don't have to do this because they have a longer time horizon than we do. But we care about very short-term events as daytraders and as professional traders.

Let's say somebody came to you and said, "I want to do this full-time and I'm funded to do it full-time, and it can go one of two ways. Which way should I go? Should I be looking at hundreds and hundreds of different stocks, looking for positions with a mathematical edge? Basically anytime something is, let's say, two times the H.V. (historic volatility), I'm going to hedge myself and take advantage of it that way. Or am I better off just focusing on 10 or 15 stocks and knowing the companies inside and out and knowing their personality and behavior and learning how to take advantage of those and forgetting about the math?"

It's the latter strategy, Larry. I don't think an individual investor can watch 50 or 100 stocks like we do and like many other professional traders do. I think they would be really over-extending themselves.

But strictly looking at it from a math edge versus a fundamental knowledge edge, is the math—

—If you're getting down to a math edge, you're talking about exploiting a very small edge, because with the advent of computers and other changes, the playing field has virtually been leveled for everybody. Most of the edge has been taken away from the professional trader on the floor. The biggest advantage that I still have, Larry, is that I don't have the margin issues that the customers have. I can buy, as we do routinely, $100 million to $200 million worth of stock. And we do it because I don't have the same margin requirements that customers do. Because of that, the individual investor needs to have a little bit longer of a time horizon, unless they're just lucky and somebody left them a hell of a lot of money.

I think most investors are not going to focus on and try to exploit that mathematical edge, because that's really the trading area of the daytrader or the pit trader. I think what the regular customer wants to do, whether they trade fundamentally or technically, is look at stocks that they know or industries that they're familiar with. We see investors doing the best by buying what they know. Like Peter Lynch always recommends, trade what you know. And I think that's good advice for any investor.

So let's jump to some specifics. When it comes to delta neutral trading, what is your opinion of someone who wants to do this professionally and full-time? Could he or she succeed at doing delta neutral trading?

Delta neutral trading, of course, is referring to positions that, at the end of that trading day, are neutral. When the market closes today, I might have long calls in Microsoft and be bullish, but I've sold some stock to neutralize my exposure overnight. And then the next morning, if the stock opens up $10, I could be very long in that position making a lot of money, yet I started from the closing point of the market last night in a neutral stance. I think when investors look at that, they say, "Well, how can I make any money?" And if you can't trade at least 10 by 20 size, it's very difficult for an individual to invest or to make money. If you're doing IBM options and you're buying five of the 115 calls and selling 10 of the 120s, it's very difficult to make money because commissions are a big factor of that trade. And then you need a fairly big move in that stock to make money. So if the investor is able to trade 10 by 20, that investor could be a delta neutral trader.

And Larry, you couldn't have imagined a better environment to be delta neutral in than today's environment. I mean we're seeing stocks every day—Unisys, Bristol-Myers, Lucent—big stocks, making extraordinary moves because the market is willing to either punish severely or reward wonderfully, depending on the news and how the market reacts to the news. I think that there are few times when being a delta neutral investor and being a back spreader, you know, buying premium, could have worked better than in this market.

But that is not going to last forever. If somebody is reading this book five years from now . . .

You're absolutely right. And it's why we tell people that you can't force the trade that you love just because you always make money as a back spreader. For instance, you are always buying premium. There are times when it's a lousy time to buy premium, in particular, of course, ahead of earnings. As you're going into that earnings event, the volatilities are sky high. The world is anticipating extraordinary things. And that's priced into those options. The option that would normally be an at-the-money option in Micron Technology, one of our stocks, might normally be $5, but before earnings it might be trading for 8 1/2.

Do you tend to be a seller into events?

I do. But I also like to buy into events if I don't think that the market has priced in enough of the risk that I think is inherent in that announcement.

Are there any guidelines that you can share with us as to what priced-in means?

Well, for instance, let's look at a stock like Micron. If the normal volatility for Micron—let me just pull it up real quick—the May 2000 options were 74 percent, April options were 113 percent, March options were 108 percent, and February was 95 percent. In other words, this is a very volatile stock. You've got a stock averaging near triple-digit volatility during that time frame. That's a volatile stock, and the stock movement of Micron suggests that as well. When you look at a chart, it moved from $35 up to $95 a share pretty quickly because the semis were red-hot.

When I'm talking about volatilities, if I said the average volatility for Micron was 75 percent, around earnings I would expect it to be up 140 percent from there or 150 percent. If it were only up 125 percent, then I would say maybe there's not enough premium in those options. I would rather be a buyer, thinking that Micron could make an extraordinary move after those earnings are announced.

You'd be a buyer of the options.

Yep, I'd be a buyer. I'm usually looking around earnings, unless it's like the most stable Commonwealth Edison kind of utility stock. I'm looking for the earnings and industry events to move the volatilities probably 140 to 150 percent higher than normal. And if they're not, then I tend to buy them.

And, Jon, if it moved 200 percent above normal, you'd be looking to be a seller?

Yes. But I would try to protect myself by buying some disaster puts if I were selling puts or disaster calls above the market so that I could protect myself and not just be naked long or short.

So you're hedging yourself no matter what?

Yes, sir.

Are you always hedged?

We are. We're always hedged.

For you, is that the key to success?

I think it is. What we try to do is be in a diverse portfolio of stocks. We're mainly in high tech and biotech. So we know that if the market is crapping out from the tech stocks, it's going to hurt all the stocks in our portfolio. But we'll probably have long premium positions in a couple of them and short premium positions in a boatload of them. This is because overall, the market—especially in 2000 and for most of 1999—has been trading at unusually high volatilities. But the market has been justifying that by rocking and rolling the way it has.

Can we jump to sentiment indicators? What do you use for sentiment indicators for the overall market? What are your favorites?

Well, what we use, of course, are the short-term indicators like the S&P 500 and the Nasdaq futures. But beyond that, we look at the measure of volatility in the market, the VIX. What we do, Larry, is we look at the VIX and think of volatility for stocks or indexes like a rubber band. And I think there's an equilibrium, for instance, in the VIX. And if I look at it, that equilibrium looks to be about 26 percent. When the volatility jumps and makes a move up into the 30s, you know, 32, 34, 36 percent, that's on the very high end of volatility and it's almost unsustainable. In my opinion, it's almost impossible for the market to sustain that kind of volatility for a broad market like the VIX represents.

Likewise, when it falls down into the low-20s, which it's done on a few occasions in the last year, then I'm a big buyer of volatility, thinking that it's going to snap back toward that 26 number. This is similar to when it's overvalued and trading at 35 or 36. Then, it's going to snap back down. Generally when we see a high VIX number, we know that the world is panicked and it needs protection. That's normally not when the market makes big moves. The market usually makes its biggest moves when the world is complacent and no one is buying put options to protect the downsides of their portfolios. And instead, they are just overwriting call options and hammering premiums.

Extreme VIX Readings: CBOE Market Volatility Index (VIX), Daily

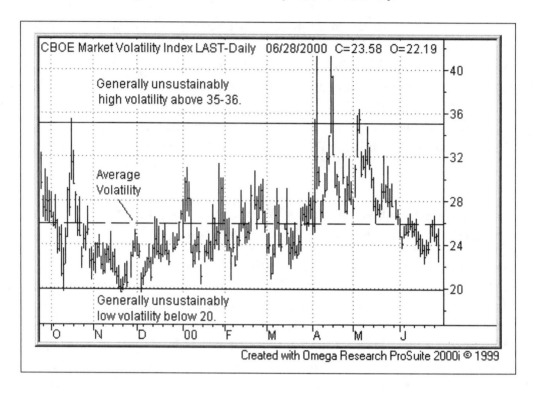

Do you believe the VIX is superior to the put-to-call ratio now?

I do, yes.

I very much agree. You know, we're talking and this is the summer of 2000. It may be an agenda thing, but the options writer for *Barron's* seems to think that the VIX doesn't work. Do you have any thoughts on that?

Well, in fact I know the options writer for *Barron's*, Erin Arvedlund, and she's a good lady. And I think she understands the products pretty well. I guess, Larry, different opinions are what make a market. Some people want to look at put-call ratios.

What I do like, as far as another indicator, is block-option trades.

Tell me what that is.

When I'm seeing blocks of options in the 500-to-1,000 option category, that's indicating to me that a very big player is getting into the market quickly. And if we think of the market as an animal like a dog, we say, "Well, the tail is wagging the dog." This is when somebody enters a big option order rather than going into the stock itself. For instance, in Sun Micro, Amazon or whatever, they might come in and buy a huge amount of call options rather than buy the stock. Why? Because they can get the trade done in pretty damn good size very quickly. If they were to go to the Nasdaq market makers to buy stock, they are afraid the market makers would run the stock up. So they might enter through the options.

Next, the options market makers all go for the stock, as they are going to hedge themselves for the exposure they just took on. And that's why I say it wags the dog in some instances. It just depends where somebody enters the market. So when I see blocks of options trading, to me that indicates that there is some big institutional player accumulating a position or selling a position, depending on what it is.

Because you can tell if a 1,000-lot trades at $7 1/2 and the market at that time was 7 1/4 or 1/2, I know that that big trade was a big option buyer, not a big option seller. You know what I mean? So chances are the crowd, the market makers, and specialists were the big sellers. And we are reactionary; we are trading defensively. The options market makers are not the guys on the offensive. We're like the catcher in a game of baseball. We have to just respond to what the pitcher throws. So like when you, Larry, and your readers are initiating trades, they are the pitcher. They are determining, they're starting the trade. Market makers are making markets. And we're making markets based on the underlying security.

When a customer order comes in, whether it's Goldman Sachs, Charles Schwab, whatever, when they come into the market, we react to it. So now I'm trading defensively. Most of our trading is defensive trading and that's why we, the traders on the floor, spread so much. We're acting defensively to a big customer who wants to accumulate options or a small customer that wants to accumulate options or vice versa. That's why we're defensively trading. And I think that when you look at these blocks of options, you can tell when a big player is entering the market and you'll see it ripple through the stock market in the next few minutes.

So basically you might be able to predict short-term price movement of stocks by looking at these large blocks coming into the options markets?

Absolutely.

And what do you use? You obviously have software to detect these types of blocks coming in.

Yes, we do. And that's what we use to provide the content on 1010Wall Street.com—our online advisory service.

Is it proprietary software or is it . . .

It is proprietary. It's stuff we've developed for ourselves to help us track this.

Do you work with Len Yates from OptionVue?

Yes, Lenny is a good guy. And we in fact use OptionVue 5 a lot. I like the way Len presents the information in the program. I think it's easy to use. I think it's good solid software, it works well, and it's reasonably priced.

As far as other sentiment indicators, do you look at anything else beyond the VIX and beyond the block options?

No, not really. I mean I tend to be a bit of a contrarian anyway, Larry. And that's why when Motorola had a big disappointment like they did a month ago or a month-and-a-half ago, I tend to be a buyer on that. Just like today with Unisys. I didn't buy it today, but I generally buy it on the second day after one of those events.

Were you buying Amazon, for example, a couple of weeks ago when some analysts seemed to talk it down?

Well, we've been in and out of Amazon so much, I can't really say for the long term that we did anything, except that my partner on the trading desk, Tom Haugh, thinks the stock is going to zero. We did sell a lot of puts into it, though, on the drop when it got down into the low-30s. Tom still thinks it's going to zero.

But you're taking advantage of the price drop?

Yes. Exactly.

Collecting The Panic: Amazon (AMZN), Daily

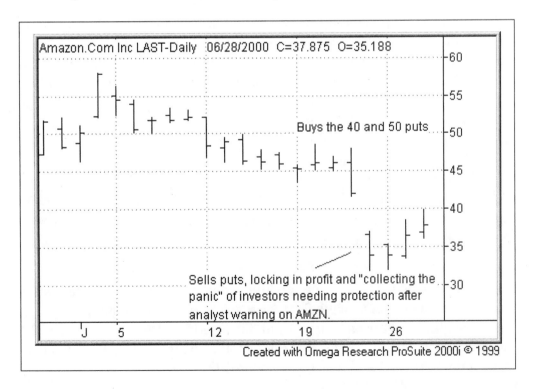

And just to reiterate, when you're selling the puts, you are hedging yourself one way or another just in case your partner is correct?

Yes, we are. Chances are—I mean Tom was long—he had been buying puts before that $7 or $8 drop (on June 23, 2000). He was buying the 45 and the 50 puts when it was around those levels. And two days later the stock dropped down there into the low 30s and he was pounding out 35 and 30 puts because now he is locking in a lot of the profit from the bigger puts and collecting the panic from the people that needed protection right as the hurricane was hitting.

Going back to money management, you were talking about this before, what is the firm's exposure to any given trade? Are you risking 1 percent of what you have under the roof, or is there a percentage? What risk are you willing to assume?

We've never actually looked at it that way, Larry. But there are some big trades that we do when we sort of have a gun to our head, in Sun Micro or in Micron. This is because these are super competitive crowds where we are competing against four different exchanges. We might take down a quarter-of-a-million share position and have to get ourselves hedged very quickly. That's not a fun position to be in. And I guess if I thought about it at that moment when we did it, it might be 10 percent of the firm. But we don't do that very often.

Like I say, unfortunately in the competitive world that we are in, we're forced to step up and do much bigger size trades than we'd like to do to keep the paper trading on our floor, the CBOE. That's where our main operation is. We have operations on all the exchanges except the Philly. But Chicago is our home base. So for most of the trades, we prefer to do them here.

Let's say I was to give you a quarter-million dollars today and you were no longer allowed to trade on the floor. Now you've got to grow these quarter-million dollars and support your family with it. What would you do? How would you trade? Maybe that's not a fair number for starting. But you are now a retail trader. What would you do today?

Investors at seminars always ask, "Could I quit my day job?" And I say, "How big is your portfolio?" I mean if you're talking about quitting your day job with a $50,000 portfolio, the question is always "Is that big enough?" And I'd say, "What can you live on?" If you're telling me that you've got only 50-grand to trade with and you want to trade relatively conservatively, then I'd say, you've got to be able to survive on a lot less than you're probably making now.

So with a quarter-million dollar portfolio, could you pretty easily make 25 to 40 percent on that? Yes. Not necessarily easily, but you could do it. For instance, you could buy LEAPS. Most of the long-term successful option folks in our brokerage firm, I'd say, do that day in and day out and they make the most consistent money. Buying LEAPS as a surrogate for buying stocks. In lieu of buying Microsoft or Motorola or IBM or any of these stocks, they're buying the LEAP in that stock. And then they're overwriting it each month or each quarter, depending on how aggressive they are with an option, one to one.

The downside is that they've really neutralized a lot of that because they've bought a $20 leap instead of a $120 stock and they can have a broad portfolio of stocks. You do the math all the time, too, I'm sure. Look at what would happen if I owned a leap on IBM at, let's say, $17 to $25. And every month I sell an out-of-the-money call one strike out of the money for 2 1/2 bucks. Two-and-a-half times 12 is a pretty nice amount of money that I'm taking in against the $25 investment.

But that, in your opinion, is the best way for the retail trader to succeed at this game?

Yes. I would say that, yes.

I'm looking at my notes here and we've covered a lot. Are there any parting thoughts or any advice that you can give to individual traders? Any thoughts on what you would tell them?

One other thing would be that the individual investor needs a broker that understands options. Otherwise they're wasting their time. And they need to understand that until there are electronic systems—ECNs if you will, for options—they can't really do everything online. When they are doing spreading, they are going to have to deal with a broker somewhere. For instance, often if you are only dealing with certain discount firms, you're kind of hosed because that broker can't give you any advice—basically by mandate of the firm. They're not going to give you any advice. And if you give them the strategy wrong, they are going to execute it and just play the tape back to you. Do you know what I mean?

Sure.

So you have to deal with an option broker who can help you with the strategies. And you don't want to educate your option broker. You want to find a good one. And when you find a good one, you'll find that they're very popular, that everybody wants to be there. And that's an important factor. You can't just go onto the cheapest online Web site and expect you are going to have great success with that brokerage firm. You are going to have to find a broker that you can call when you are doing a spread, so you are not just paying the offer and hitting the bid. You are probably giving up 10 percent of the investment on that and you need to narrow that a little bit. A good broker should be able to do that.

And the other thing is, just as this book is doing, you need education. Before you make any trades, we always tell people to do a lot of paper trading. But before you really want to dive into options, you want to get some education. Not everybody can afford a $2,000 or a $3,000 seminar. That's not the issue. However, you do need to get educated.

Do you have a favorite book?

I've got a book coming out this fall.

What's the name?

It's *How I Trade Options* by Jon Najarian. It's going to be published by Wiley in late 2000.

That sounds exciting. I'm looking forward to seeing it.

I hope so, thank you.

I don't know if you agree, but Natenberg's book (*Option Volatility and Pricing: Advanced Trading Strategies and Techniques*) in my opinion is one of the best. I've read through it so many times. And even though it doesn't tell you what to do, he leads you in the right direction.

Oh, absolutely. Sheldon Natenberg's book helps investors. That's a good book.

Okay. Again, this is a pleasure.

It's my pleasure, too, Larry. Thank you.

GREG KUHN

PASSIONATE PLAYER

By Kevin N. Marder

Greg Kuhn is simply one of the best stock traders I've ever met. In running up consistently superb, long-term results with his hedge fund, Thorough-bred Partners, LP, Kuhn breaks most of the rules that many investors worship blindly.

Buying a stock as it makes a price high, religiously nipping losses in the bud, adding to winning positions, ignoring a stock's rich valuation, listening to the market's message and not the message of others—these are all traits that Kuhn practices with precision.

Having been greatly influenced by Bill O'Neil, Kuhn is a classic chartist, fo-cusing on the patterns themselves and eschewing the indicators that can be de-rived from them. When it comes to general market timing, he relies on the tried-and-true, namely an analysis of what the big averages and leading issues are saying.

Interestingly, Kuhn's methodology is living proof that someone keying on just chart patterns and earnings growth can reap outsized rewards year after year.

Kevin N. Marder: How did you get your start in the trading business? Were you a broker first, like so many successful traders?

Gregory J. Kuhn: Yes, I started out as a stockbroker in 1985 with Thomson Mc-Kinnon Securities, which at the time was one of the top 10 firms. I think they were No. 10. They considered themselves to be the best-kept secret on the Street. When it turned out that senior management was skimming off the top and the company was about to go under, Prudential Securities bought them out. This was after I left. I spent 18 months with them and then jumped over to Shearson Lehman Brothers, which is now part of Salomon Smith Barney.

From there, I really started getting into the market. Rather than concentrate on selling, I decided I wanted to get into the trading end of the business. I felt the best way to do that without any prior experience was to get as close to trading desks as I could in New York. So I left Shearson Lehman in 1989 and went to New York and got a job with Wheat First Securities, which is now part of First Union. None of the firms I was with are known by the same name. They were all gobbled up by somebody else. The only way I could get close to these trading desks was to get a job as a broker. That way, I could at least be in the city, make some money, earn a small living, and then go around and interview for trading positions.

I was getting pretty close to hooking up with somebody when, in August-September 1990, Iraq invaded Kuwait. The market went down the tubes and everyone put a hiring freeze on. Here I was, ready to make a move to trading, and no one wanted to hire me. So I came home one day and told my wife that I was taking a calculated risk and I was going to leave my job and start my own money management business with the handful of clients I had as a broker.

Up to that point, I had been using Bill O'Neil's principles to trade stocks and I was doing very well for some of the clients that I had in the first half of 1990. That was just before the market sold off, and I was actually able to get clients out of the market at the top. I felt like I could really give this a go with some of these people since I was actually managing some of these accounts on a discretionary basis. But I was only being paid a broker's commission. Although I wasn't the best salesman, I think the sales experience did help in running my business . . . you know, being able to interact with the public. So I had had about four years experience as a broker before I started.

As a trader, what would you consider your time frame to be?

The intermediate term. I look to hold a winning position for a few weeks to a few months. I don't do any short-term trading or daytrading or anything like that. So when the market is weak, rather than try to squeeze out a couple of extra dimes by trading the short-term time frame, I move to a 100 percent cash position, take some time off, walk away, and wait for another market cycle to reset. Probably one of the toughest things to do is sit there and do nothing unless there's absolutely something to do. You go through these little spurts where the market is acting great and you have all these positions on and you're making money and you're into it day after day. Then all of a sudden, the market corrects, you get out of your positions, and you end up with a 100 percent cash position, waiting until the tide turns. I guess it's hard for a lot of people to kind of turn it on and turn it off. It just takes a lot of practice.

Were you able to capitalize on the 1991 bull move that began in October 1990?

I was. I did it just by following some of the basic principles that O'Neil laid out, such as the follow-through day concept, which was very clear off the October bottom. I also noticed that a number of stocks were setting up by building bases. The most fascinating thing about it was that I had just gone to the first O'Neil seminar about six months before that. And at the seminar, they were going over all the chart patterns . . . and showing the ones that worked . . . and what you should look for. And coming off that bottom in October and heading into November-December, I was seeing these cup-with-handle formations. They were just flowing left and right on great stocks with great earnings. It was a beautiful thing because stocks were setting up and, as they were in their base-building mode, you could see that the earnings growth in these companies was still accelerating. So it became a very easy decision in narrowing down which ones I wanted to buy based on seeing this accelerating growth rate. And I would just wait for the patterns to complete before buying them. So I was able to take advantage of that right into the end of 1990, and of course into 1991.

What are the basic criteria you look for in your buy candidates?

The first thing I do when I screen through a daily or weekly chart book is to look at the actual chart formations. It's the first thing I'm looking for because timing is the most important part of what I do. Everything else can be right, but if I ill-time something, it costs me money. When I get into a stock, I want it to work so that I'm at a profit by the end of the day that I buy it. So I'll scan thousands of charts a week and I'll just look at the chart formations. I am looking for specific chart patterns.

Do you look at a company's fundamentals in addition to its technicals?

Yes. Just as important, I also look at several fundamental things in a company. Namely, I am looking at a company's earnings growth and revenue growth. My initial screening process is on the technical side, simply because each week I want to be in touch with which groups and which stocks are actually on the move. But just looking at the chart is only half the picture. The other half, and just as important, is what's going on with the company fundamentally. Specifically, I look at what's going on in a company's income statement. I don't care so much about its balance sheet, because when you're looking to invest in growth stocks, what's on the balance sheet really doesn't matter. For example, a company's book value has no bearing on my decision-making. However, on the income statement side, if the stock's acting well and the company has a superior new product, then it should show up on the company's bottom line. I focus on a company's annual and quarterly earnings growth. What I really want to see is, at a minimum, 30 percent growth on an annual as well as quarterly basis.

However, some companies don't have a long enough track record of annual earnings. For instance, some newer companies may have only started earning money in the last few years. In that case, I'm really deferring to the last few quarters in terms of its earnings. Again, what I want to see is 30 percent earnings growth at a minimum, but preferably a lot higher . . . the higher, the better. Even better than that, I want to see the earnings growth rate over the last several quarters accelerate.

What about revenues?

I also look at a company's revenues to make sure they are strong. Again, I am looking for revenue growth of at least 25 percent over the last couple of quarters. I measure this by comparing one quarter to the same quarter of the prior year. When it comes to the annual stuff, I'm looking at the earnings growth as opposed to anything else. Additionally, and sometimes just as important, I look at a company's after-tax profit margin to see if it's improving. Ideally, if a company's quarterly earnings growth is expanding over the last couple or few quarters, you also want to see the after-tax profit margin increase percentage-wise. This is a very good measure of how profitable the company's bottom line is and how efficiently this bottom line is being managed. On the other hand, when it comes to some of the newer, more dynamic industries like Internet, telecommunications services, and biotechnology, a lot of these companies won't have any earnings. So the thing to do there is defer strictly to the company's revenue growth, which is what the fund managers have been focusing on. What I really want to see with Internet stocks is revenue growth of at least 100 percent in the last two to four quarters.

What about companies with no growth? Do you still consider them for purchase?

With the biotechnology stocks, a lot of times the better moves develop as part of a group move. A lot of these companies not only don't have any earnings, but they don't have any revenue growth, either. As long as the whole group is moving, the chart patterns are sound, and the stocks have very high relative-strength rankings, then it would be okay to go with biotechnology stocks *sans* looking at the fundamental picture.

In a nutshell, that's what I look for. I think too many people either get caught up in the technical side or the fundamental side. With me, I like to have all these factors in place. It doesn't mean you can't use only a chart or only the fundamentals to make your decision. But I think in order to increase your probabilities of finding a big winner, you really ought to have all these factors in place.

As I said, if you only have the chart, you only have half the equation. The other part of the equation is the company's fundamentals. You can trade off chart patterns, but in order to have the confidence to hold the stock for a bigger move, the company really has to have a strong bottom line and a great new product that is ending up on its bottom line. Basically, it's a total combination. People wonder why they're not in some great stocks. They only look at the chart pattern and as soon as a stock gets into a little trouble, if they don't know what's going on with the company, they won't have confidence to hold onto the stock.

What do you want to see when you look at chart patterns?

The main thing I want to see on the chart is a base of at least five weeks in duration. A base is a sideways period of consolidation. Buying a stock just as it emerges from a base limits my risk, since the top of the base should act as support for the stock in case I'm wrong.

I'm looking for three different kinds of bases: either a cup-with-handle formation, a flat base, or a double bottom base. If you look at O'Neil's historical studies, I think he came up with a number—about 80 percent—that tells you what percentage of big winners have a cup-with-handle pattern before they start to move. These are the bases that work over and over again.

Is there any minimum time length that you want to see a cup-with-handle form in?

Yes. I would say, at a minimum, six weeks for a cup-with-handle. It's got to take the appearance of a cup. You can imagine that if it's only six weeks and well-formed, the cup's got to be pretty shallow. Basically, those small ones will form in sort of an interruption period in a market's trend. You have a nice trend forming and you get an interruption sort of like we had in January 2000. The Nasdaq Composite had this 10 percent correction and went sideways for a

Cup-With-Handle Base: Nokia (NOK), Daily

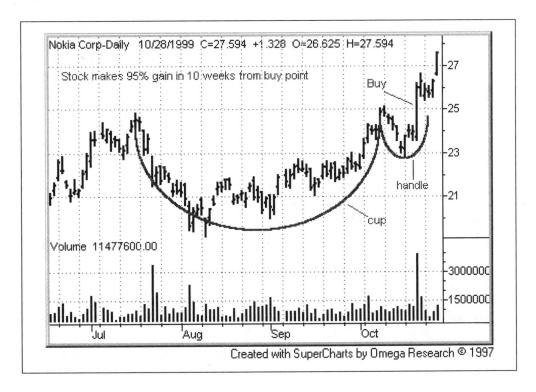

Nokia Corp-Daily 10/28/1999 C=27.594 +1.328 O=26.625 H=27.594

Stock makes 95% gain in 10 weeks from buy point

Buy

handle

cup

Volume 11477600.00

Created with SuperCharts by Omega Research © 1997

month before it swung out of there again. And that's where you'll see a shallower or smaller cup-with-handle form. The stock will form the pattern and go up out of that. Normally, the cup-with-handle is much deeper and longer.

And as far as the flat base goes, are you also looking at only six-week bases?

A flat base can be as short as five weeks. A lot of times you see a flat base after a breakout from a bigger chart formation. For example, you see a stock come out of a four-month, cup-with-handle formation. What happens is that it will break out of the handle and, for some reason, the market's still in somewhat of a corrective

Flat Base: JDS Uniphase (JDSU), Daily

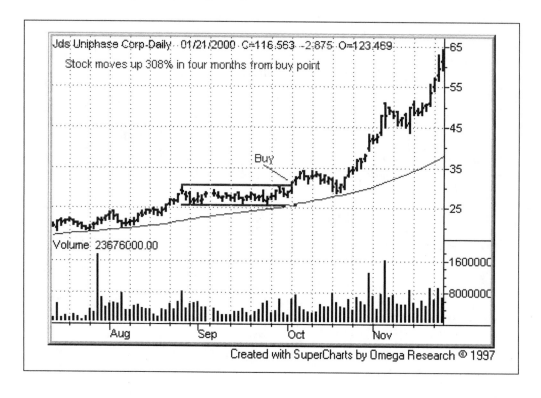

Jds Uniphase Corp-Daily 01/21/2000 C=116.563 -2.875 O=123.469

Stock moves up 308% in four months from buy point

Buy

Volume: 23676000.00

Created with SuperCharts by Omega Research © 1997

period or a bear market. And the stock will just move sideways in a tight pattern for five weeks before it swings out of there again. That's often when you see a flat base. Basically, what it does is give you another shot to get on board. Once the weight of the market comes off, then the stock's ready to go. So that's why they can be a little short. All other bases should be at least six weeks in duration.

And the third pattern you like is the double bottom?

Yes. The double bottom is a rare cup-with-handle. The main difference is the look of it. In the cup-with-handle, you have more of a rounding bottom, whereas in the double bottom you get this sharp rally back toward the old high and back down toward the low. In a cup-with-handle, the stock will get increasingly quiet and spend more of its base-building time down around its lows so it will give you the appearance of a nice cup. The double bottom will look more like a "W" and have more of a jaggedness to it around the bottom. It won't spend a lot of time down there. It will sell off, rally up, sell off again. Some of the better ones have a sort of shakeout move, where the second low will go below the first low but will only spend a couple days down there and shoot right back up. And then on the double bottom, instead of waiting for the breakout of the handle to buy, you can use the midpoint of the "W" as your buy point. But more often than not, I do see double bottoms form a handle. They will come through the midpoint of the "W" and back to the old high and you'll still get a little, one-week pivot area after a handle forms. And if you use your imagination, it almost looks like a cup-with-handle.

So you're really a pattern player as opposed to an indicator player?

Right. I don't like to refer to it as technical analysis. It's really just chart analysis—analyzing supply and demand pressures.

What do you look at on a chart, then? Obviously the price bars and the volume bars . . . but what else do you want to see there?

Moving averages are important. First of all, I always want to see a prior up trend before a pattern forms. This will tell you that the stock is already being accumulated. There is interest in the stock and, let's face it, a stock is only going to make a big move if we can get the institutional community to jump on board. But in addition to price-and-volume action, a stock's got to be above its 200-day moving average. The breakout point's got to be above the stock's 50-day moving average and, in most all cases, above its 21-day moving average. What will happen is that, as a stock builds its base and moves back to its old high—which is often its breakout point—it will automatically be above all of these moving averages. In the base, I like to see the 50-day moving average or, even more important, the 21-day moving average, turning up before the stock starts breaking

Double Bottom Base: America Online (AOL), Daily

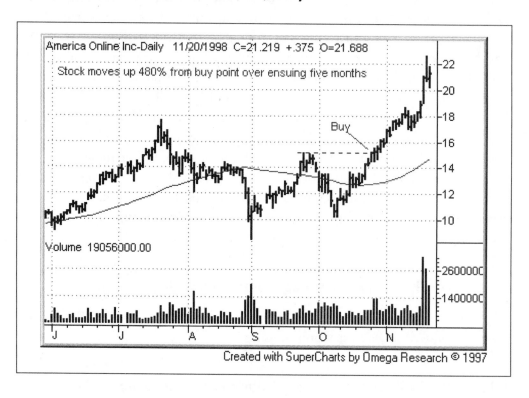

through a pivot area . . . before it's really buyable. If the moving averages haven't turned up at that point, that's a good tip-off that the base isn't quite complete.

Sometimes it can get a little tricky when you're looking at a handle. For instance, it might appear to be a handle, but then the stock tries to break out, the breakout fails, the stock immediately falls back, and it then forms a second handle. In hindsight, this ends up being the "real handle." So I usually see moving averages as a helpful tip-off as to whether the stock is really ready to take off at that point.

Is there anything else that you'd like to see on a chart besides moving averages, price, and volume?

No, that's it. Am I missing something? Were you leading me to something?

What about the relative strength line?

I guess I should be looking at a chart as I'm talking about this (*chuckles*). Yes, the relative strength line is definitely important. This is an indicator that measures how a stock has performed versus an index, such as the S&P 500. It's plotted on the chart as a line. An upward-sloping line corresponds with a stock that has out-performed the index, i.e. the market, and a downward-sloping line relates to an underperforming stock. As the stock breaks out, I want to see the RS line either confirm or lead the stock into new high ground. It doesn't always have to lead the stock to a new high; in fact, most times it will not. If it does, it's an added plus. At the least, I want to see that RS line up near its old high. Once I've taken a position in it, and I look at the chart that night after it breaks out successfully, I want to see that it's confirming the move into new highs.

As far as volume goes, what are you looking for in a buy candidate?

If you have a cup-shaped base or double bottom base, you want to see volume dry up for several days around the lows of the formation. But as the right side of that cup is being formed, you want to see volume increase. Then, as the base's handle forms, you want to see volume dry up again. When it breaks out, you want to see volume on the breakout day increase by at least 40 percent above its recent average. In fact, if you look at all big-winning stocks, the weekly volume should have increased over the prior week. The weekly volume is another thing I watch at the end of each week. If it's lower than for the prior week, it may not be the strongest situation. Almost all of these big-winning stocks have bigger volume on the breakout week. But of course you have to wait until the end of the week to determine that. That helps me to determine at the end of the week if this thing has a chance of really succeeding or whether it might fail. That alone, however, would not necessarily get me to sell it.

One other thing: I also look at a stock's relative strength rank. If a stock has a relative strength rank below the 80 percentile, I won't even consider it regardless of the pattern. There is one exception: if it was a new issue within, let's say, the last six months. The RS rank would be skewed by that because it's a 12-month measure of price performance. Most of the weight is put on the last three months, yet it still has a 12-month weighting. Most of the stocks I buy have a relative strength of 90 or above. So that's another good way of narrowing down your selection process. A lower RS rank tells me that the stock hasn't led the market long enough to increase my probabilities of jumping on a stock that will continue to lead. If the RS rank is higher, it suggests that a stock has been leading the majority of stocks in the market. That just increases the odds that it will continue to do so in the future.

Speaking of selling, what are your general parameters for telling you when to get out of a stock?

Interestingly, I have more sell rules than buy rules. When I first started out, I developed a checklist of sell rules. Each night I would go through and determine if any of the sell rules were triggered. If they weren't, then I stuck with the stock. Most of them incorporate the action between the stock's price movement and the volume because a lot of what I'm looking for here is the supply/demand equation. So I use this checklist, essentially making a stock jump through all of these hoops at the end of the day. And if it could do that, then I thought I had a good situation on my hands. But as soon as one of the sell rules would be triggered, I wouldn't necessarily sell it; I'd wait for further confirmation. If a combination of sell rules was triggered, then I would know that this was a stock to get out of.

Could you share a few of those sell rules with us?

Yeah. One of the rules has to do with distribution. For example, let's say you have a stock that's about 70 percent extended from its most recent base breakout, and the volume had been good up to that point. All of a sudden you'll see extremely heavy volume on one day, perhaps even the heaviest volume day since the advance began. After being up significantly during the day, the stock will either close up slightly, stall out and close unchanged, or actually reverse and close down, but on heavy volume. That churning action and distribution is what you normally see as the stock is running out of steam at that point. However, that doesn't always have to mark the exact top of the run.

Let's say the stock goes up 100 percent. As long as I capture three-quarters of that move, my work is done. And that's what these sell rules are designed to do: to keep you in the majority of the advance since no one is going to get out at the exact top. In fact, it's a lot easier to get out on the way up when there's still some buyers interested in the stock. As it is, they're waiting for the thing to break down. In a situation in which I don't get some of these signals on the way up—like a distribution signal—I also have rules that tell me to get out if the thing starts to break down. Sometimes I won't always get those rules on the way up, so I end up having to sell on the way down. One of these would be if a stock breaks down, for example, on a 300 percent increase in volume over average daily volume. Another would be if a stock breaks a 50-day moving average on a 200 percent increase in volume. Things like that would get me out of the stock. Without any questions, I would just bail.

Any other basic pointers?

The main thing in deciding whether to hold a stock or sell it is the price-and-volume action. This is my first line of defense. Ideally, what you want to be able to do is take the volume histogram at the bottom of the chart and shove it up underneath the price chart. It should fit like a puzzle. Up days should occur on up volume, pullback days should occur on declining volume. If you can see that trend persist, ignore everything else at that point. That is the ideal situation, and is telling you the stock is still being accumulated. Although it's not always there, occasionally I do get a stock in which I stay for the whole move based solely on following that analysis. Eventually, the stock goes into some kind of climactic advance. Let's say it takes two months for a stock to go up 70 percent. Then all of a sudden it goes straight up and the balance of the move is another 25 or 30 percent in three days. That would be climactic. And sometimes right at the final end of the move it will gap up in price. It will close higher, but there will be a nice gap there on the last up bar. And you want to sell right into that.

In another situation, a stock has favorable price-and-volume action. You don't get any distribution at the top and you don't get low volume at the top. In fact that day, that gap day, may even occur on one of the biggest volume days since the advance began. That's where big volume would be a negative, because that would be a sign of climactic action. Now, with that said, it would only be a short-term negative because sometimes there's still very good volume up at that level. The stock may still build another base, and longer-term it may still be okay. But I don't want to sit through the correction. I want to take my profit and wait for the base to rebuild and get back on if it's going to go again.

So you don't often sit through a correction in a stock, hoping to play the thing out for a bigger gain?

Not if I want to get paid on a regular basis. Once it looks like the move is over, I personally do not like to sit and try to hold out for anything bigger. I'll get off board. I know that if the thing is going to go again, it's got to build a whole new base—so I can get a chance to take a breather, step back, and repurchase the position. There's no reason why I need to hold onto the whole thing hoping that the thing actually hangs in there. I'm just not that good. I'd rather get off board and let the market tell me where to get refocused for the next advance. I do this by watching which stocks hold up during a corrective period.

As an example, a stock has a nice run-up of 50 percent or so coming out of a base, and you get on board. Would you be tempted to sell the stock if it drops 20 percent off its peak when it eventually corrects?

I'd usually be out, yes. If other leaders are breaking down, you can start feeling that something is amiss. At that point, you're also likely to see signs of distribution in the big averages begin to develop. This is characterized by a down day in price on increased volume from the day before. That's a sign that the market is running out of steam. So I will start selling when the thing looks like it's coming off a little too much. Another rule, which I don't see often, involves a stock peak-ing after an extended advance. A stock will experience its largest down day since the advance began. That might be on big volume or light volume.

So most of the time you're going to be out before the stock drops 20 percent off its peak?

Sometimes I follow these rules and I'm out a little earlier. That's fine with me. I mean I can drive myself to the nuthouse trying to sell every stock at the top tick, which is impossible.

You know the saying: The only people that buy the bottom tick and sell the top tick are liars.

One thing that I do after a stock breaks out is to hold through short-term corrective periods. After a stock breaks out, you have to be willing to sit through the stock's first pullback and that can be a little painful. That's because, if you think about it, initially you're up maybe 20 to 30 percent. And on that first pullback, maybe you've given back half of that as the stock corrects. You worked so hard, you did all your work, the thing breaks out, runs up, and there's this nice gain. Without having a set of rules, your initial thought may be, "Ah, I'm going to nail this down. I'm going to take it." But ultimately that might be the biggest winner in your portfolio. So selling at that point may be selling it too soon. The stock's up that much and then it retraces 50 percent of the breakout move. Now you're only up 12 percent on the stock, let's say. You've got to be willing to hold through that. I'll sit through that as the stock tries to regenerate for another thrust higher. But once it's made a tremendous move of 60 to 100 percent or more, if it's giving me some of these signals, I'm not going to stick around.

As far as money management goes, what percentage of your portfolio will you allocate to one position?

Six percent.

Will you start off with a 6 percent position or do you like to build into that?

I like to build into it. I prefer to put that 6 percent position on by the time the stock's broken out. I've already followed that stock up and I may have looked at it for three weeks as the base is being built. I think it's important to see how a stock trades before I even buy it. I mean that's not always possible, but each stock has its own little character. I like to watch the bid-ask spread and see how liquid it is and see how it's trading. So I watch all this stuff as the base is being completed. For example, let's say it's a stock in a cup-with-handle formation. I know where I'm at in the market, the market's acting fine, the stock is a high RS stock, and it's in one of the leading groups. I'll look to see if the stock pulls back to form the handle. If it does, and if volume is light as it starts to turn up on the right side of the handle, I'll start buying it right there to build my position even before it breaks out. I may do that in thirds. By the time it breaks out, if I had to buy a 25,000 share position, the last third is being put on in the breakout as opposed to trying to buy 25,000 shares on the breakout, which is not an easy task.

This brings me to another point. One of the things I am also looking at in buy candidates is which industry group the stock is in. The stock's got to be a leading member of one of the leading groups, in most cases. I'm looking for those companies with superior product lines that are leading their particular group, a group which at that point in time happens to be where institutional investor interest is. Interestingly, just by looking at the charts, you automatically end up in the right groups. They will take you to the right groups.

Do you use leverage much?

I do not.

Why?

I've spent many years building my money management business. I've been entrusted with the money from many people and I don't want to take the risk of using leverage even at times when I feel like I should really be slamming it. One of my theories was that if I used leverage and I doubled the return that I had, it would be very difficult to build a money management business. It would be hard for me to decipher between a client who is a legitimate client versus someone who is looking for a hot money manager. If you end up getting a client who is looking for a hot money manager, as soon as you have a rough patch in the market they're gone. They leave. And that whole process is very disruptive to running money. So it's much easier to manage money and build the size of the fund more with the turtle approach than with the hare approach. Everyone is happier and it keeps the gains more consistent and the volatility down.

Do you pyramid up into your winners? In other words, do you add on to a winner as the stock moves up?

No. It's a tricky thing to do. Again, it's more prudent when you're running money for other people to have your risk spread out somewhat. So I prefer to keep my positions even all the way up. In some cases I will double up on a stock, but I won't get it to a point where I have all the money pyramided into a narrow list of names. Of course that will cut down on the returns, but it's just easier to deal with. Keeping the volatility down makes my job a lot easier when I'm managing money for other people.

What sentiment indicators do you look at?

I look at the CBOE put/call ratio, usually just the total ratio. That can be a tricky thing, but it essentially ends up being better than a lot of sentiment gauges out there because a lot of them measure attitude as opposed to what people are really doing with their money. The drawback to the put/call numbers is that, over time, the levels of optimism and pessimism—the levels at which you see turning points in the markets—change. And what was once considered a level of extreme optimism six years ago isn't anymore.

Any other sentiment indicators besides the put/call ratio?

No. In fact as time has gone on, I've used that less and less and tried to focus on reading the market. I've gotten better over time. It's just that the sentiment numbers look like a real easy thing to use. As human beings, we migrate to the easiest thing. The hardest thing is to figure out how to read the market, how to look for signs of accumulation and distribution. With a lot of practice I was able to do it. It took years to get comfortable with that way of looking at the market. It happened because I had a passion for what I was doing and I wanted to figure out the best way to make money in the market with the least amount of risk. I gathered this was a way to do it, just by reading the market. So now I don't look at those numbers as much as I used to because they can be misleading. One of the ways they can be misleading is that sometimes if a trend persists, attitudes or action in the market can persist for that entire period of time.

What do you mean by that?

For example, if an up trend has persisted for months, you may see the put/call ratio stay at a very high level of optimism for, say, the last six, seven weeks of the move. Then you get to a point where the crowd is right . . . I mean there are spots where the crowd is right for a time, so there is just no reason to get hung up on it. Eventually the market will peak and the best way to determine exactly when it's going to happen is by looking for signs in the market itself.

So it really sounds like you place much more emphasis on what the market is doing, as opposed to other indicators, whether they be sentiment indicators or—

—I would say at this point I put all my emphasis on that. Some of the other things are great peripherally and they kind of give me an early warning. For example, if I saw a lot of optimism in the market, I would be in more of a heightened awareness state looking for distribution signs in the market itself.

Yet ultimately you are going to ignore what the sentiment indicators say if the general market is doing something different.

Yes . . . hands down.

The one topic we have not covered has been general market direction. Can you tell us exactly what you look at?

Every major bottom that has led to either an intermediate-term advance or a new bull market has been accompanied by good price follow-through in the indices within days of a low. That's referred to as an O'Neil follow-through day and that's when one or more major indices advances by at least 1 percent on increased volume from the prior day. The follow-through day should occur within four to 10 days of the exact closing low. The most potent signals usually occur between the fourth and seventh day off the lowest close. Anything outside of that has a higher failure rate. You can get a follow-through day 13, 14, or 15 days after the exact closing low of a down trend, but these are more failure-prone. The follow-through day indicates that the sellers are out of the way. Selling pressure is gone. When an index advances by more than 1 percent on increased volume that soon after a closing low, it indicates that all of that selling pressure has been alleviated—fresh buyers are going to carry the market higher.

So once I get that signal, I'll immediately start buying stocks that are ready to break out. Sometimes that signal will be accompanied by no stocks ready to break out, some stocks ready to break out, or maybe a lot of stocks ready to break out. Basically, once you get that signal, you want to let the market bring you back in from the cash position that you should have built up during the prior down trend. There's no reason to get 100 percent invested on that follow-through day. Let the stocks confirm it for you. On occasion, one of these signals will actually fail. The beauty of it is that the market will fail within a few days of the failed signal in most cases. So you'll never be in this position where you've gotten over-invested based on this one-day signal.

How likely is it that one of these follow-through day signals will fail?

According to O'Neil, they confirm an intermediate-term bottom about 80 percent of the time.

And what do you look at as an indication of a top?

On the top side, you're looking for distribution in one or more of the big averages, which is characterized by an unchanged or down close on increased volume from the day before. The main selling will occur on the way up or right around the area which ultimately ends up being the peak. And that's sometimes why you initially see light volume on the way down from the peak. If you're waiting for the market to be down 15 percent before you sell, it's just way too late. You'll get anywhere from three to five of these distribution days within a two- to three-week period after the market's already topped. You'll also see some leaders that have made extensive moves start to break down on hard volume, and recent breakouts begin to fail. If all that's clustered together in a very short period of time, that's your signal to be totally out of the market.

We discussed the general market at a bottom and the general market at a top, right? Did we discuss leading stocks at a top?

At an important, intermediate-term top in the market, you'll not only get distribution signals in the indices themselves, but the leaders will start to break down simultaneously . . . recent breakouts will fail.

Your enthusiasm for what you do is quite rabid.

Well, it's very gratifying to figure out a strategy and see it through to fruition. I've just had to pour my whole life into building my money management business over the last 10 years. Because I've done that, I've sacrificed a lot of other things. I've given up other opportunities. I don't golf because I haven't had time to really get into it. So when you stop, and you have some spare time, you'd better have some other hobbies that you can be involved with, whether it be doing yard work, or gardening, or whatever. Because otherwise you'll have this temptation to always be involved in something and you really don't have to. It's just a whole balancing act.

As a money manager, it's very gratifying to have people investigate what I do and go through this whole due diligence process on their own. I have clients from all over the country. Then they finally make this decision to put their faith and trust in me and send me money. To be able to come through for them, to make them money consistently and let them know through this that they made the right decision . . . it's just so gratifying for me. To actually have someone make this big decision to send me their money and to be able to actually come through for them is very meaningful for me.

It's just amazing to me to look back over the last 12 years, see where I've come from, and see the success I've actually developed in the business that I've built. I turned a goose egg into a thriving, little business. There's no magic pill. You look at people who are successful in life and you think, boy, it would be great to be that successful. Gee, I wonder what that person's motivation was? Well, the motivation for a lot of successful people, in almost all cases, is not money. It's that they had a passion for what they were doing and the money was just a by-product of that success.

What would you recommend to aspiring traders?

The only thing I can recommend to aspiring traders is simply this: Understand that there is no magic pill, other than hard work and perseverance. As much of a cliché as that may sound, it's simply the truth. One of the most important things in trading the markets is finding that critical balance between a good level of confidence in your trading and a real sense of perpetual humility.

Thanks very much, Greg.

DAVID KUANG

THE COMEBACK KID

By Kevin N. Marder

It takes most traders at least several years to become successful—let alone become a top trader.

Not so with David Kuang.

Despite a calamitous start that included a $20,000 loss in his first nine days as well as his boss's comment that he was "redefining the definition of bad luck," Kuang skyrocketed up the learning curve.

In only his second full year of daytrading, Kuang earned $1.8 million. In each of the next two years, he duplicated this seven-figure feat despite trading for only a fraction of each year.

To put Kuang's success into perspective, for the 6 1/2-month period ended July 15, 2000, golf great Tiger Woods had earned $4.9 million, or more than double the amount of his closest competitor on the PGA tour. By comparison, Kuang had pocketed $6.5 million!

Interestingly, some daytraders would consider Kuang's strategy, which focuses on stocks experiencing extraordinary movement, to be steeped in risk. Kuang, on the other hand, believes his odds of success to be high.

Kevin N. Marder: How did you first become interested in the stock market, David?

David Kuang: When I was growing up in Europe, we used to look at a lot of newspapers. One of them was the *International Herald Tribune*, which my father used to show me every day. And then at MIT, I was able to pursue finance studies at the Sloan School. I got to do some undergraduate research in expert trading systems and technical analysis. The interest has always been there.

Did you actually start trading while you were in college?

No. I didn't have a lot of money and I was more interested in other pursuits at the time. I think it was something that I was interested in, but not something that I was throwing myself into during my college years.

What happened when you got out of college? Did you get a job in the investments field?

I had a couple of job offers. They were slightly different. One was an opportunity to trade options and the other involved securities litigation, securities litigation being when shareholders sue companies for sudden stock price drops. The securities litigation job was more of a consulting/analyst position. I thought that would be more interesting because it would allow me to go to either law school or business school. And if I was still interested in trading, I could go into trading.

So I decided to pursue securities litigation, which I did for a year and a half. Then, after working for many long hours, I decided I really wanted to trade, primarily because of the instant gratification, the meritocracy, and basically the fact that you can be your own boss. So that was how the first couple of years evolved following my graduation.

What was your major at MIT?

Originally, I went in as a chemical engineering major. After not doing so well at engineering, I pursued finance. My undergraduate degree is a management degree, but I particularly focused on finance courses . . . a lot of stats, a lot of probability, a lot of math.

After your 18-month stint at the securities litigation job, where was your next stop?

I really wanted to leave that job quite badly. So I was willing to take almost any job possible in New York City. I had a friend at Smith Barney who mentioned a company called Datek. Back then, they weren't a brokerage. They were purely a daytrading operation. I didn't know anything about them.

They waived the first interview since I had flown myself out for the meeting, which showed them I was serious and interested in the position. And then the so-called second interview consisted of one 15-minute meeting. The head of the firm liked my watch and actually tried to buy it from me before he offered me the job. So that was pretty simple.

And what was that job all about?

Daytrading . . . purely SOES (the Nasdaq's Small Order Execution System). You had to take the Series 7, 63, and 24 exams and you started trading as a registered representative.

Were you trading the firm's proprietary account?

Yes. This was back in December 1996.

Back in the days when they used to refer to these types of trading rooms as SOES rooms.

Yeah. SOES rooms . . . SOES bandits.

Right.

Within three days they sat you down, gave you a computer and a million-dollar account, and you started trading.

Did you have to put up any money of your own to get started?

No.

With just a couple of days to work with, the training they gave you must have been pretty minimal.

It was.

Back in 1996, because it was the seminal days of what I call the New Era of Daytrading, the market was a lot less efficient. You could really benefit from looking at Level II changes. Is that the way your initial strategy came about, or was there something else you started focusing on back then?

I think, back then, liquidity was a little worse because only market makers could participate. As a result, momentum was a little bit easier. Back then, we were able to actually do SOES momentum very clearly. I think now, with the introduction of ECNs, plus a lot more liquidity, plus a lot more participants in the market-place, momentum still exists. However, there's a lot of noise. Small buyers and small sellers will come in and momentarily cloud the market on the Level II.

So I think you're right, Kevin, back then Level II was a lot easier to interpret. However, as for how you use that, it's changed now. People are making more money now than three or four years ago. That's because there's more liquidity now. We're able to take larger size with less risk.

When you refer to SOES momentum, what are you referring to?

Three or four years ago, the primary strategy people used to make money—and they still do today—was to find a stock moving upward with strong bids. We would buy stock at the offer on SOES. As the offers were lifting, we would sell our stock at the offer price back to the market makers on SelectNet.

You were at Datek for a couple of years?

I was an employee, a registered rep, for nine months, after which I had made enough money where I was given the option to become a customer . . . a customer basically being someone who traded their own account through Datek's technology and paid Datek commissions.

So you began doing that, then?

Right.

Did you have success in the beginning?

Ah! *(Laughs)*. I have some great stories. My trainer, my mentor whom they assigned me to, was not so good, not very conservative. My first day I wrote 87,000 shares and within my first nine days I had lost $20,000. It was a really tough time. The head of the firm once came over and said "David, you are redefining the definition of bad luck." I remember one time I came in on a Tuesday and I had 1,000 shares of a stock down 12 points on bad earnings.

Wow.

Then the very next day I went home with 2,000 shares of an airline company that was very strong. And their plane crashed that night.

Sheeez.

So, you know, things were really rough. It took me about three months to really get on my feet and begin to consistently make money every day. After six months, I had broken even. After nine months, I had made a lot of money.

So in the beginning, they had said it was okay to take home positions overnight?

Back then there used to be a lot of position-taking overnight. I think one of the reasons was because of the lack of liquidity.

And from there, you traded your own Datek account through that same trading room?

Yes. I was a customer at Datek for about six months. And then I left Datek and came to what is now known as Tradescape, or Momentum Securities. Momentum Securities is the brokerage arm of Tradescape.

I remember that in those seminal days back in 1996, you had to trade from a SOES trading room, since you couldn't trade from home and get instant executions. Nowadays, in 2000, you can trade from home just about as easily as at one of the trading rooms. Obviously you see some sort of advantage in trading among other traders versus doing it at home alone.

Actually I've done both. I was out in L.A. for a year, trading from home. The real difference is the ability to take large size with a comfort level. Regardless of your connection, any investor could take a couple hundred shares or a thousand shares of a position and not have to worry about too much slippage or a slow-speed connection that's really going to cost them a lot of money. In March and April 2000, we were taking 30,000-, 40,000-, 50,000-share positions in stocks . . . $5 million to $10 million worth of stock intraday.

Basically, the issue came down to making sure we have the best execution with the best tech support. Since we trade a half million shares a day, even if it's 10 milliseconds faster, that adds up to a couple thousand dollars a day if we're not careful. So the reason why I came back after taking a year off was to pick up my trading again and really make sure I had the best technology. It's really a comfort level issue. I think you can trade from home with a high degree of success. It's just that if you want to take it to the next level of success, it's important, for me at least, to have a comfort level with tech support and technology.

What's the typical size of your order?

The minimum is 1,000 shares . . . sometimes 500 shares if you're just trying to get a feel for a stock. And then, as your position size builds, the minimum size obviously increases. So you might have 1,000-share orders going in up to maybe a 10,000-share position, at which point you might increase it by 2,000 or 3,000. It really depends on your stock and the amount of liquidity and the situation.

I take it that you do add on to your winners as they rise.

Actually, I almost never add on to my winners, only in certain situations. But I do not believe in rot-and-hold. I'll say that right now. I believe in being patient and waiting for very good opportunities. Basically, I could spend 90 percent of the day just watching the market. But within the other 10 percent of the day, there's usually a couple of really good opportunities where you could buy a large amount of stock within a short price range within a short amount of time at a very good price.

And that's what we use the technology for. We'll be patient and wait. We won't just average down into a position. We'll specifically try and identify a turning point or a buying opportunity which maybe will last 20 seconds. We'll buy as much stock as possible, and as the stock goes up we will then kick out shares. That's how I trade.

So you're operating with another one or two traders as a team, then?

Yeah, I have a trading desk. I primarily work with one other trader.

Once you identify the opportunity, are the two of you just trying to buy as much in 1,000-share lots as you can?

He has a totally different style of trading and that's why I work with him. He gives me a different point of view. I usually try and buy as much as I can because I usually have enough capital where I can buy all the stock that's out there. At Tradescape, or at this firm at least, most of the good traders do not sit together. Very bad results can occur from having very big traders sit next to each other.

Let's get back to the speed of your connection for a second. One reason that you like being over at Tradescape is that you've got the tech support there. So when something goes wrong, you can just raise your hand and someone will come right over to your workstation. The other thing is that the connections are just a teeny bit faster.

Typically, if you trade from home, unless you have a direct connection like with a T-1 line, a lot of places go through the Internet. And with the Internet, you lose maybe 20 or 40 milliseconds on the data transfer.

In terms of your overall strategy, what are your buy criteria?

It's pretty simple, actually. I look for inefficient situations, places where stocks are overbought or oversold based on order imbalances or panic or sentiment or market conditions. I do not try and play news. That's the biggest criterion. I don't think that I'm the smartest person in the world and I'm not going to compete with these institutions that are selling stocks on earnings or buying stocks on earnings. I'm looking purely for situations where maybe a retail order has come in and is driving a stock down.

Herzog is an example of a market maker who does a lot of retail. If Herzog is selling, selling, selling, driving a stock down in the morning because he has a morning order to sell, and I can identify on Level II that he's close to finishing his selling, I will begin to accumulate stock. The odds are very high that as soon as Herzog is done with that retail order, the stock's going to go back up.

Do you use any sort of overbought/oversold oscillator to help you in that, or is the information all gleaned from Level II?

Mostly from Level II. I look at tick charts and I try to identify rapid price movement. That's my key criterion. I need to see rapid price movement. Basically, this is a price move that, if it were to continue for a couple of hours, the stock would go to zero. That's an example of an unsustainable price move.

Common logic would say that if you see a stock drop that fast and the move was to continue, in a couple of hours it would be at zero. It's not sustainable. So there has to be something: either there's news, it's going to stop and turn, it's going to continue going down . . . something's going to happen. That's what I think special daytraders look for . . . situations where they know something is going to happen. Once you identify that, there's profit potential.

Does that sort of setup occur with nearly 100 percent of your trades, or do you have other types of setups that you're trying to find as well?

No, there's a lot of other types of setups. You can play the multi-day play, look for momentum in the morning, shorts in the morning. There's a wide variety. But I would say 90 percent of the high-profit trades that I do are those situations . . . looking for overbought or oversold situations.

Do you use five-minute bar charts to determine that sort of extraordinary movement?

We currently have one-minute charts. But if you can get hold of tick charts, those are great.

Which do you prefer, tick charts or one-minute charts?

I really like the tick. That's the great thing about being in the office—we can access tick charts with a minimal amount of upload delay.

In that particular setup, then, it's a matter of you waiting until there's some type of price reversal occurring. So if something's speeding higher and it looks like you've identified some sort of unsustainable price movement, you're not going to buy as the thing continues. You're going to take a short position when you see some sort of opposite movement, right?

Correct. On the way up, if it looks very, very strong, I might pick up a couple thousand shares. But I will not take any sort of significant size. I'm still *reeeally* looking for that top . . . I'm looking for signs where, right before the top, I can really load up on a short position.

Sometimes if it looks really dangerous and it looks like the stock could continue a lot higher, I'll step back and just wait for a secondary top. An example would be if it's run up 20 points, comes off 3 points really fast, tries to make a new high, fails to make that new high . . . I'll hit all the high bids.

Everyone seems to have a different take on this next point. Some traders, in a reversal situation, don't want to see one bar reverse. They want to see one bar reverse and then they want to see the following bar take out the low of the previous bar. Do you like to see that sort of confirmation or is it not that important?

It sounds so complicated. I've never thought of it that way at all. I purely think of stocks in terms of price levels.

What are your general thoughts on shorting?

I have two things to say about shorting. First, I think shorting is very dangerous. You can make a lot of money very fast. But you can also lose a lot of money, because of the uptick rule, the short-sale rule. Invariably, you'll find yourself out of the money before you're in the money when you're shorting a stock. I don't recommend that to people who are interested in getting into daytrading as a primary strategy. I've gone through a lot of pain shorting and it's not fun.

Secondly, I think it's very important to think of stocks in terms of their price levels. If you know there are sellers at a certain price and buyers at a certain price and if you can identify those support and resistance levels, you can often get really good price execution. If you're waiting for five-minute bars to overlap and cross and close gaps, you're giving up a lot of slippage. You might be waiting for an extra half-point for the stock to cross some bar when you know there are a lot of sellers and you can get that extra half-point.

And that's what looking at Level II gives you.

Exactly.

Do you look at the different ECN books, like the Island book, to see where the other bids and asks are beyond the Level II?

Correct. Looking at the ECNs is extremely important. They give you a true measure of the bids and offers. Market makers don't always honor their quotes because they're allowed a certain time delay to update their quotes. But the real bids and offers are often established by the ECNs. So it's important to utilize the Level II to identify the ECNs and see where the true limit orders are bidding and offering stock.

As far as an unsustainable price movement goes, is this something that lasts a minute or so?

It's over different time frames. It could be over a minute, it could be over 30 minutes, or it could be over a day. I'll give three different examples. First, on July 12, 2000, Ciena (CIEN) went from 170 to 156 1/2 in about five minutes. There was a rumor about accounting.

Another one is Research Frontiers (REFR), when the market was collapsing in April 2000. I bought 10,000 shares at 10 that morning. In five days, the stock goes from 30 to 10. Is it going to go to negative 10 in another five days? No. Absolutely not. There is going to be a reversal there somewhere. That's a classic example. You don't even have to be a daytrader. You could be a swing trader. You could be an intraweek trader. You could have made a lot of money on that one.

Again, the thing that tells you exactly when to get in is Nasdaq Level II. You're seeing the orders stack up, and you say "gee, it looks like things are going to reverse here."

Yes. There's one other piece of technology we have here which helps a lot. It's scanning technology. Scanning technology is really important. It frees up our time by scanning the market for profit opportunities that we're interested in, so

Unsustainable Price Movement: Ciena (CIEN), 5-minute

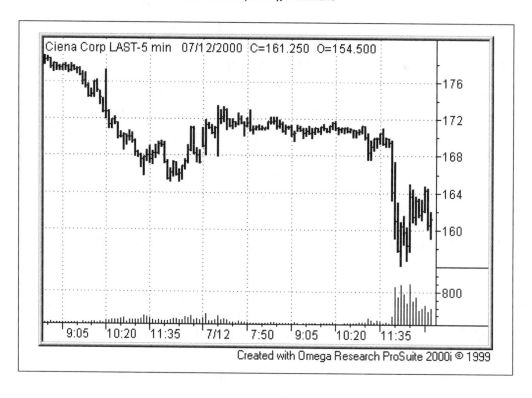

that we don't burn out. We can relax in the morning. It shows us which stocks are moving and then we can trade those stocks. And then if nothing's moving during the day, we can relax and rest and do our research. I think to successfully daytrade, it's important to use some sort of scanning technology.

Out of all the trades you make, what percent would be on the short side?

A year ago, it was 90 percent. Now, it's maybe 10 percent.

Is this because you've determined that the odds are better on the long side?

Unsustainable Price Movement: Research Frontiers (REFR), Daily

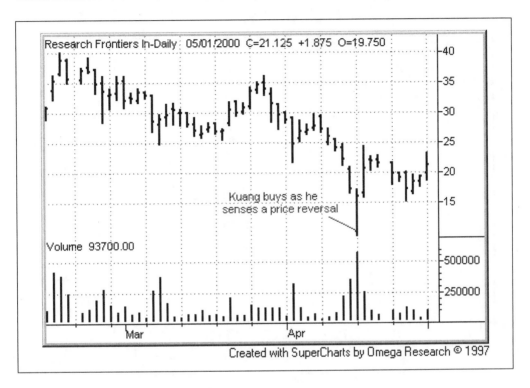

Yes.

Approximately how many trades do you make a day on average?

Right now it's about 100 roundtrips a day.

I'm a little surprised since you'd given me the impression that you were sort of kicking back waiting for that primo setup to happen.

I'll give you an example of a primo trade where you just burn tickets, but you make a lot of money. New Era of Networks (NEON) on July 13, 2000 from

Unsustainable Price Movement: New Era Of Networks (NEON), 5-minute

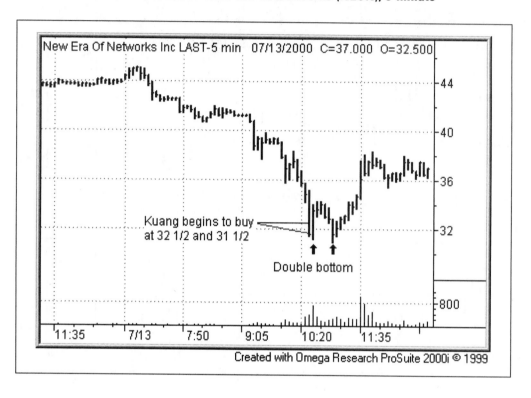

7:00 a.m. EST began collapsing from 45. I began buying at 32 1/2 down to 31 1/2. In that situation, I was buying 20,000 shares, 30,000 shares . . . looking for that double bottom, which it established. That was one situation where I did begin to buy on the way up, because I wanted it to establish that secondary bottom.

Did you buy as it was coming down the first time or on the retest?

It bottomed on the first bottom, where I sold it on that first little blip up because I knew it was probably going to retest its low. When it went down again, I cleaned out my position just to be careful. And then at the turn, I took out all the offers . . . took out everything. So that's a situation where we did a lot of trades, a lot of volume, but in one stock . . . in one situation.

Was there anything specific that told you to get in on that first leg down?

Unsustainable price movement.

Was there something that was keying you, like on Level II, that this was an opportunity?

Yes. Yes. You can identify the buyers and sellers. You can begin to tell when bids are coming in.

The momentum is changing.

Yeah, you can tell. I also look for support across several days. If you go to a daily chart of the stock, 32 or 31 1/2 is a definite support level. In hindsight, it's pretty obvious. I try to keep my daytrading as simple as possible.

Do you create a hit list every night for the next day of stocks ready to break out?

I don't do research. I used to really believe in doing research. The problem with research is that it gives preconceived notions going into the stock market, which changes minute by minute and day by day. What invariably happens when you focus on putting your stock list together and your news list together and your hit list together is that you end up missing out on opportunities that aren't on your list. You might want to look at these five stocks today, but if these five stocks don't move, or even if they do move, you're giving up an opportunity of a better return on a better situation in a better stock.

I see so many people create hit lists. And they do well. However, the amount of time and energy that they spend on it [isn't worth it] and it pigeon-holes their focus for the new day. So I really don't do that. I tell all my traders "don't read newspapers, go home, get some rest, think about your trades, think about how you can trade better, how you can execute better, don't try and predict which way the stock's going to go."

Some traders will only take a trade if it has a minimum reward/risk ratio. Do you have a ballpark ratio you work with? I know some players look for a 2 1/2-to-1 ratio, or a 3-to-1 ratio.

Yes. I use a 4-to-1 ratio.

Do you get into a trade and know where your exit point is instinctively? Do you do it on a point system, whereby you never risk more than a point?

I think in terms of points. When you think in points, it gives you a little bit more leeway to be wrong.

Is it always 1 point, for example?

It depends on the stock. If it's a highly liquid stock, I'll give it a quarter-point, maybe an eighth. If it's a stock that's going down 10 points, I'll give it 2 points, 3 points. But the whole ratio should be roughly around 4 to 1. I like a 4-to-1 ratio.

When you're looking at a setup, how do you figure out what to base your reward expectation on?

By looking at the bids and the offers. Depending on the price at which I bought stock, I look to see how many bids I would have to hit in order to get out. On the upside, I look at the number of offers that have to lift before I can sell my stock at a profit. Depending on that price range, I can determine the appropriate reward-to-risk ratio. If I feel that the price at which I would like to sell my stock is within the potential rebound price range of the stock, then I would consider the reward-to-risk ratio legitimate.

I'm assuming that you don't take positions home overnight.

Not really.

Do you like this time frame over others because of the instant gratification? Or is there something else you enjoy about doing so many trades in such a slim time frame?

I think the real happiness factor stems from knowing that my odds of success are so high . . . that our edge in our profession is so high relative to other time frames of investing.

So you think it's easier to make money in the daytrading time frame than the swing time frame or intermediate time frame? Or maybe "easy" isn't the word. How about "consistent?"

I think consistent is the word.

What are your selling techniques? For example, on a pullback after a run-up.

That's a really good question. I try to identify a resistance level . . . a price level where I feel people are definitely going to be selling. Let's say a stock goes from 70 to 63 and I know there are a lot of sellers at 68. First, I'll give myself one price haircut at 67, which is where I'm assuming all the other daytraders are going to sell. I'll then give it one more haircut to a lower price, which is where I sell. I try to identify where retail is going to sell or daytraders are going to sell. And I want to be right in front of that. I'll also use Level II to identify how high these guys are willing to pay within a stock rebound.

When you say "where the daytraders are," what are you referring to?

Looking at the Island ECN. That's a classic example. It's primarily used by a lot of daytraders.

And as far as the retail crowd, would that be your bigger market makers, like Merrill and people like that?

Also sometimes Spear, Leeds will go through REDIBook, the ECN. You try to identify which ECNs are coming to the offer.

What are you paying in commissions?

Right now I'm paying approximately $10 per thousand shares.

That's a penny a share. Is that critical to your success, or merely important to your success?

I think the average daytrader worries way too much about the commission rate, about getting the best deal. If you have a good system and you're happy and you're making money and you're not writing 50,000 shares or 20,000 shares or even 10,000 shares a day, stick with the system . . .stick with the technology that enables you to make money.

The commission should always be secondary. Now with that said, if you're a daytrader whose trading is going to the next level where you're doing 100 trades a day, 100,000 shares a day, commissions add up. It's starts adding up by an extra $1,000 a day in commissions. At that point in time, I would recommend people begin looking for comparable technology at a cheaper commission rate. But for the average daytrader, don't fret too much about it. Learn good trading technique first and get some decent technology.

How do you determine what the axe, or dominant player, is in a stock? Is there anything that tells you this is the guy that's controlling this issue?

I think a lot of daytraders are taught to trade high-volume, high-liquidity stocks, like Cisco (CSCO) and Sun (SUNW) . . . or maybe even high-volume secondary stocks, such as Yahoo! (YHOO) and Akamai (AKAM). I think it's very difficult to determine the axe in these types of stocks because there's so much liquidity and so many market makers going in and out. But even in those stocks, there are certain situations where one or two market makers will obviously be making a stand. Those types of identifiable situations occur not when a stock is going up, but when it's going down.

Here's an example. A stock goes up 15 points. You'd think it would come off. People are hitting bids. Merrill Lynch is soaking up stock on the bid. That's when you identify it . . . when the stock is moving contrary to his position and he is holding the stock. In lower liquidity stocks, it's much more obvious. On a stock with a 2-point spread, you'll have Herzog's offer at 1 1/2 points below anyone else's offer. I'm not saying he's the axe, but at that moment in time, he definitely wants to sell.

As far as your performance goes, how have you done over the last three years?

In 1998, I made $1.8 million. In 1999, after I returned from some time off, I traded for four months and did $1.5 million. This year through mid-July, I'm up $6.5 million. I might add that you don't always use all of your capital to trade every single day. I only used a half-million in buying power today, for example.

Do you have any advice for newer traders that are just getting into this game? Is there anything that you think they need to know before they get started, or things to be aware of?

There are three things. First, be careful whom you learn from. Make sure you learn something which is good for you . . . a style which is good for you . . . something which you are comfortable with. Make sure you don't just follow blindly what someone says. Sit back and think about the logic behind the trading strategy . . . very, very important. If you're never comfortable or you never fully understand your trading strategy, you'll never grow as a trader.

Second, don't try and make a large amount of money right away. Learn how to make money consistently as soon as possible, every single day . . . a way which is comfortable and safe . . . very, very important . . . because that's what enables you to survive this business and then to grow on that trading strategy and expand your trading strategy.

Third, and foremost: Have fun. If you're not having fun, you're going to burn out, you're going to do something stupid, and you'll lose a lot of money. Be sure the enjoyment factor is still there for you. Identify it. It's different for everyone. It could be the thrill of finding a good opportunity. Or it could be making a lot of money. Whatever that thrill is, identify it and appreciate it. And I think that leads to success.

Also, here's something that's very important. If you're starting daytrading, make sure that you've set enough money aside so that you don't have to worry about rent and food and bills for three to six months. If you trade with that hanging over your head, it can really put a lot of strain and stress on you. You'll try too hard or you won't be patient enough and you'll lose money.

Okay.

I think everyone should try it if they have an opportunity to try it.

Thanks very much for your time, David.

ON THE CUSP

One of the wonderful things about Wall Street is that new talent is constantly surfacing above the noise. The following three gentlemen, though young in age, are just beginning to hit their stride. Two run hedge funds with solid returns; the third has made himself a millionaire from daytrading. What we found interesting is that even though they do not have the same seasoning as some of the veteran traders we interviewed, they do share the exact same disciplines and in-depth knowledge that's needed to reach the top of this game.

DAVID BAKER

THE WHIZ KID

By Kevin N. Marder

David Baker represents the new breed of daytraders that journalists love to hate. Over a three-year period of time, Baker grew a five-figure trading account into a seven-figure account by daytrading, both on the long and the short side. What makes Baker even more impressive is the fact that, in spite of his age, his knowledge of the markets and understanding of market dynamics is equal to some of the finest traders I've ever had the privilege of meeting.

The test of all great traders is how they respond to adversity. Baker showed his true mettle by snapping back from a 50 percent drawdown early in his career. To do this, he completely withdrew from trading for months, preferring to spend nearly every waking hour examining his prior trading mistakes. During this wood-shedding period, Baker totally reformulated his money management plan, including a revision of his approach to cutting losses and limiting risk.

Baker emerged from this hibernation reinvigorated and eager to do battle. Armed with a fresh approach backed up by many hours of research, he quickly rebuilt his trading account—and never looked back.

Kevin N. Marder: Dave, how did you first become interested in trading?

David Baker: Early in my college years at the University of California, Irvine, a friend introduced me to the market. After he described it to me one day, he took me down to a brokerage firm and, with his guidance, I opened an account. About two hours after leaving the brokerage office, I ran home and bought a stock based on my friend's tip. I watched that stock go up 15 percent in two days and I realized it was something I wanted to pursue. Later on, another friend took me under his wing and introduced me to options trading. We made some money and then eventually lost it. I then realized I had to do my own research. I had just quit my job and had my initial investment remaining, thanks to a few winning trades. I took some time off from trading and began reading a lot of different books on options and stocks, trying to figure out how it all worked.

So I spent the summer after my freshman year in college studying the market. When I finally picked my first stock, it did well, but it took a couple of weeks to make a meaningful move. The next stock I bought moved within 90 minutes of when I'd gotten into it. At that point, I realized that buying a stock that moved was something I wanted to do every day. I wanted to find a stock that would move a couple of dollars every day instead of having to panic each day and hold something overnight. At that point, I realized that there was a lot less stress trading that way. It's a lot easier to sleep when you don't go home with any positions, especially things that are speculative that you're not familiar with.

How did you develop your early technique?

I learned a lot of how daytrading works through some friends I'd met in a chat room on the Internet. They gave me the basics and a small course to teach me what they did. They were scalpers mostly . . . they were going after small gains. The first two daytrades that I made were stocks that probably moved from $20 to $25 in one day. So that's what I was looking for.

Were the friends that you had met in the chat room scalping for eighths and quarters?

Yeah. After a couple of months of on-and-off gains and losses, I realized that that was too risky because the risk-reward ratio was too great. I was risking too much to be picking up a quarter-point.

Were you financially supporting yourself through your daytrading at this point?

In the beginning, I was living mainly off my savings from my prior job. Not too long after I started, I began to live off my trading, since I'd had a couple of good winners right from the beginning.

You were still in college, though.

Yes. By my sophomore year, I had scheduled all of my classes so that I would only be in class after the market closed each day. That way I would have time to watch the market during trading hours. By then, I had moved out of my parents' house, was living on my own, and was totally supporting myself through my daytrading.

You mean you put yourself through the last three years of college at the University of California at Irvine, then, paying your tuition, books, rent, and all living expenses, just through your profits as a daytrader?

Yes. But after I was trading for a couple of months, I had a little trading tragedy where my account shrank by at least 50 percent, if not more.

And you consider that to be a little tragedy?

Well, at least it didn't wipe me out! (*Chuckles*). I had to take a break because at that point I had been through scalping and that was very stressful. Having a big loss when you're used to taking a lot of small gains really kills your mentality and makes it difficult to not be afraid to pull the trigger next time. At that point, I took a little break of about three months to figure out a new trading style. During this period of time, I paper-traded mostly. And then I lined up some financial backing to re-enter the trading world. I still had part of my account left.

At that point I got back in and looked for something that was better than scalping, but was still considered daytrading. I wanted to find a strategy that would give me gains of 1 to 5 points instead of just small gains. I had read all of these books about the psychology of trading and risk versus reward, and I realized I was risking too much versus what I was making. So I changed my style and paper-traded stocks and futures for a little while. All along, I had been doing some options trading on the side to generate income . . . a lot of covered calls and naked puts. Then I moved back into daytrading again.

How did you bring your account down by 50 percent? Was it one or two trades?

It was sort of a chain reaction. It all started when I placed my first market order on a hot-moving stock one day. By the time I got a confirmation that my order had been filled, the stock was already down 5 points. And I had bought a significant number of shares. At that point, I didn't know what to do and panicked and just sold it and took a big hit. Following that, I fell into that trap of trying to make back what I had lost. And so I got burned a couple more times, not for the same reason, but just because I was panicked, trying to make back what money I had lost, and not taking good trades.

As a daytrader, you're basically looking at five-minute bar charts, right?

Yes. For my intraday setups I use five-minute bars, but as my trading has matured I have shifted my focus to include more daytrades based on breakouts from daily charts. For those trades, I use a combination of daily bars as well as five-minute bars.

Do you go short as much as you go long?

This is dependent upon market positions. When the market is strongly trending upwards, I'm hesitant to take many short positions because I'm always afraid of buyers coming in on the dips. If I'm shorting a stock based on a breakdown from a daily pattern, as opposed to an intraday pattern, it's a different story. In this case, the short is based on something that has been forming over a greater period of time . . . it's been building up. When daytrading futures, I'm not hesitant to take short positions.

So what do you look for in a daytrade?

I have two patterns that I love to trade. The first is when a stock is consolidating either near the high or low of the day, which is similar to what Kevin Haggerty refers to as a Slim Jim. I look for stocks that have usually spiked in the early-morning part of the trading day and then they consolidate on lower volume. They then make a strong-volume move out of the consolidation. I look for consolidations that have gone on for at least 40 minutes in a range that's anywhere from 1/2 point to 2 points, depending on the price of the stock. I look for those to break out in the same direction as the original trend. So if they're consolidating near their high, I'm looking for them to break out to the upside. Before I enter, I will usually wait for a follow-through because I've been caught by too many false breakouts.

When you say "follow-through," what do you mean?

I either look for the opening of another five-minute bar to eclipse the high of the previous bar—

—the previous bar being the breakout bar.

Yes, the breakout bar.

So that's the first pattern that you like to trade. What's the second?

Consolidation Breakdown: Terayon Communication Systems, Inc. (TERN), 5-minute

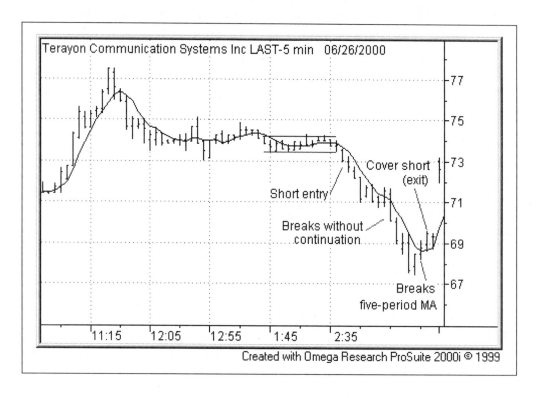

In the second case, I'll put a position on when a stock's bouncing off the same trend line over and over again. I use the same simple moving averages that I use on a daily chart, the 5-, 10-, and 20-period. Some stocks that trend higher or lower throughout the day move along one moving average.

Are the 5- and 10-period moving averages the most common?

Yeah. When a stock's move starts to accelerate, I look for the shorter-term moving average to pick the stock up and carry it higher. And I use that as a trend line for the rest of the day. I watch for breaks in those trend lines as sell signals.

So if you see an upwardly trending stock touch its five-period moving average line, you would be buying it once it touches the moving average line?

I look for a bounce off the moving average line, because it's not a mechanical system. It's very common that a stock will dip below the line by 1/8 or 1/4 point, so I don't use a system like that. It's a combination of watching the bounce and watching the Level II quote system and the time-and-sales data as the orders go through. This gives me a feel for the continuation of the move. I don't like to open any positions based solely on a feeling, or because I simply think that it's headed higher. Instead, I like to see some kind of pattern on the intraday charts beyond simply a trend. For example, strongly-trending stocks often tend to enter intraday consolidations, or form shelves. I look at these patterns as pauses before a continuation. I prefer to enter a position on a breakout of such a pattern. Something key to my trading is avoiding blatant speculation. Thus I won't just buy when the stock enters a consolidation on the belief that it will move higher. I want to see the breakout.

What are you looking for on the Level II quotes? If the stock's trending higher, are you looking for a lot of people on the bid side?

I want to see a lot of people on the bid side, and not just a lot of shares from one market maker or ECN. I prefer to see several—the more, the better, because the amount they're bidding is not always reflecting the number of shares they have. And I look for large bids as well as the bid size greater than the ask. I also want to see the ask side slowly disappear as the orders go through. The best thing I like to see is a lot of trades at the asking price . . . an acceleration of trades at the asking price. I want to see all of that combined with strong volume on the five-minute bars. Strong volume is my favorite indicator.

Do you confirm your decision to enter a trade by looking at bigger time frame charts?

Yes. Before I buy anything, I always glance over at the 30-minute and daily bar charts to look for resistance points. This is because if a stock had a lot of trouble going through a certain price maybe five days ago, and the breakout point is just under that price, I'm not going to take the position until it goes through that price.

Let's step back for a second. You said that you want to see more than one person on the bid side. Is it more important to see a lot of different bids or just a couple of bids with 10,000-share lots?

If it's a significant number of shares, like 10,000, then I'm happy to see two or three. However, I rarely see this. If it's a lot of small orders of 100 shares or 500 shares, I want to see a lot of buyers. It always catches my eye when the big brokers are buying, too, as opposed to the market makers and ECNs, which are where many daytraders route their orders.

And the big brokers are who? Goldman—

—Merrill Lynch, Goldman, DLJ. If I see them bidding for 50,000 shares, I know that it's more than just a daytrader trying to scalp an eighth.

What are the daytraders looking at?

They're probably looking at the most active ECNs and market makers, like Knight/Trimark, Island, Instinet, Redibook, and Attain. Most daytraders that I know use these systems to place their trades, and not the big brokers that I'm on the lookout for.

Where would your sell point be on these trades?

If it's a trade that I took because it was a breakout from a consolidation, and if I get in too early and it's a false breakout, even after a second bar I will hold it un-

The Baker Five-and-Dime Method: SDL Inc. (SDLI), 5-minute

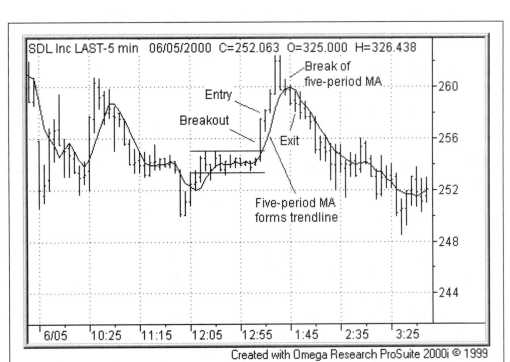

til it breaks the bottom part of the trading range that it's been in. Now if a stock's been trending for three or more five-minute bars, I like to try to draw a trend line, usually after three bars, which is enough points to draw an adequate line of some kind.

Or I'll use a system that I have developed over the last few years which I call "The Baker Five-and-Dime Method." What I've noticed is that if the five-period moving average on a five-minute chart carries a stock higher, the next greater one, the 10-period, will act as a secondary support. So if something has been trending higher and I've been in the position for maybe 30 minutes and it breaks through the first moving average that was carrying it, I use that as a signal to sell. But then I wait for some sort of confirmation like a break of the next moving average, such as the 10-period. Of course, all of this depends on how much I'm up on the position. If I'm up 1 point, and the chart is starting to show weakness, I may exit the position on a small break of the five-period moving average.

I also have a 4-point rule, where I will sell, or at least place a stop on, at least one-half of my position on a profit of 4 points.

So in this example, all price has to do is dip down below the 10-period for a few seconds?

Actually, I would prefer to see it close below that level and then continue roughly 1/4-point lower. I tend to be a more aggressive seller on the more volatile stocks. If I enter a stock based on a setup from an intraday pattern, I'm more willing to lock in profits quickly. If I open a position based on a longer-term setup from the daily charts, I'm willing to wait through more volatility, because the trend lines I'm using have been built over more time, theoretically making them stronger. But it honestly depends on how much I'm up on the position. I'm much happier to get out with no loss at all than to gamble for a couple of points, because there's always another opportunity. I would prefer to start with a fresh trade than to have to make a decision when I'm at a loss.

Do you always use that technique—a break of the trend line or a break of the next higher moving average?

That's my favorite technique. But at the same time, if I notice that the entire market is collapsing, and I have a long position in some high-flying stock, I'll tend to start worrying a little more and be more willing to pull the trigger and sell something if it starts to pull back. I look at points, not percentages. So if it's a $200 stock and it's up 5 points or it's a $10 stock and it's up 5 points, I still look at it the same way. I don't wait for a certain percentage dip.

Do you look at both time-and-sales and Level II when you're thinking of getting out of a position as well as when you're considering entry?

Yes, always. If I'm in a long position, I'm always looking to see if people are pulling away their bids even though the price isn't falling. Sometimes if there's three 10,000-share bids, all of a sudden there's just one party bidding. And then I watch to see if the trades are going through at the bid or the ask, particularly if it's next to a whole number, like 10, 20, 30, 40, 50. Those often cause problems, especially if it's near 50, 100, or 200. For short-term trading, I always notice that those numbers cause problems.

So when you see a lot of bids start to dry up, you're thinking the thing's really going to head lower, right?

Yeah. I always have my sell order ready as soon as I have the confirmation of my fill. I'm pretty much looking to get out if the bids are drying up. I don't want to be the last one out.

Would you short a stock based on the same criteria that you would buy a stock if the trend on that *day* is down? Or do you have to see that both the intermediate-term trend (a few weeks to a few months), and short-term trend (a few days to a few weeks), are both down?

I'm not too concerned with the short-, intermediate-, or long-term trends. But I still look at the 30-minute and daily charts and I draw my support and resistance levels on them. And I make sure that I'm aware of where all of the moving averages are, especially the 50-day and 200-day. Otherwise, I use the same criteria. I would prefer to short a stock that's been moving down that day. I never try to call tops and bottoms—I've learned bad lessons from that.

When you speak of "the trend," are you referring to the trend of that day?

Yes.

If it's before the open of trading, and it looks like there will be a big gap-up opening in the averages, do you consider that to be an up trend even though the day hasn't yet begun?

In the first hour of trading, if there is a gap and everything's moving higher, I'm looking to catch the momentum of the first 15 minutes or 30 minutes of trading. And then I look for reversals. Over the years, I've noticed that these reversals occur earlier and earlier in the day. A stock will gap up 10 points and then suddenly fall. I really like to play the reversals when the entire market is reversing. I'd rather not go against the trend. Never fight the trend. If I didn't do anything in the opening 30 minutes, I usually look for flip-top openings. That's where the stock spikes up, spikes down, and then crosses the morning high again, or vice versa for shorts. I like to enter when price takes out the morning high. I know of a lot of daytraders who don't watch the rest of the market and don't care about it at all. But I like to watch the Nasdaq futures just to get a feel. I primarily only use momentum techniques in the first hour of trading, otherwise I focus on reversals and flip-tops.

When you play the open, and let's say Sun Microsystems is expected to open 5 points higher, do you ever get in right when the first trade happens 5 points higher because you think it's going to move up another couple of points?

Depending on the stock, sometimes I'll get in during pre-market trading, especially if the stock has been trading in the pre-market for long positions at the asking price all morning. As my trading has matured, I prefer to avoid speculating and I'd rather wait for a confirmation. I almost never place market orders, let alone at the open. If I feel the momentum is there, I consider buying in the first five minutes. I try to let five minutes go by just to see—

—if the move's going to extend a little bit.

Yes. And if I'm going to trade something at the open, I want to trade something that has a wide average daily range. This is usually whatever the popular stock of the week is . . . whatever the hot sector is. Those stocks usually have a huge range because everybody's trading them. So if a stock only moves an average of 1 point a day . . . I mean I'm not going to try to trade a drug stock at the open while some telecom stock trades every day with a range of 10 to 20 points.

So, when you trade the open, you're looking more for the flip-top than anything else.

Yeah. My favorite thing would be reversals. Either there's some carryover from the day before when the market closes at its high of the day and then runs up a little more before it sells off, or vice versa. In some cases, there's some profit-taking after a big run-up . . . but it will just be a small amount of profit-taking. After a while you can almost tell how much it's going to be.

And so after it opens down a little bit you're going to watch it reverse. Now would you enter one tick above that day's high?

That would be my goal. In the first 30 minutes, you can see a complete flip-top, where it opens up, moves down, then takes out the morning high. You can see all of that occur in 30 minutes now—if not less—and often in three- or four-, five-minute bars.

To short a down flip-top opening when price initially moves down, comes back up, then goes down again, you're going to short a tick below the early low?

Not necessarily. I don't have a very mechanical system, I guess. But, yes, somewhere roughly around that area.

Will you ever short it before it takes out the morning low?

I used to do that all the time. But I learned a couple of expensive lessons doing that, thinking that it would have to go lower.

It doesn't always take out the low.

No. Sometimes it goes 1/8 or 1/4 below, but I try to wait for it to go at least 3/8 below the earlier low.

A lot of people are looking at that same trade then, which is why it doesn't work.

Probably.

So your favorite way of playing the open is a reversal type of trade, right?

I guess my two favorite ways would be catching the momentum, when everyone just wants to buy something right at the open. You can see the orders rushing in right when the market opens at 9:30. I like to bid 1/16 over everybody else, get ahead of them, and ride it up for a couple of points. Or the flip-top. I love the flip-top because everybody sells, thinking they got out at a higher price, and the stock falls 2 points. And all of a sudden it reverses, and then they realize that that was all the profit-taking there was going to be. And everyone thinks they missed the train and has to jump back in. So you catch that momentum and sell it at someone else's expense.

How many stocks do you typically follow at one time?

I keep a list of about 30 to 40 stocks on my screen every day that I consider to be the most popular flavors of the month. I use these to hunt for intraday setups, as opposed to my other list, which I daytrade based on longer-term setups. This latter list is comprised of stocks that show the most trading activity as they approach their old price highs.

Are there some stocks you trade more often than others?

Yes. I followed Knight/Trimark for months. I didn't initially look at it as a daytrade. But after following it for awhile, I noticed that it repeated the same patterns over and over. For roughly 60 to 65 days straight, I traded it every day based on almost the same pattern. You always notice recurring patterns in the same stocks. Every stock has its own personality. So different trends and different patterns work differently for different stocks.

You saw the exact same thing happening in Knight every day for 65 days?

Yes.

I'm in suspense. What was the pattern?

After it made a morning move, it would break out from a consolidation. Also, you'd often see it sell off toward the close, and then gap up the next morning at the open. It would then run up for a couple of minutes and then consolidate, so I would set my audible alerts just outside of the trading range.

Some days it would break out higher, above the consolidation, and some days it would break down lower, below the consolidation. You didn't know which way it would go.

Yes. And most of the action always took place in the last hour, so you could wait all day.

Do you look at any indicators for general market direction? Or, since you're a daytrader, aren't you basically just looking at how the Nasdaq futures are going to open each morning before the open?

Yeah. For my early-morning trades, all I care about is what's happening right in the first 15 minutes before the market opens. For a lot of my daytrades or my swing trades, I like to see stocks that are mimicking the charts of the Nasdaq or the S&P. A lot of tech charts look exactly like the Nasdaq charts, so when I see a bounce in the broader market, I'll see the same bounce in the same type names.

In the Nasdaq futures, you mean.

Well, the Nasdaq futures as well as the Nasdaq Composite. For the pre-open, I use the futures because they trade close to 24 hours a day, whereas the Composite doesn't. That gives me the best indication of how people reacted to the news from the previous day's close and overnight. Intraday, I watch the futures. I've always thought that they were a leading indicator . . . they move a lot faster than the Nasdaq Composite.

Now, why wouldn't you be looking at the NDX, the Nasdaq 100? That's really more of a pure play on tech than the Nasdaq Comp.

Usually, when I'm looking to see where I think the Nasdaq in general is going to be, I look at the big-name tech stocks. They used to call them the Four Horsemen or the Five Jewels. Some of those stocks make up a large percentage of the index.

You mean like Intel and Cisco?

And also Microsoft, JDS Uniphase, and Oracle. Those are the five that have the largest weighting in the Nasdaq Composite.

So you're saying it's better to look at the Four Horsemen or Five Jewels?

I like to see where the leaders of the day, the current market leaders, are going, rather than look at the NDX. I don't see the charts of the Composite and the NDX as being that much different. Most people see the Composite in the newspaper and on television. If that's what everybody else is watching, I want to know what they're looking at. Lately I have been focusing more on the futures, as leadership in the Nasdaq continues to change each day. It's so important to let your trading evolve with the times. What worked three years ago 95 percent of the time might only work 50 percent of the time today. Just the other day, I was in two long positions in the tech sector and I started to see the Nasdaq futures take out their intraday support level. After seeing a continuation to the downside, I started to close out my positions. By the end of the day the same stocks that brought me a profit of several points broke down and closed negative.

Do you spend much time looking at market sentiment indicators like put-to-call ratios, the VIX, things like that?

I look at them when they're at extreme levels. There was a time when a 20 on the VIX was a sell signal and a 30 was a buy signal. I compare them to the charts of the indices. You can see where reversals have occurred relative to those indicators.

As far as money management goes, how much of your account do you put in one position?

I base my trades on the number of shares. I usually rank each stock on a scale of 1 through 4. This tells me if I should buy 300, 500, 800, or 1,000 shares for a daytrade. The stocks that I'm more familiar with, that I've traded a lot more, whose trends I feel that I know better, I'm more willing to call a "4," which would be 1,000 shares. Something that is more volatile, and which I consider to be riskier, I would take a smaller position in. I don't have a percentage that I use. I base it on shares.

Do you add more to a winning position as it moves higher?

No. I am willing to cost-average down in a daytrade. This is where a combination of gut feeling and the charts come into play. I don't think daytrading can be a mechanical system. There are other underlying factors at any moment that tell you to hold on or to sell.

Are there any trading books that you've found particularly interesting?

My favorite book is Thomas Bulkowski's *Encyclopedia of Chart Patterns.* Initially, the only books I'd wanted to read were about chart patterns. I read Jeff Cooper's books and I learned a lot from them. I narrowed down some of his patterns to the ones that I liked. Later on, after I'd stopped trying to find all the different patterns, I started to read more about the psychology of trading. Since one's emotions play a greater role in the daytrader's decision-making process, I found that that was pretty interesting. There's a lot of psychology involved in trading, which is why I like Alexander Elder's *Trading for a Living*. It covers the topic quite well. Trading takes a certain personality.

Do you see yourself doing anything but trading for the rest of your life?

One day I would like to run a hedge fund, Kevin, but I guess I always want to be involved in trading. I can't see myself doing anything else.

Thanks, David.

MANUEL OCHOA

STEALTH

By Marc Dupée

Manuel Ochoa has established himself as one of the rising stars in the hedge fund business. Early in his career, MAR Hedge recognized the performance of his global macro fund, ranking it third in the world among global macro funds for its performance in 1997. He currently runs three funds and has achieved consistently high annual returns, putting him on the map as one of the best young hedge fund managers. *Futures Magazine* called Manuel Ochoa, now 31, "one of America's hottest new traders."

Ochoa applies both longer-term, trend-following, and swing-trading techniques in the futures markets, focusing on financial futures, specifically, T-bonds, S&Ps, and currencies. He relies on a discretionary approach for many of his market decisions, but at the same time employs mechanical trading systems he has developed in many markets to reduce the overall volatility of his portfolio.

He launched his trading career while still a finance student at the University of Southern California (USC) in the late 1980s and drew inspiration from finance professors, one of whom traded currencies full-time.

Ochoa began researching trading strategies at the USC computer labs, combining coursework with his research, and learning about price behavior and market correlations that subsequently laid the groundwork for both his future trading systems and discretionary trading approach. While earning his degree at USC, he also began trading.

"I traded the S&Ps early in my career with a seat-of-the-pants approach. Needless to say, it was a bad experience: I was losing money. I opened an account and lost all of it. I started learning from there."

After college, he spent two more years researching, testing, and trading his own account using a short-term, discretionary approach before becoming a consistently successful trader. He then shopped his performance to land his first investors and now has primarily banks and large institutions as clients.

Ringing a similar bell to other success stories, Ochoa's early failures served as catalysts that led to the design and development of the trading systems and portfolio diversification and risk-management models that serve him in the markets today. His years of studying and trading have gifted him with an ability to "sense" the market and to interpret what the market is "thinking," keeping him in step with, or one-step ahead of, major market movements and price swings.

Marc Dupée: Tell me about the hedge funds that you manage.

Manuel Ochoa: The style of trading that's done is called "global macro," as opposed to other styles like "event driven," "distressed securities," or "market timing."

How would you define the global macro style of trading?

Instead of trying to pick winning stocks, for example, you just try to determine whether the market's going to be going up or down. What you do is buy the whole basket of stocks, like the S&P 500 futures. So you're making a macro call instead of making a micro call like a stock picker would.

Which markets do you trade?

All the major global financials, like the U.S. stock market, U.S. bond market, European stocks, European bonds, Asian stocks, and Asian bonds.

Do you trade indexes on all of those?

Yes.

And do you trade at different exchanges, too, or mostly in the U.S.?

I trade on all different exchanges.

What criteria or parameters do you use to decide when to get into a market?

Basically, I use a blend of technical indicators and fundamental data that come out pretty much every day. You just start getting a picture of what's going on, and what the markets are thinking, and then you start seeing when people begin to get real scared when bad news hits. You then see how that interacts with price action. On the other end of the spectrum, you see people begin to get really euphoric when a batch of bullish economic reports comes out. You see how price action acts in conjunction with those reports and then you see patterns begin to develop. Basically that's how you get a feel for what your strategy is.

For technical indicators, could you give an example of a recent trade in currencies, bonds, or a stock index? Could you qualify what the fundamental overtones were and provide us with specific parameters that got you into the trade?

Recently, you saw some interesting price action in the S&Ps. Recently, it has been the Nasdaq stocks that were getting sold off hard due to profit-taking. And then bearish comments coming out from various sources have accelerated downward price movement in the Nasdaq.

You're talking about that three-day decline from its March 10, 2000 high through March 15, when the Nasdaq fell as much as 11 percent?

Yes, and then you look at the S&P 500 and see that it's basically got downward pressure but it hasn't really taken out any major recent support levels. That's telling you that the sell-off is basically a function of rotation going on. There's money leaving high-tech stocks, but a lot of the money is going back into the stocks that haven't been doing as well, like in the S&P 500 and the Dow Jones. That's a tip-off.

So then you look to see if there's a catalyst that's going to come out to cause any kind of rally. On March 16, 2000, the producer price index (PPI) report came in pretty much as expected. There weren't any big surprises in it, and that was a catalyst for a sigh of relief. Selling was concentrated on the Nasdaq. That was a good trade setup to go long S&Ps and it worked out. It doesn't always work out. Sometimes you're wrong but those are the times that you want to be trading because when you're right, those are the times when you're really right.

Were you long on March 15, 2000?

Yes.

So when the Nasdaq was selling down hard on March 13, 14 and 15 . . .

Then I started buying June S&P futures. I saw the S&Ps were still in a congestion zone and hadn't really taken out the recent lows.

The lows around Feb. 28, 2000?

Yes, those lows right around there. If we had taken those lows out afterward, I would have thrown in the towel. But I knew there was going to be a bottom somewhere right around there. And it worked out. It doesn't always work out, though. Sometimes you're wrong.

Twenty points on the S&Ps is a lot.

Reading The Market Ahead Of A Catalyst: June 2000 S&P 500 Futures (SPM0), Daily

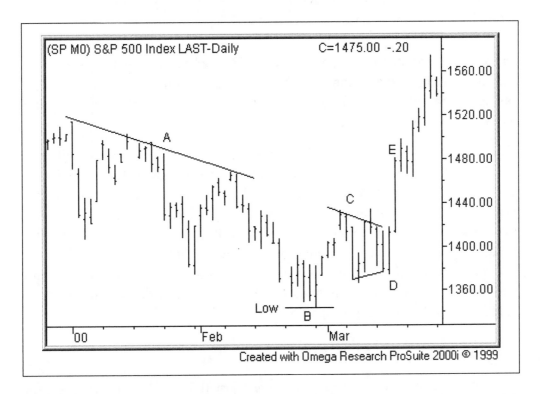

The S&P futures bounce off a longer-term trendline (A to C) but fail to take out the low at (B). The S&Ps hold in a congestion zone between (C) and (D) as the Nasdaq sells off as much as 11 percent from its March highs in the three days prior to an economic report "catalyst." This divergence implied a rotation from tech into S&P 500 stocks, where Ochoa established long S&P futures positions. On March 15, 2000 at (D), one day prior to the release of the Producer Price Index report (PPI), the S&Ps rise in anticipation of a friendly (non-inflationary) PPI as the Nasdaq extends its slide. At (E), the S&Ps soar an unusual 65 points on the PPI report.

If you can't risk at least 20 points per S&P contract, you probably shouldn't be trading it because the best S&P traders are the guys that can put big enough stops where they're not going to get stopped out all the time. Either that or you'd better start trading S&P E-Minis. If the guys are risking $2 or $3 per contract, I guarantee you that, assuming they're even profitable, they're nowhere near the profitability level of the guys that are risking $20.

You said that you had started buying June S&Ps when the Nasdaq was selling down hard and as the S&Ps held in a congestion zone prior to the PPI release on March 13 and 14. What were you looking for in terms of your price objective or your price target?

Originally, I was looking for a 1430 profit target. But then the market rallied so much on March 15, the day before the PPI, that we already had had a $35 rally, a bigger-than-average profit at that point. I looked at my other positions and looked at how much money I already had on the table. And then I sensed that the market was already anticipating a friendly PPI report. So part of that discounting process may have already started. Usually, that's the way it will work. But this week was the exception because it didn't work out that way. In actuality, I would have been better off holding out, because the next day we got that huge rally in the S&P, where it was up $65.

You got out before then?

Yes. I got out the day before that, because I just thought, "Wait a second. The market looks like it's already discounting a good PPI report."

You mean the $35 rally on the day before the PPI was due to the S&Ps discounting the news?

Yes, it was already anticipating. There were a lot of people who were already anticipating a friendly PPI report.

So you were afraid they would "buy the rumor and sell the news?"

Yes, I was afraid it was already getting *too* discounted. So I said to myself, "You know what, I've got a feeling this is going on, so I'm getting out at the close." So

I got out at the close. In retrospect, that was the wrong thing to do, because the next day it rallied even more.

Did you jump back in?

No, I didn't. But, you know, you don't trade based on moves that happened like those in the past two days. This is because those types of moves only happen once a year. So if you're trying to be a consistent money maker, you don't trade for the things that usually *don't* happen, you trade for the things that usually *do* happen. That was unusual price action that we got on March 15 and 16.

How do you usually place your price-target objectives, then?

You know, recent highs and lows. Sometimes, you just trail the stops. And sometimes there isn't even a price objective. My price objective was the recent high in the 1430 area.

You mean on March 15, 2000?

Yes. It all depends. It's like the pitcher and the batter. Each pitch is never exactly the same as the one before it.

How do you place stops?

Most of the time, it's a question of recent volatility. If you know the recent volatility on the S&P is fluctuating and the average daily range over the last couple of days has been $25, you have to assume that from one day to the next it will be somewhat close to that same level of fluctuation. So you extrapolate that. Other times, you can get lucky. You can use a tighter stop than that based on just chart points and the number of potential catalysts in the next 24 hours.

By catalysts, you mean . . . ?

Like a report. If a report comes out and it's bullish, for example an inflation-friendly producer price index report, you know your stop is not going to get hit because you're going to be right, immediately . . . and the S&P 500 futures will blow back or will gap up on the open, anyway. So it's a combination of different setups. You can trade S&Ps on a purely mechanical basis, but there are certain things that you'll never be able to do as well as actually being able to understand what's going on and really seeing why things are moving and what potential moves are going to come up in the future. You can't program that into a trading system.

If the stops that you place are not mechanical . . .

Some of them are.

But it sounds like they're mental stops. It also sounds like you'll qualify them if the context and tone of the market has changed . . .

Yes, basically, it's a discretionary process. That's what it is.

Your stops are discretionary?

Yes. Sometimes it's for a technical reason that you take a trade, sometimes it's a mixture of technicals and fundamentals. But the best way to trade S&Ps or any market is that you only trade it at the times when you know there's a report coming out . . . and if you're right, the market is going to immediately move in your favor. This is as opposed to just putting a trade on, you know, from one random day to the next, where you don't have any market-moving event and you're just sitting there in the market hoping that it's going to edge up your way.

Do you have rules for stops?

As I said, I use the average true range, where I know that I'll have to use at least a $25 stop because that's been the average range in the last couple of days in the S&P.

So you'll use the average true range from wherever your entry point is. Will you be out of a position if it drops below that?

Yes, and sometimes I'll just use chart points I like . . . where if you know that it makes a new low on the S&P, and you know that the reason it's going to be making that new low is because bearish data came out on the PPI, then even though the average true range was, let's say, $25, you know that in actuality you don't have to use $25 stops. This is because most likely it's just going to keep going against you if it goes past, say, $12 and $13 below your entry point. This is because you know what's going on. A lot of fundamental investors—there's a lot of them out there—are going to look at that PPI data and they're going to get scared and they're going to start selling stocks. The S&P will be down 40. So why wait until it's down 25 when you can get out when it's only down 12?

Do you sometimes have an initial risk on a swing trade that is larger than or close to your profit target?

Yes, because of the random price movement in the markets. If you place your stops too close there is a good chance that you will be stopped out of too many trades. In the end, you wind up trading with tight stops that all get hit, leaving you with a big loss.

Sounds like your trading is extremely discretionary. Do you have any hard-and-fast technical rules that help get you in and out of trades, or some type of system? I know you're a big developer of systems.

Yeah. I do a lot of systems trading but, to tell you the truth, I really only apply it to the smaller commodity markets where I don't have a good knowledge of the fundamental backdrop. That's mainly what I use systems trading for.

In which markets?

All the commodity markets, you know, like crude oil.

What's the overview of that mechanical trading system?

It's a combination of momentum and counter-momentum strategies. For a trend, I would put up a 25-day moving average and then trade whatever it's telling me, whether the trend is up or down.

So if it stays above the 25-day moving average, you stay in?

Yes.

How would you define a counter-trend?

In a counter-trend, I'll use an oscillator like an RSI. If the RSI gets up too high, then I'll start peeling off the long contracts.

Do you use any type of system like that in the markets that you're more familiar with, like the S&Ps?

I use them in the currencies. But in the bonds and the S&Ps, I pretty much stick with the patterns I was telling you about before . . . a discretionary type of trading.

It's a discretionary approach to trading based on your knowledge of the markets, the news, and your opinion of the news?

Yes.

In a sense, it's more fundamental.

But I use technicals, too. It's a combination.

Where do you get your fundamental information from and how do you qualify it?

I look for people who know more about the economy than I do and I just read their reports and kind of get a feel for what they're thinking. Those people, such as analysts at major brokerage houses, are widely read by a lot of big fund managers. Then I'll look at Bloomberg financial news . . . they've got stories all the time. You get a feel for who is doing what, who is good. You just get estimates, consensus estimates.

Do you tend to stick with the consensus?

No, not really. I don't really make my opinion one way or another. I just look for differences from the consensus, like what the actual numbers are versus the consensus. Then you see the price reaction to it and it gives you a snapshot of what's going on. So many times when the bonds have a bearish number they spike down and that's it. They'll spend the rest of the session coming back up again because that news was already discounted. So, even though the number came in more bearish than expected, if you see that the market starts rallying back you know that everyone that wanted to sell has already sold. And then you get these slow moves back up. And then if you're short you probably want to cover and try to get short again at a higher price.

Getting back to your stops, do you ever use a percentage loss of your portfolio as a stop-loss level? Is that ever one of your rules?

Down a certain amount? Yes. If I ever lost more than 10 percent in one month I would probably shut down for a month. That's never happened to me.

That would probably be over several trades. But do you have a percentage loss rule for any one trade?

Yes, I usually don't like to risk more than 2 percent on any one trade.

What about on the upside? Do you ever average up when things are going your way?

Not usually, no. I normally don't because that creates a lot of volatility. Usually if you're going to be out, you're not in a market that's moving strongly in your favor and usually when you get markets like that nowadays, you have these violent corrections in between. So if you're averaging up, that strategy is not nearly as good as it used to be. There are too many speculators in the market.

So what happens?

If you're averaging up before a correction, you don't know exactly when it is going to occur, and ultimately you end up taking major heat. You have a temporary loss on your portfolio. You might get out of there, because it keeps going up the day after, but you take more of a loss than you'd like to. I've got clients who follow their equity on a daily basis. Next thing you know, they're on the phone asking me why I lost 3 percent in one day. I know people that do it, but that's not my style. I don't like to trade like that because you're trading based on having a one-way move and usually it's not that easy. You always get profit-taking in the interim, and even on these strong rallies you get these strong corrections in the Nasdaq.

Then you get hammered.

Yeah, then you get hammered and puke everything during the correction. Then, the next day, it starts going back up again after it got you out.

A lot of the stuff you describe is reading the market in terms of gauging the sentiment of the market. Do you have any favorite sentiment indicators that you use?

Not really. I used to look at the put-to-call ratio, but that's been distorted. You've got a lot of hedging going on there. You've got a lot of synthetic strategies going on. It's not a clean measure anymore. I wouldn't use it anymore.

You sometimes talk about the shotgun approach and the rifle approach. Can you expand on that a little bit? Which one are you currently trading and why?

The shotgun approach would be the macro approach. The rifle approach would be the micro. The stock pickers are using the rifle, and the macro is for guys like me that don't know . . . we don't have the ability to pick out companies. I don't want to know. All I want to know is whether the whole market is going to go up or down . . . and I'd buy a little bit of volatility just to catch the train. You know, it would be great if I could do both, but there's just not enough time to be able to do both of those well.

Can you give us a feel of what you do, in general?

Most of my clients are institutional clients that are looking for diversification in their existing bond and stock portfolios. They're looking for guys who are going to be able to make some money if the market starts going down or sideways. They're looking for an alternative investment, which is the category that guys like me fall under. It's not for somebody who doesn't have a regular portfolio already. Our clients usually have regular portfolios and they're looking for something different to round it out more. It's not usually a good idea to put all your money in something like this first.

How did you fall into having banks give you a million dollars? You're young.

I'm 31 years old.

How long have you been trading this account size? And how did you get your start?

I got my start while I was in college in the late '80s. I was a business major at the University of Southern California and my finance professors got me interested in how markets work and why markets do what they do. And I started from there. Then I began trading and I lost all of my money. The first time I traded, I opened up an account with something like 10 grand and lost all of it. I kind of started learning from there. (*Chuckles*).

So what would you do differently today if put back in that same position?

I would have waited a lot longer before risking real money in the market. I had just begun trading. You're eager to start. It takes a while before you can have a chance at making money. I would have studied more. I would have paper-traded more and done more simulated trading. I was just too eager. Most people start trading with too small of a bankroll. In other words, they don't have enough capital to start trading.

After you lost all of your money, how did you end up getting a bank or institution to give you a million dollars?

I managed to get some more capital and I traded that for about five years. I decided that's really what I should be doing. Then I just shopped my performance around for a few years after doing it for myself on a small scale. And I got a couple of investors. The more investors you get, the easier it is to get the next one. Nobody wants to talk to you when you're small.

So it was difficult to get your first break?

Yes, very difficult.

You described how you've developed a discretionary style to your global macro trading. How did you arrive at the current foundation of your trading strategy?

Observation and testing.

Are your systems something you don't discuss or is there something you can tell us, without giving anything away?

Basically, they're trend-based, trend-following systems. You're not trying to guess or make any type of judgment on the market. You're just following the system to jump on or off the train. There's nothing special about that. A lot of people use it. The only reason I do that is it helps round out my risk-reward portfolio. It helps lower my volatility. Some days when I'm really wrong on my discretionary trading, I'll make money off my trend trading. I've found that they tend to balance each other out pretty well. There's nothing special about it, though. There are a million guys that do that. I don't try to sell myself based on that. Anybody can do that. It's easy.

What type of easy, trend-following systems are you describing?

Oh, they're like pre-packaged, man. Just buy TradeStation. They have something on the order of 30 pre-packaged ones in there, ready to go . . . breakouts, RSI, etc.

Are there some that you think are better than others?

No, they're all based on the same principle: trend following. They're just different variations. They're all trying to do the same thing. Some years one does better than the other, then vice versa the next year. There's nothing special about it. It's real easy. The only comment I have about that is that most people don't have the discipline to follow the systems. That's the only thing of interest to say about that. People just don't follow it. They don't have the discipline to do it.

Many traders are uncomfortable with trading systems because they feel like they lack control over their trading.

If a trader feels uneasy using a system it's probably because he doesn't understand the nature of it. There are certain advantages and disadvantages to systems. The advantage is it gives you a tool with which you can use to approach the markets every day, a specific trade plan that you can execute and make a profit with in the long run.

But you also have to realize that most systems are only right about 40 percent of the time, so it can be very difficult to follow your system during losing periods. If the trader doesn't understand the nature of his system he will almost surely quit using it and end up taking a loss.

I adopted a systems approach because I saw patterns that developed over the years. Tradable patterns can be very simple. For example, when a market makes new highs there is usually follow-through. Or if the market makes a new high and then fails, it usually makes a big move the other way. To execute these patterns, I programmed them and started trading them. Once a system is up and running, I can use my time to research other ideas.

Can you compare the success of swing trading systems with the average trend-following system?

Swing trading has a higher winning percentage of trades than trend-following. Swing trades should average at least 60 percent winners because you are taking small profits very often and you need those to cover the occasional loser. Trend following has a much lower percentage of winning trades because you are trying to make most of your money in one or two big trades. You're going for the home run, so to speak. The rest of the trades are losers and small winners.

What is your time frame? Or do you have varying time frames?

My time frame varies. Shorter-term and longer-term . . . I kind of just pick a little bit of each one. That's the best way to do it; instead of being strictly long-term, or short-term only. The problem with that is that you get erratic performance. And if you're a money manager like me, after a year of not making money, clients begin to get impatient and they start leaving. You're better off making a little bit every year and keeping them.

You trade across a range of markets and in different time frames. Can you give an overview of the importance of diversification, both in terms of markets and time frames?

Diversification is important if you are systems trading because you don't know where you are going to make your money in the future. There are only a couple of markets that make very big moves each year, simply because the supply-demand situation doesn't fluctuate that much on a year-to-year basis.

However, once in a while you do have a major shift in the outlook for a market which causes the big moves that systems traders can profit from. One way to improve your chances is to diversify the time frame of your systems. You can have a system that looks back at the last 50 days of data to make its decision, and then you can use one that only looks back at the last five days. The advantage is that you can trade moves that are five days in length and also the longer ones at 50 days. These systems will behave differently and their losing periods are much less likely to occur at the same time than would two systems that look back 50 days. This way, you smooth out your returns.

You're better off varying your time-frame strategy and diversifying . . . you get better results. Speaking of results . . .

My average annual return is around 20 percent.

What happened differently in 1998 from your better-performing years when you were up 47 and 27 percent? And what did you learn from that?

In 1998, I started trading tech stocks. The problem was that, instead of scaling into it, I made the mistake of just piling into it at once. Unfortunately, just after I started trading them, I went into an immediate drawdown. That was the problem. So the moral of the story is that whenever you are going to start trading a new style, instead of just piling in one day, you're better off taking it piece by piece, in little pieces.

In other words, if you find a new system, like for example you trade bonds, and you decide that you're going to trade 10 contracts per signal, you're better off kind of easing into it over the course of, say, six months. You start trading more and more contracts per signal. So at the first buy signal that you get, you might take two or three contracts. And then maybe a month later, you add some more contracts or start trading six-lots, instead of starting to trade 10 right off the bat. What happens is that everything is cyclical. You go through up trends in equity and drawdowns. I had the very unfortunate luck of immediately going into a drawdown. It hurt my performance. That was a learning lesson.

What kind of software do you utilize?

I use custom software that I had programmed and I also use some off-the-shelf software. It depends on what I need. If I need very complex calculations, I'll use my custom software. For easier tasks, I use the other software . . . whatever it takes to get the job done.

Are commissions and slippage a big factor in your trading?

Yes, definitely.

Which markets do you find the most difficult for getting good fills?

You know, the thinner markets, some of the smaller commodity markets. And Nasdaq futures. The slippage there is, wow, $500. It's real big. And that's per side. A thousand dollars round turn.

Then do you enter with market orders in the Nasdaq futures?

Sometimes, yes.

Why don't you use limit orders?

Because the contract is so big, $1000 doesn't even mean anything. It is just like the juice . . . you've got to pay for the right to play. The contract is a $400,000 contract. One of the worst things you can do is be right and not make any money.

What size account do you think somebody should start with?

People shouldn't start trading unless they have at least 50 grand. Otherwise, you're not diversified enough.

What would you tell someone new to trading?

To trade a couple of different markets for diversification . . . to have starting capital of at least $25,000, which would be for trading E-Mini contracts.

Thank you very much for sharing your ideas, Manuel.

You're welcome, Marc.

Jim Whitner

Only the Humble Survive

By Marc Dupée

Removed from the bustle and frenzied distraction of an urban environment, Jim Whitner has emerged as one of a new breed of money managers to watch. The quiet and solitude of the bucolic Blue Ridge Mountains in Virginia help Whitner focus and zero-in on emerging technologies and economic trends that become the winning trades of his Stargazer One hedge fund.

Unfettered by the noise of the Street, Whitner spends long hours researching and voraciously reading to arrive at independent judgments of the driving forces and enterprises that are shaping the economy. In its debut year in 1999, the fund achieved a 170 percent return.

This has always been his way. For the several years leading up to the launching of his hedge fund, Jim scrupulously researched the world's greatest traders and studied industry trends, company fundamentals, and chart patterns to uncover what the best-performing traders and stocks had in common. He also gained real-world experience trading and managing his family's money. Learning from his mistakes, he developed the analytical model he now uses in his hedge fund to get into the right stocks at the right time.

A competitive amateur equestrian, Whitner is as meticulous with his stock picking as he is in training for a horse race. For instance, in his preparation for the Paul Mellon trophy of the Foxhunters' Chase in 1999, Whitner walked the 3-1/2-mile course so many times that he commented, "I know it so well that, by now, I walk for the sheer pleasure of it."

Jim is unassuming. Like most successful traders, he is extremely risk-averse and displays an interpersonal humility that, he believes, must be extended to the market. For one of the greatest dangers, Whitner feels, is to allow success to blind a trader as to what the market is saying at any given moment. Paraphrasing Intel's Andy Grove, Whitner sees that "In the markets, only the humble survive."

Marc Dupée: Jim, tell us about your hedge fund.

Jim Whitner: What we have is, by definition, a hedge fund. But I like to refer to it as an investment partnership, because in the traditional definition of a hedge fund, you'll go long and short. We're not really very good at going short. We don't like to experiment with our clients' money, so in learning how to go short, I'd rather lose my own money.

How would you define the focus of your fund, and how well has that approach worked for you?

In 1999, we did 170 percent. I can only give you that figure as a track record, since we started the fund in 1999. But during that single year, we also did 15 percent in the third quarter during which the market got clobbered. The Nasdaq was up 2 percent, the Dow was down 7 percent, and the S&P 500 was down 6 percent in that same period. We did this by using an investment strategy that not only helped you make money, but helped you protect your money in a correction. Our fund is a small, mid-cap growth stock fund. We set it up that way because we felt we could add a lot of value to a sophisticated investor's portfolio by giving him exposure to what we call the "entrepreneurial growth in the U.S. economy." Everybody has their own definition of market cap, but we like to define that area as the "sweet spot" of the small, mid-cap segment. That is, we focus on stocks with a market value between $300 million and $5 billion as the territory between small-cap and big-cap. We'll buy stocks within that range, but we might even hold them until they grow as large as $12 billion. If you hook into a Dell Computer, Microsoft, or Cisco, you're not going to sell that gorilla prematurely if you can help it. The small, mid-cap area is a dynamic area. That's where all these new companies that are coming to market with these new products and services are. It's where the new industries are developing.

How did you get started investing in the stock market?

I was an econ major in college. That happened to be the one area in which I was getting good grades. From economics I gained an interest in the stock market. My family needed some help with their personal finances and they asked me to help them out. Through that, I got a lot of exposure to the markets. Then I went to business school in the late-'80s and we did a lot of case studies and I realized that I really loved doing research. And I developed a real interest in analyzing companies. The more I read and learned, the more I realized that the classical education you get from the classroom about the stock market isn't going to make you very successful.

That's what I expected to hear.

Yeah. So I decided that I was going to read everything that has been written since the turn of the century about the successful money managers. I'm an avid reader, so I took off. I read everything I could about Warren Buffett, Philip Fisher, Peter Lynch, Gerald Loeb, Bill O'Neil. The more I read, the more I began to understand the dynamics behind the market.

What did you wind up with when you began to synthesize the strategies of these legends?

I started with a value perspective because I had always idolized Warren Buffett . . . and I still do. I think Warren Buffett is one of the greatest investors of all time. However, I think his value paradigms don't work very well in the new economy. But what he did through 1998 was just amazing. The way he managed the risk in his portfolio was head-and-shoulders above everybody else.

But it sounds like your thinking evolved over time.

As I progressed in my reading, a number of things started to become a lot more obvious. I started to get a greater appreciation for technical research as opposed to the purely fundamental approach I started out with. I began to understand how fundamental and technical research could work together to help me capitalize on certain trends in the markets.

How did you arrive at the foundation of your trading strategy?

I read Bill O'Neil's book. His investment model, CANSLIM, was the foundation. I liked his approach because it encompassed the views of a lot of the great past money management approaches. But it was a starting point. One of the most important things I've learned is that you have to constantly refine your investment model as the markets evolve and develop, and as new industries come into focus.

How do you go about that refinement?

I constantly study the past performance of big winners. For example, I'll go back and study the big winners of 1999, whether or not I owned them. I'll analyze all their charts. I'll study the companies' fundamentals, technicals, and group confirmation. One of the things we've discovered in our research that deviates from the pure O'Neil approach is that you've got to back off the primary focus on earnings in many cases. You had a number of companies that were huge winners whose earnings were not very strong. But what distinguished them was that they had a new product or service in markets that had huge growth potential. Wall Street was taking notice of these companies. A significant number of big winners did not have very strong earnings or revenue growth relative to other companies that also made big moves. Qualcomm's revenue numbers weren't that exciting at first. As economies change and new industries come into focus, you're going to realize that there are different criteria that help you separate the winners from the losers.

Early in your career did you make any big mistakes that shaped your current approach?

In the beginning I wasn't very good and had just average returns. I was trying to blend growth and value strategies together. I was also listening to others' opinions too much. One of the things that really helped my performance was that I stopped reading everything I could about what was going on in Wall Street and avoided the weekly articles that appeared in Forbes. That's not to say that the information wasn't worthwhile. Rather, I decided that I had to rely upon and make decisions on the basis of my own research. If I was going to follow anything, it was going to be research and information sources that were in harmony with my approach. In this business, you have to manage information-overload. In the information economy, we all have to deal with that. I realized that I needed to maintain a focus. I learned that successful money managers of the past were focused. They didn't let the noise of the Street distract them.

You mentioned earlier that you analyze past winners in order to build a model of what will be successful in the future. Tell us about how you applied that model in 1999. What exactly did you look for in a stock in order to produce the 170 percent return you realized?

We try to focus on those industries that are benefiting from fundamental trends in the economy. We're looking for companies that are bringing new products and services to market and that have the potential for tremendous growth over the next few years. We also want to see that growth evidenced in their quarterly earnings and revenue numbers. We're looking for companies that are experiencing dramatic growth as a result of a new product or service or new industry trend.

That probably requires a lot of research, doesn't it?

Definitely. You have to focus on the dominant trends unfolding in the economy right now, whether it's broadband data applications, e-commerce, or e-business. Once you understand what's going on in those areas, you can relate to telecom equipment companies, Internet software, Internet security solutions, ISP hosting, ASP service providers, and wireless broadband applications. You can even get into biotech and genomics. With this model, we're looking for companies that are part of dynamic industries whose growth is driven by powerful economic trends. I look for companies that are evidencing this growth through very strong quarterly earnings and revenue numbers. Then we'll check on the story on these companies and see how they fit in with their industry groups.

What do you do with this model that seems to focus primarily on fundamental analysis?

We'll use technical analysis to help us pick our buy and sell points as well as to manage the risk. Let me use a couple of examples to illustrate how we do this. My two biggest winners of 1999 fit the criteria very well. One was MicroStrategy and the other was i2 Technologies. These were two stocks that had significant earnings and revenue growth. The enterprise software group was hot. It was one of the big leading groups in the market. These were two companies with strong fundamentals and the technical situation looked very promising. So we started building positions in them.

What did you like about the technical situation? Let's start with i2.

We were catching these stocks breaking out of good, solid bases. That's always the key. You don't want to chase extended stocks, stocks that have already risen a substantial amount from their bases. Those are going to be the first to pull back against you. If you can start off from a winning position, then you're much more able to ride out the next correction. We first bought i2 on Oct. 27, 1999. It had

i2 Technologies (ITWO), Daily

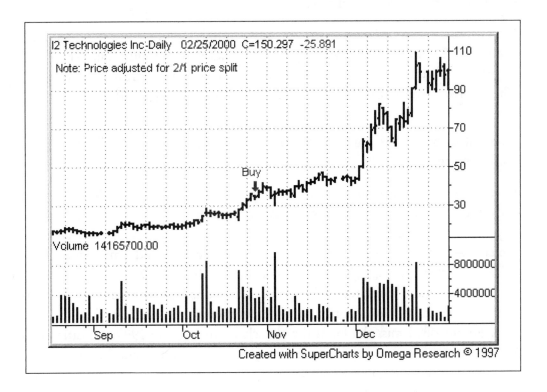

broken out a couple of days before on big volume out of a base around 23 or so. Then it formed another little base and broke out again. It jumped from 29 to 31 and that's where we took our first position. That was a pretty good breakout. The market was just getting ready to take off. i2 was a company with mutual fund ownership running at about 35 percent of the float at the time, and they were well-covered by a number of good brokerage firms. They had just recorded a real solid quarter on the earnings. In the previous quarter, earnings were up 300 percent and revenues were up 53 percent. For the previous couple of quarters they had exhibited very strong quarterly revenue numbers.

What about MSTR? Similar setup? Looking at the chart I can see that the stock broke out in late November.

MSTR was a similar setup. We actually started buying MicroStrategies on September 23, 1999, which was right in the middle of the third-quarter market correction. If you look at it on a weekly chart, it was just starting to break out. They had very strong earnings and revenue numbers on a quarterly basis.

That's interesting that you mustered up the confidence to buy MSTR during a market correction.

One of the things that's important about the investment model is that if you go back and study the characteristics of past winners, it's so much easier for you to step up to the plate and open a position in the next good idea that fits your parameters—even in a correction. You've seen it happen time and time again. If you understand that a company fits the parameters of the past Dells and Microsofts, you feel a lot more comfortable doing this. That's one way in which money managers manage the risk in a portfolio: They put money into the best ideas they can find. Admittedly, I missed a lot of the biotech advance of late 1999 and early 2000 mainly because it was really hard for me to wrap my hands around those companies when they were going from 20 to 80. That's not to say I didn't think they could be big winners. Rather, the issue was more in managing the risk.

In other words, you couldn't see examples of past winners that the hot genomic group within the biotech sector resembled, right?

That's it. We didn't understand this particular industry as well as we understood Internet-related companies. But we're starting to learn a lot about biotechs and we'll be in a position as we go forward to step up to the plate.

What industry trends do you see on the horizon that you imagine you might be participating in down the road? Earlier we touched on the subject of biotech. Do you see yourself getting into that?

Base Breakout: Microstrategy (MSTR), Daily

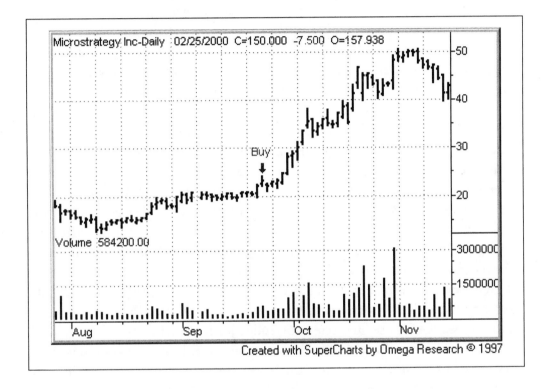

Well, if you just look at what happened in the biotech stocks in late 1999 and early 2000 and consider how they showed tremendous strength in the January 2000 market correction, it reminds me of the big trend in Internet stocks back in 1996 and 1997 when Yahoo! and America Online came on the scene. Remember those nasty corrections we had back then? They weren't beaten up much at all! They held their own. You could say they were trading at huge valuations relative to their earnings numbers back then. The biotechs seem to have started to come into their own. They're starting to gain a lot of recognition on the Street. Technology is rapidly making dynamic changes in the research-and-development process.

Now let's talk about how you go about dumping your losers . . . if there are any.

(*Laughs*) Yeah, there are losers. The thing is, risk management is the most important part of our investment strategy. We set a stop 8 to 10 percent below where we bought our first position. We will walk into the position. Let's say we want to own 8,000 to 10,000 shares of a stock. We might buy 3,000 shares, wait for it to jump up 2 points to buy another 3,000 shares, and then another two points to buy another 3,000 shares. So we'll average in. This way, we're committing the smallest amount of capital to the position each time we buy some shares in the stock. The idea is that when we initially jump in, we're committing a small amount of our capital so that when we take a loss, it's a smaller loss. There are exceptions to the rule, of course. When we feel like the market is starting to turn and we're getting into a bull market, we'll just all of a sudden go full margin. We'll just max out. But even when we do that, we'll treat each individual position on its own merit. We're not afraid to sell them. (*Whitner snaps his fingers quite loudly.*)

The most important thing you can do in managing money is to manage the risk of each position. It's more important than all your research. If you go back and study some of those guys like Paul Tudor Jones, Dreyfus, Bill O'Neil, you'll find that they were all obsessed with managing the risk of their positions. It all goes back to that very simple concept: If you cut your losses short and let your winners ride, you're going to make a lot of money in the market.

What are your criteria for selling?

First, it's the stop. In addition, we'll use the 10-, 30-, and 50-day moving averages as additional exit indicators. We'll look at the stock crossing the 30-day MA. If it's starting to hit the 30-day MA and it's not very extended, we'll usually get out. Another significant selling signal is when the 10-day MA starts to turn below the 30-day MA. A lot of times when a stock climaxes after an advance and it just starts to fall apart, you'll see the stock break below the 30-day MA. And then you might see it bounce back up, and then you'll see the 10-day MA start to break below the 30-day MA. Usually, I find that by the time the 10-day MA drops below the 30-day MA, the stock has lost its institutional support.

Where does the 50-day MA come in?

If the stock hits the 50-day MA, that's usually the big warning signal.

Can you give a scenario as to how these moving averages work together in order to help you exit a losing trade?

The idea is that these stocks we get into are trading above their 30-day MA and they should continue to trend up above the 30-day MA. Say you have a large amount of appreciation in a certain position. Say you're up 100 percent; you bought the stock at 80 and it goes to 160. Then you come into this correction and the stock pulls back to 140 and it's hitting the 30-day MA. We probably wouldn't sell it if it's holding up better relative to other stocks in the market and its sector. Your big winners will tend to form another base in a correction and trade sideways. They'll be the first to break out on the next rally. When you start to see stocks fall below the 50-day MA across the board, that's a pretty negative kind of signal and it's also a very negative indicator for the health of the market. When the market falls apart like that, you'll want to go to cash.

Do you have any particular indicators you like for market timing?

Well, one of the things I do is focus on the interest rate outlook. I'll try to have a feel for what the Fed is doing and how the market is reacting to their decisions. I'll just look at the daily charts and look at moving averages for the major indices. I like to look at the indices as a group. We like to look at the Dow, the OEX, S&P 500, the Nasdaq Composite, and the Nasdaq 100 and see how they're behaving as a group. I also look at what the leading industry groups are. If all the leaders start to fall apart, I know it's time to take my money off the table.

Let's talk about your trading psychology. You keep a detailed record of winners you've studied which gives you the confidence to enter new positions when you see stocks that fit that model. You've also mentioned that you're isolated from the rest of the world. You don't read other people's opinions and you live way out in the boonies. Tell us a little about your whole thought process when it comes to trading.

Let's make an important distinction. I read profusely. I read all day long, seven days a week. A lot of the reading I'm doing is on different industries and companies. What I avoid is other people's opinions. It's not that I don't respect their opinions. But they just cloud my judgment. There are a lot of smart people out there and they all have systems that work for them. And I love to sit down and talk to people about the market. But I'll be the first to say that I don't know what the market's going to do tomorrow or over the next two quarters or over the next five to 10 years. I've got some pretty good ideas of where I think the growth is based on the current economic situation and certain fundamental trends in the economy. And I've got a pretty good idea of where I might want to put my money to work. But it's very important to keep an open mind, be flexible, and try not to predict anything.

I think it's important to be humble. To borrow a quote from Andy Grove—who said, "only the paranoid survive"—only the humble survive in the stock market. As soon as you think you're smarter than the market and smarter than everybody else, you're going to get your head handed to you. As soon as I buy into a position, I totally go on the defense. I'm more concerned about losing money in a position than I am winning it. Like Paul Tudor Jones, I'm obsessed with defense.

Your obsession with risk extends to where you live, doesn't it?

Well, actually the reason I moved out here has nothing to do with the stock market. We live in probably some of the most beautiful country in the world. It's Middleburg, Virginia, which is in the foothills of the Blue Ridge Mountains. It's actually a very historic area because a lot of Civil War battles were fought here.

Probably more Americans died in the surrounding area than in any other place in the world. It's also big horse country. I love to ride and train.

Do you find that isolation helps you?

If you were to ask me where I'd move next, I would tell you that I wouldn't move back to New York. If I did live in New York, I would operate in isolation from the market establishment. The reason is that I want to let my research tell me what to do and not listen to the gossip on the Street. You look at Warren Buffett living out there in Omaha, Nebraska, okay? He achieved all that success living out there. I think that's a perfect example of how guys are able to get away from the Street and do their good-quality research and succeed. That's not to say the Street is a bad place. It's just that for my particular type of personality, the isolation works for me. I'd say I've almost become kind of a hermit over the last five years. A lot of my friends who live in other parts of the country complain because they never hear from me. It's really because I get so absorbed in my work.

I take it that you must put in a lot of hours.

One of the great aspects about the market is that there are always another couple of good ideas coming down the pipe. The only catch is, you've got to do your research. If you're going to invest in these markets, you've got to be willing to put in the time and effort to do the research. I probably do 60 or 70 hours a week of mostly research. It's something I enjoy doing.

Thanks, Jim. Best of luck to you.

Same to you, Marc.

Final Thoughts

The world of the top trader reeks of mystique and intrigue. Unlike the glamorous persona depicted by the media, the outstanding trader must constantly deal with a sea of conflicting emotions and extreme ups and downs, all the while railing against a set of odds stacked firmly against him or her. It is our hope that this book sheds fresh light on the strategies, emotions, and thought processes associated with the best.

Many aspiring traders believe that a sound strategy is all it takes to succeed in the world of trading. If only it was this easy!

Those readers in search of the mysterious "Holy Grail," some sort of elusive indicator or trading system that promises to deliver fat profits to a trader's door step, will no doubt come away from these pages disappointed. The Holy Grail simply doesn't exist. The outstanding players in this book reached the top not by possessing a Holy Grail, but rather by developing and maintaining an edge over their competition. In itself, understanding that there is no such thing as a Holy Grail is one of this book's most valuable lessons.

Those who had hoped to learn more about specific trading strategies will no doubt be able to walk away from this book with a greater knowledge of how the top traders do it. If you're like us, you will, in short order, seek to apply some of the techniques discussed inside—be they entry setups, exit criteria, or pyramiding methods—to your own trading.

Meanwhile, there are those who were drawn to these pages purely out of a desire to learn more about the intangibles—that sense of *je ne sais quoi*—that go with being a top trader. It is you whom we suspect will glean the most from these chapters.

Along these lines, it is our expectation that this book's coverage of these "big-picture qualities"—among them discipline, flexibility, persistence, patience, desire, passion, and humility—will give you a keener grasp of exactly what it takes to become a top trader.

Interestingly, by the time we had wrapped up our interviews, it became clear that, despite these traders' differing strategies and backgrounds, a number of common threads ran throughout. The most obvious to us was an all-consuming passion for the markets. Comments such as "When I walked out onto the trading floor, I thought it was the greatest thing I ever saw in my life" are typical of these traders' near-obsession with the markets. Others confessed to being "trading junkies" or made comments such as "there is no place you'd rather be: it's a narcotic." Still another trader is so obsessed with trading that he reads about the market while driving.

But while these traders' love of the markets appears on the verge of obsession, their passion is anything but reckless. In fact, of all the qualities needed to put a trader on top, we noticed that "discipline" was the one that came up the most in our conversations. Here, discipline means to have a trading plan and to "follow your plan in all kinds of market environments."

Tied in to discipline, outstanding traders share a level of risk aversion that compels them to adhere rigorously to a loss-management plan. Simply, they're not afraid to pull the trigger on a trade gone sour, take their loss, and move on to the next trade. As one trader put it, "I would rather have a mediocre strategy and a good money management system than a good strategy and a mediocre money management system."

Indeed, we came into this project knowing that discipline is important in developing success as a trader. Somehow, though, hearing it from some of the world's top traders drives the point home like no other! Thus, by the time this project was completed, we became convinced that discipline is the end-all and be-all. With it, a trader has a chance at being an outstanding performer. Without it, he hasn't a chance.

It makes sense to think that a big ego goes hand-in-hand with being a great trader. For us, however, one of the biggest surprises of this project was the realization that these gentlemen cast their egos aside when it comes to battling the market. Early in their careers, they realized that the market is smarter than they; to trade egotistically is to trade foolishly. They learned, sometimes the hard way, that a large ego has no place in the mindset of a highly successful trader.

Once we understood the make-up of a top trader, we came to the following conclusion: Certainly, the biggest downfall for most aspiring traders is a belief that they know more than the market. Learning how to throw in the towel on a trade, then, is absolutely crucial.

Perseverance was another quality that permeates the careers of these players. They hunker down during trying periods, redouble their resolve to win, and do not accept failure under any circumstances.

All of these top performers struck us as being less interested in the monetary spoils of their profession and much more interested in the game itself. They trade because they want to see their trading plan succeed. The money they make, then, is a by-product of the proper execution of their trading plan and the spoil of the achievement of successful trading.

Ultimately, the litmus test of any book about trading is its effect on the reader—not only in the present, but also in the future. With this in mind, we are confident the reader will find it worthwhile to revisit these pages from time to time so as to reinforce the concepts and ideas presented herein. We know that we will.

Passion, discipline, competitiveness, humility, flexibility, perseverance, and the ability to learn from mistakes are the recurring characteristics that emerged from these interviews. These are the traits that bring these gentlemen unusual success in the markets. These are the characteristics that allow a trader to step away from the rest of the pack, to develop instinct, a certain sixth sense, about the markets.

These are the qualities that put a trader on top.

Other Books from
M. GORDON
PUBLISHING GROUP
www.mgordonpub.com

HIT AND RUN TRADING
The Short-Term Stock Traders' Bible

JEFF COOPER

Written by professional equities trader, Jeff Cooper, this best-selling manual teaches traders how to day-trade and short-term trade stocks. Jeff's strategies identify daily the ideal stocks to trade and point out the exact entry and protective exit point. Most trades risk 1 point or less and last from a few hours to a few days.

Among the strategies taught are:

- Stepping In Front Of Size—You will be taught how to identify when a large institution is desperately attempting to buy or sell a large block of stock. You will then be taught how to step in front of this institution before the stock explodes or implodes. This strategy many times leads to gains from 1/4 point to 4 points within minutes.

- 1-2-3-4s—Rapidly moving stocks tend to pause for a few days before they explode again. You will be taught the three-day setup that consistently triggers solid gains within days.

- Expansion Breakouts—Most breakouts are false! You will learn the one breakout pattern that consistently leads to further gains. This pattern alone is worth the price of the manual.

- Also, you will learn how to trade market explosions (Boomers), how to trade secondary offerings, how to trade Slingshots, and you will learn a number of other profitable strategies that will make you a stronger trader.

160 PAGES HARD COVER $100.00

STREET SMARTS
High Probability Short-Term Trading Strategies

LAURENCE A. CONNORS AND LINDA BRADFORD RASCHKE

Published in 1996 and written by Larry Connors and *New Market Wizard* Linda Raschke, this 245-page manual is considered by many to be one of the best books written on trading futures. Twenty-five years of combined trading experience is divulged as you will learn 20 of their best strategies. Among the methods you will be taught are:

- **Swing Trading**—The backbone of Linda's success. Not only will you learn exactly how to swing trade, you will also learn specific advanced techniques never before made public.

- **News**—Among the strategies revealed is an intraday news strategy they use to exploit the herd when the 8:30 A.M. economic reports are released. This strategy will be especially appreciated by bond traders and currency traders.

- **Pattern Recognition**—You will learn some of the best short-term setup patterns available. Larry and Linda will also teach you how they combine these patterns with other strategies to identify explosive moves.

- **ADX**—In our opinion, ADX is one of the most powerful and misunderstood indicators available to traders. Now, for the first time, they reveal a handful of short-term trading strategies they use in conjunction with this terrific indicator.

- **Volatility**—You will learn how to identify markets that are about to explode and how to trade these exciting situations.

- Also, included are chapters on trading the smart money index, trading Crabel, trading gap reversals, a special chapter on professional money management, and many other trading strategies!

245 PAGES HARD COVER $175.00

HIT AND RUN TRADING II
CAPTURING EXPLOSIVE SHORT-TERM MOVES IN STOCKS

JEFF COOPER

212 fact-filled pages of new trading strategies from Jeff Cooper. You will learn the best momentum continuation and reversal strategies to trade. You will also be taught the best day-trading strategies that have allowed Jeff to make his living trading for the past decade. Also included is a special five-chapter bonus section entitled, "Techniques of a Professional Trader" where Jeff teaches you the most important aspects of trading, including money management, stop placement, daily preparation, and profit-taking strategies.

If you aspire to become a full-time professional trader, this is the book for you.

212 PAGES HARD COVER $100.00

THE 5-DAY MOMENTUM METHOD

JEFF COOPER

Strongly trending stocks always pause before they resume their move. *The 5-Day Momentum Method* identifies three- to seven-day explosive moves on strongly trending momentum stocks. Highly recommended for traders who are looking for larger than normal short-term gains and who do not want to sit in front of the screen during the day. *The 5-Day Momentum Method* works as well shorting declining stocks as it does buying rising stocks. Also, there is a special section written for option traders.

SPIRAL BOUND $50.00

INVESTMENT SECRETS OF A HEDGE FUND MANAGER
Exploiting the Herd Mentality of the Financial Markets

LAURENCE A. CONNORS AND BLAKE E. HAYWARD

Released in 1995, this top-selling trading book reveals strategies that give you the tools to stand apart from the crowd.

Among the strategies you will learn from this book are:

- **Connors-Hayward Historical Volatility System**—The most powerful chapter in the book, this revolutionary method utilizes historical volatility to pinpoint markets that are ready to explode.

- **News Reversals**—A rule-based strategy to exploit the irrational crowd psychology caused by news events.

- **NDX-SPX**—An early-warning signal that uses the NASDAQ 100 Index to anticipate moves in the S&P 500.

- **Globex**—Cutting edge techniques that identify mispricings that regularly occur on the Globex markets.

225 PAGES CLOTH COVER $49.95

CONNORS ON ADVANCED TRADING STRATEGIES
31 Chapters on Beating the Markets

LAURENCE A. CONNORS

Written by Larry Connors, this new book is broken into seven sections; S&P and stock market timing, volatility, new patterns, equities, day-trading, options, and more advanced trading strategies and concepts. Thirty-one chapters of in-depth knowledge to bring you up to the same level of trading as the professionals.

Among the strategies you will learn are:

- **Connors VIX Reversals I, II and III (Chapter 2)**—Three of the most powerful strategies ever revealed. You will learn how the CBOE OEX Volatility Index (VIX) pinpoints short-term highs and lows in the S&Ps and the stock market. The average profit/trade for this method is among the highest Larry has ever released.

- **The 15 Minute ADX Breakout Method (Chapter 20)**— Especially for day-traders! This dynamic method teaches you how to specifically trade the most explosive futures and stocks everyday! This strategy alone is worth the price of the book.

- **Options (Section 5)**—Four chapters and numerous in-depth strategies for trading options. You will learn the strategies used by the best Market Makers and a small handful of professionals to consistently capture options gains!

- **Crash, Burn, and Profit (Chapter 11)**—Huge profits occur when stocks implode. During a recent 12-month period, the Crash, Burn and Profit strategy shorted Centennial Technologies at 49 1/8; six weeks later it was at 2 1/2! It shorted Diana Corp. at 67 3/8; a few months later it collapsed to 4 3/8! It recently shorted Fine Host at 35; eight weeks later the stock was halted from trading at 10! This strategy will be an even bigger bonanza for you in a bear market.

- **Advanced Volatility Strategies (Section 2)**—Numerous, never-before revealed strategies and concepts using volatility to identify markets immediately before they explode.

- and much, much more!

259 PAGES HARD COVER $150.00

METHOD IN DEALING IN STOCKS
Reading the Mind of the Market on a Daily Basis

JOSEPH H. KERR, JR.

This gem was originally published in 1931 by Joseph Kerr has been expanded and updated to reflect today's markets. This book is considered to be the bible of interpreting both daily market action and daily news events.

150 PAGES PAPERBACK $35.00

TO ORDER CALL:
1-800-797-2584 or 1-213-955-5777 (outside the U.S.)
OR FAX YOUR ORDER TO:
1-213-955-4242

OR MAIL YOUR ORDER TO:
M. Gordon Publishing Group, 445 S. Figueroa St.,
Suite 2930, Los Angeles, CA 90071

www.mgordonpub.com

All orders please add $6 + $1 each add'l item; Priority Mail: $10 + $1 each add'l item;
Airborne Int'l: $25 for shipping and handling.
California residents include 8% sales tax.

FREE REPORT
Maximize Your Trading Profits Immediately!

David Landry, TradingMarkets.com Director of Research, has put together a set of simple money management rules to help all traders become more successful in his report *The True Secret to Trading Success: Simple Money Management Rules That Will Make You a More Profitable Trader!*

To obtain this report, send your request along with your name and address to:

M. Gordon Publishing Group, Inc.
445 S. Figueroa Street, Suite 2930, Dept. H2
Los Angeles, CA 90071

Or

Fax your information to 213-955-4242.

Your report will be mailed immediately.

ABOUT THE AUTHORS

Kevin N. Marder, an equity trader since 1986, is president of Los Angeles-based Marder Investment Advisors. Previously, he was editor-in-chief of TradingMarkets.com and a co-founder of CBS MarketWatch, where his market comments were broadcast over the CBS Radio Network several times daily. Marder has been written about in *Forbes,* the *Los Angeles Times, Red Herring,* and *Online Investor,* among other publications.

From 1990 to 1995, Marder provided equity research services to a hedge fund and developed fixed-income portfolio analytic software for use by institutional portfolio managers and brokerage firms. Marder is a contributing author to the Prentice-Hall book, *Computerized Trading.*

He received an MBA with honors in Investments and Corporate Finance from the University of Southern California.

Marc Dupée is futures editor of TradingMarkets.com. A trader of stock index futures and currencies, he got his start in the financial markets on the floor of the Comex.

Previously, Dupée developed business curriculum for the University of California, Berkeley Haas School of Business and created documentary programming for CNN and NBC.

Dupée received a B.A. in Political Economy from the University of California, Berkeley and an International MBA from the University of San Diego. Dupée is a U.S. Coast Guard-licensed captain and has circumnavigated the globe on sailing vessels.